THE POLITICS OF MUSLIM
IDENTITIES IN ASIA

THE POLITICS OF MUSLIM IDENTITIES IN ASIA

• • •

EDITED BY IULIA LUMINA

EDINBURGH
University Press

Edinburgh University Press is one of the leading university presses in the UK. We publish academic books and journals in our selected subject areas across the humanities and social sciences, combining cutting-edge scholarship with high editorial and production values to produce academic works of lasting importance. For more information visit our website: edinburghuniversitypress.com

Edinburgh University Press Ltd
The Tun – Holyrood Road
12 (2f) Jackson's Entry
Edinburgh EH8 8PJ

First published in hardback by Edinburgh University Press 2022

Typeset in KoufrUni by
Cheshire Typesetting Ltd, Cuddington, Cheshire

A CIP record for this book is available from the British Library

ISBN 978 1 4744 6683 7 (hardback)
ISBN 978 1 4744 6684 4 (paperback)
ISBN 978 1 4744 6686 8 (webready PDF)
ISBN 978 1 4744 6685 1 (epub)

CONTENTS

Contents

NOTES ON CONTRIBUTORS

Irfan Ahmad is Senior Research Fellow at the Max Planck Institute for the Study of Religious and Ethnic Diversity in Göttingen. Previously an Associate Professor of Political Anthropology at Australian Catholic University and Senior Lecturer at Monash University, he has also taught at the University of Amsterdam and University College Utrecht, The Netherlands. He is the author of two monographs, *Islamism and Democracy in India* (2009; 2010) and *Religion as Critique: Islamic Critical Thinking from Mecca to the Marketplace* (2017). He is the editor of *Anthropology and Ethnography are Not Equivalent: Reorienting Anthropology for the Future* (2021), *The Algebra of Warfare-Welfare: A Long View of India's 2014 Elections* (2019) and *(Il)liberal Europe: Islamophobia, Modernity and Radicalization* (2017). A columnist for *Anthropology News* in 2018 and founding co-editor of the *Journal of Religious and Political Practice*, he sits on the advisory boards of *Public Anthropologist*, *South Asia: Journal of South Asian Studies* and *International Journal of Islam in Asia*. In 2020, he gave a Ted-x Talk titled 'Twins Unknown: Islamophobia and Domophilia'.

Syed Imad Alatas is currently pursuing his PhD in Sociology at the University of North Carolina-Chapel Hill, United States. His research interests include the sociology of religion, gender and youth. His Master's thesis at the National University of Singapore (NUS) focused on female Muslim NGOs in Malaysia and their discourses on women's roles and gender relations. Prior to commencing his Master's studies, he worked at the Middle East Institute in NUS, where he oversaw the institute's publications and was in charge of the internship programme. He has written on anti-Semitism in Malaysia and Indonesia and adolescent masculinities for the Asia Pacific Social Science Review and the Southeast Asian Social Science Review, respectively. Imad has also published a chapter on interfaith harmony in *Budi Kritik* (2018), a collection of essays on intellectual life, religion, ethnic identity, and political activity of Malays in Singapore. Outside academia, he has written for Malaysian online publications such as *Free Malaysia Today* and the *Malay Mail*.

Nazry Bahrawi is Assistant Professor of Southeast Asian Literature and Culture at the University of Washington. He specialises in the comparative study of texts, theories and traditions of Indian Ocean cultures between the Malay Archipelago and the Middle East. His research is informed by discourses in world literature, decolonial theory, translation studies and ethnic studies. He has published in *Critical Muslim, Journal of Intercultural Studies, Moving Worlds, CounterText, Journal of World Literature* and *Literature and Theology*.

Syafiq Hasyim is Lecturer and Director of Library and Culture at the Indonesian International Islamic University (UIII). He is also lecturer at the Faculty of Social and Political Sciences, UIN Syarif Hidayatullah Jakarta. From March 2020 onwards, he is visiting fellow at the Indonesia Studies Programme of the ISEAS – Yusof Ishak Institute. He obtained a DPhil in Islamic Studies from the Free University, Berlin, Germany, and an MA in Islamic Studies from Leiden University, The Netherlands. His latest publication includes *Fatwa and Democracy: Majelis Ulama Indonesia* and *Rising Islamic Conservatism in Indonesia: Islamic Groups and Identity Politics*, co-edited with Leonard C. Sebastian and Alexander R. Arifianto (2021). He has also published chapters in numerous edited collections including *Secularism, Religion and Democracy in Southeast Asia*, edited by Vidhu Verma and Aakash Singh Rathore (2019), and *Freedom of Expression in Islam: Challenging Apostasy and Blasphemy Laws*, edited by Muhammad Khalid Masud, Kari Vogt, Lena Larsen and Christian Moe (2021).

Imrul Islam works for The Bridge Initiative, a research project on Islamophobia, in Washington, DC. His research focuses on South Asia, specifically the ongoing crisis in Myanmar and the erosion of refugee and minority rights in India, Bangladesh and Sri Lanka. His work has been published in the *Atlantic Council, The New Arab, Sojourners, The Blueprint* and *The Daily Star*. Imrul holds an MA in Conflict Resolution from Georgetown University and certificates in Mediation (Community Boards) as well as Refugee and Humanitarian Emergencies (Institute for the Study of International Migration at Georgetown University, ISIM). He is also an advisor for participatory action research by Rohingya youth, in collaboration with the Political Settlements Research Programme at the University of Edinburgh.

Iulia Lumina is an independent researcher based in Singapore and focuses on the intellectual history of the Global South. She graduated from the School of Oriental and African Studies (SOAS), University of London, where she specialised in the anthropology and politics of the Middle East, Southeast Asia and the comparative study of Islam.

Nazneen Mohsina is Senior Analyst at the Centre of Excellence for National Security of the S. Rajaratnam School of International Studies (RSIS), Nanyang Technological University, Singapore. She holds an MSc in International Relations from RSIS. Her research interests include contemporary debates about identity politics, inter-ethnic or inter-religious relations and how domestic and international politics shape one's religious/ethnic identity. Nazneen specialises in religion and politics in South Asia, particularly India and Bangladesh. Her commentaries have been published in various media such as *Channel News Asia, South China Morning Post, South Asian Voices, Lowy Institute* and the *Diplomat*. She has also presented papers with the British Association for South Asian Studies, the Institute of South Asian Studies in Singapore and the Washington Institute for Near East Policy.

Matthew J. Nelson is Professor of Politics at the School of Oriental and African Studies (SOAS), University of London. His research focuses on the comparative and international politics of South Asia, with an emphasis on non-elite politics, constitutional politics, the politics of Islamic ideas and institutions, and democracy. Before coming to SOAS, Matthew taught at UC Santa Cruz, Bates College and Yale University. At SOAS, he is a founding member of the Centre on Comparative Political Thought and the Centre on Conflict, Rights and Justice. In 2009–10, he was the James D. Wolfensohn Family Member in the School of Social Science at the Institute for Advanced Study (IAS) in Princeton; in 2011 he was a Resident Fellow at the Woodrow Wilson International Center for Scholars (WWICS) in Washington, DC; in 2014–15, he was a Resident Fellow at the Zentrum für Interdisziplinäre Forschung (ZiF) in Germany. Matthew has also served as an elected board member for the American Institute of Pakistan Studies (AIPS), the South Asia Council of the Association for Asian Studies (AAS) and the Religion and Politics Section of the American Political Science Association (APSA). His current research focuses on comparative constitutional politics and the politics of sectarian and doctrinal diversity in Islamic law and Muslim education.

Nathan Gilbert Quimpo is Adjunct Professor (semi-retired) in Political Science and International Relations at the University of Tsukuba and Hosei University in Japan. He has taught at the University of the Philippines, the University of Amsterdam (Netherlands), Sophia University (Japan) and Toyo University. Before turning to an academic career, he was a long-time political activist in the Philippines. Arrested and detained as a political prisoner a few times by the Marcos regime, he later fled to the Netherlands where he became a political refugee. Nathan is the author of numerous books, including *Contested Democracy and the Left in the Philippines after Marcos* (2008) and *Subversive Lives: A Family Memoir of the Marcos Years* (co-authored with Susan F. Quimpo, 2012; 2016). He has published articles in *Comparative Politics, Pacific Review, Asian Survey, Southeast Asian Affairs, Critical Asian*

Studies, Journal of Asian Security and International Affairs and the *Philippine Political Science Journal*.

Joanne Smith Finley is Reader in Chinese Studies. Her research interests have included: the evolution of identities among the Uyghurs of Xinjiang, Northwest China, and in the Uyghur diaspora; strategies of symbolic resistance in Xinjiang; Uyghur women between Islamic revival and Chinese state securitisation of religion; PRC counter-terrorism measures in Xinjiang as state terror; and political 're-education' in Xinjiang as (cultural) genocide. She is author of *The Art of Symbolic Resistance: Uyghur Identities and Uyghur-Han Relations in Contemporary Xinjiang* (2013) and co-editor of *Language, Education and Uyghur Identity in Urban Xinjiang* (2015). She has published numerous journal articles, including recent contributions in the *Journal of Genocide Research* and *Central Asian Survey*. Joanne serves as an expert country witness in Uyghur asylum cases in the UK, Europe, the US and Canada, and she advises legal firms, refugee support organisations, government departments, non-governmental organisations and think-tanks.

INTRODUCTION:
SITUATING THE POLITICS OF MUSLIM
IDENTITIES

Iulia Lumina

The study of Islam and Muslim societies in Western scholarship often revolves around theoretical and analytical frameworks that either essential-ise or reduce Islam and Muslim identities to false dichotomies (folk versus elite, great versus little, traditional versus modern). Addressing the diversity of Muslim conduct and Islamic practices, scholars have paid particular atten-tion to what constitutes Islam as an analytical category and how to carry out studies of Muslim societies across the many disciplines within the social sciences. In anthropology, a discipline concerned with the particularities of culture, the debate has addressed the relationship between the diversity of local Muslim practices and a universal conception of Islam. Islamic studies scholars have shown particular interest in scripture and theology, privileg-ing a law-informed approach to normative Islam, while sociologists have investigated Muslim societies through the frameworks of modernisation and secularisation theories. Most scholars implicitly or explicitly assume a normative Islam based on 'sacred law', but this approach conceals the fact that Islamic practices are socially and historically mediated across different localities.

A historical overview of the compilation of the Qur'an and the develop-ment of jurisprudence schools with their various methods of interpretation reveals the contestation at play in establishing the guiding principles of Muslim conduct. It shows that Islam 'is both inherited and actively created' (Hughes 2013: 10); in return, Muslim practices and identities are varied and contested. Nonetheless, since the nineteenth century, revivalist movements have advanced discourses that seek to reinstate an imagined authentic Islam, which obscures social and historical complexities and often reduces Muslim identities to normative religious precepts. The perception of Muslims as 'super-Islamised beings' (al-Azmeh 2003) has rather been a historical con-stant, informed equally by essentialist frameworks, Orientalist fantasies and modern quests for authenticity characteristic of post-colonial identity politics.

[1]

A holistic attempt to describe Muslim society considered Islam as a blue-print for social order (Gellner 1981). Gellner presented the sociology of Islam as an oscillation between tribal folk tradition and the great tradition of the learned ulama. His predicament was that the reformed, fundamentalist Islam of the city ulama becomes the prevalent form of Islam (Gellner 1990). It is important to note that Gellner fit this development in the grand scheme of transformations brought by the modern industrial-capitalist civilisation. Unlike earlier accounts, he did not see a contradiction between Islam and modernity and considered the phenomenon of scripturalism to be highly modern, which he compared with the Protestant experience in Europe. Gellner believed scripturalism was an alternative to nationalism; Clifford Geertz (1971) argued that it facilitated nationalism and revived older patterns of belief, which led to the ideologisation of religion.

The nation-state became the legitimate political entity all over the post-colonial world and influenced the ways in which Muslims imagined their state and society. While inheriting colonial legal and institutional structures, the nation-state offered 'the means for realising long-cherished dreams of religious and social transformation on a society-wide scale' (Hefner and Hovartich 1997: 6). Hence, new imaginings of community and identity were set into place, reclaiming, reconciling or suppressing certain cultural and religious elements within new state structures. New struggles for legitimation and recognition unfold as the contestation of power involves a diverse range of actors. The ulama, Gellner's champions of modernisation, were often co-opted into the state structure, gradually lost their monopoly on society and finally became just one competing voice asserting visions of society and politics. The flourishing of debate and contestation ensured the fragmentation of religious authority and political polarisation. In this light, Gellner's focus on fundamentalism as the essence of the universal Muslim society cannot account for the diverse political and religious currents across the Muslim world. It is clear that we are talking about Muslim societies in the plural, whose common themes derived from Islam unfold in specific socio-political contexts (Zubaida 1995).

The Politics of Muslim Identities in Asia – covering nine case-studies from Singapore, Malaysia, Pakistan, Indonesia, Bangladesh, Philippines, India, Myanmar and China – is a testament to the diversity of Muslim identities and practices. The volume explores how Muslims articulate their religious identity vis-à-vis the state and society where they live and how their subject positions relate to specific social and political contexts. The chapters analyse Muslim identities as active articulations by Muslims themselves and how Muslims, or certain ways of being Muslim, are rendered as the internal Other in society at large. The emphasis on agency in the discussion of religious identities is meant to contrast with the view that religion, and specifically Islam, necessarily involves coercion and a lack of critical engagement. The chapters demonstrate that different identities do not only stem from theological differences, but also from the ways in which Muslims respond to and are framed by their respective political and social environments. The articulation of identities is a social phenomenon, being clearly a function of both external and internal factors, stemming from different groups' sense of belonging, as well as the individual choices, intents and aspirations that shape one's meaning and purpose in life. The chapters in this volume are not exhaustive in treating identity politics in each country; rather, they historicise Islam and present case-studies that de-essentialise Muslim identities. The objective is not to raise Islam to the level of relativity, but to provide context-based examples revealing the contradictions and complexities that have preoccupied scholars across the social sciences. Before introducing the chapters and the thematic discussions that unfold throughout this book, I take a theoretical detour through the conceptual approaches to the study of Islam and Muslim societies in order to place the anti-essentialist ethos of this volume within the broader scholarship.

Studying the 'Human and Historical Phenomenon of Islam'

Over the past few decades, anthropologists and sociologists have debated much about what constitutes Islam as an object of study and developed different approaches to examine Muslim societies. Moving away from understanding Islam as a total social fact (Gellner 1981) or explaining the variety of cultural styles across the Muslim world as localised manifestations of a universal Islamic consciousness (Geertz 1971), there has been overwhelming consensus in opposing the idea of a monolithic Islam, instead favouring various *local Islams* (el-Zein 1977; al-Azmeh 1996). While this is not the place to rehearse what is arguably the most instructive theoretical debate in the anthropology of Islam,[1] I will briefly outline the key conceptual insights that have led to the historical and anti-essentialist study of Islam and Muslim societies.

Shortcomings have been identified in studying Islam as 'culture', 'religion' or 'civilisation': as *culture*, Islam is understood as a timeless, unchanging entity, which enables the trope of authenticity and return to the ideal or true Islam. Muslims have often been 'made to yield [. . .] a total and totalising culture which overrides the inconvenient complexity of economy, society and history' (al Azmeh 2003: 23). Moreover, in the aftermath of 9/11, political Islam has been understood as the effect of an archaic Islamic culture (Mamdani 2002), mistakenly establishing a link between violence and Islam. The 'culture talk' that distinguishes 'good Muslims' from 'bad Muslims' – instead of terrorists from civilians – understands 'individuals (from traditional cultures) in authentic and original terms, as if their identities are shaped entirely by the supposedly unchanging culture into which they are born' (Mamdani 2002: 767). Studying Islam as 'culture' not only dehistoricises

---

[1] An extensive analysis of this debate can be found in Shahab Ahmed (2016), *What is Islam? The Importance of Being Islamic.*

the construction of Muslim identities, but also prevents us from situating the study of Muslim societies within their contemporary conditions.

As *religion*, Islam is seen as anomalous or exceptional for lacking the separation of religion and politics that is characteristic of Christianity. In turn, this has led to Islam being considered incompatible with modernity and Muslims unable to modernise at the expense of tradition. Several authors have contested the Eurocentric idea of a universal concept of religion, turning instead to the particular intellectual and historical shifts that created the normative concept of religion (Asad 1993; Fitzgerald 2008; Salvatore 2009; Ahmad 2017). Having been modelled on the trajectory of Christianity in Europe, 'religion' has been restricted to the institutional power of the Church and to the private sphere. This framework, therefore, positions Islam in stark contrast to the formula of a modernising, secular public sphere, turning to essentialist cultural explanations in order to understand such a deviance.

Challenging the presumed incompatibility of Islam with modernity, some scholars have proposed to study Islam through the civilisational framework of multiple modernities, which has led to a reinterpretation of tradition as changing and dynamic process (Salvatore 2009). This approach not only provincialises the idea of modernity but also allows for a multiplicity of Islamic modernities. However, where such a multiplicity is recognised, the various articulations of Islam and modernity are accounted for in terms of the variety of cultures making up Islamic civilisation, drawing a distinction between 'religion' and 'culture'. Marshall Hodgson's influential work defined this distinction as Islamic/Islamicate, the first pertaining to Islam in a religious sense, while the latter refers to larger cultures and societies influenced by Islam (as discussed in Ahmed 2016). Hodgson (1993) pioneered a sociology of Islam that recognised not only modernising processes within Islamic civilisation, but also their centrality in world history. Nonetheless, he set 'the pious core of Islam-proper in opposition to *adab*/culture' (as discussed in Ahmed 2016: 170), which Ahmed ultimately found deficient for understanding inter-Muslim difference. This is of particular importance for the study of Islam in Asia, which should not be understood as an Islamicate variable to what is often considered the Arab Islam proper (ibid: 172–3).

Therefore, Islam as 'civilisation' is also conceptually problematic, especially when we consider that, in the late nineteenth century, Muslim intellectuals also articulated the idea of an Islamic civilisation as response to the racialisation of Muslims as inferior by the European empires (Aydin 2017). While seeking to 'articulate Muslim belonging in a universal humanity' (ibid: 10) and create political solidarity at the level of civilisation, the idea of an Islamic civilisation[2] was an abstraction build on an amnesia concerning the cosmopolitan Muslim empires (ibid). Lastly, Samuel Huntington's (1993)

---

[2] Cemil Aydin (2017) argues that this was the foundation for Muslim reformism and pan-Islamic thought in the early twentieth century.

infamous 'clash of civilisations' thesis is another gross generalisation – with tragic consequences – that assigns identities according to essentialist understandings of 'culture' and 'civilisation'.

In light of the above, it can be said that the major obstacles to a historical and anti-essentialist study of Islam and Muslim societies are the Eurocentric nature of the social sciences,[3] as well as the normative power of the modernisation theory, that inspired analyses of Islam and Muslim societies through positivist differentiations between the categories of 'culture', 'religion' and 'politics'. Instead, scholars warned us against the presumed self-evident distinction between such categories (Fitzgerald 2008: 7; Ahmed 2016: 73) and proposed to place the study of Islam within 'articulations of structural relations' (el-Zein 1977: 250). Moreover, since the search of a theoretical definition of Islam obscured 'flesh and blood Muslims [. . .] visible only through cleverly contrived representation and essentialised types' (Varisco 2005: 29), scholars turned their attention to the lived experiences of Muslims and invited us to consider the native's point of view (el-Zein 1977), unmediated by anthropological interpretations of cultural or religious symbols. This defining theoretical shift began with the recognition that Muslims objectify their religion (Eickelman and Piscatori 2004), moving from a state of 'religiousness' to 'religious-mindedness' (Geertz 1971), and was finally realised in Talal Asad's influential definition of Islam as a discursive tradition (1986: 14). Recognising that the 'various Islams' approach does not take into account relations of power, Asad explained the diversity of Islamic practice in terms of the disciplinary power of religious discourses. What was earlier considered to be the core – that is, normative, orthodox Islam – was placed by Asad in a relational context of structural articulations. Therefore, Islam is finally historicised by treating orthodoxy as a relation of power (ibid: 15) and not as the true essence of Islam.

We arrive, at last, at an understanding of Islam as 'a human and historical phenomenon' (Ahmed 2016: 72), whose study should focus on the expressions by Muslim actors rather than a scholarly search for an abstract universal definition. Beyond the study of Islam as 'culture', 'religion' or 'civilisation', new approaches have shifted the focus to 'the way knowledge, culture and power are shaped by Muslim actors who draw on a combination of traditional and modern repertoires and enact largely original patterns of sociability, solidarity and civility' (Salvatore 2013: 12), while paying attention to 'the historical conditions that enable the production and maintenance of specific discursive traditions' (Asad 1986: 17). Therefore, the right question to ask is: how do historical conditions influence the ways in which Muslim actors draw on traditional and modern repertoires? Conversely, what are the contingent politics and mechanisms through which Muslims are portrayed as Other? It is precisely these questions that the chapters in

[3] A recent volume that expands the sociological canon is by Syed Farid Alatas and Vineeta Sinha (2017), *Sociological Theory Beyond the Canon*.

this volume address, while this introduction makes the call for *situating* the politics of Muslim identities in their specific historical, social and political contexts.

The Politics of Muslim Identities in Asia aims to contribute to the anti-essentialist scholarship that illustrates how Muslims constitute themselves as modern subjects. Soares and Osella (2009) have proposed the notion of *Islam mondain* 'to apprehend some of the complex ways of being Muslim in the contemporary world in which Muslims reflect on being Muslim' (12). The focus on everydayness reveals modalities of Muslim self-fashioning that do not necessarily privilege religion, but intertwine with other spheres of existence, which are often in line with a neoliberal ethic. Similarly, Bowen (2012) insisted on studying the ways in which individual Muslims derive meaning not only from the 'set of interpretative resources and practices' (2012: 3) that Islam offers, but are also guided by intentions, emotions and the social significance of their ways of being in the world. This methodological everydayness calls for 'a new cosmopolitanism that embraces the diversity of ideas, practices and hopes of a globalised world' (Mirsepassi and Graham 2015: 84). In this spirit, Marsden and Retsikas caution us that 'Islam is deeply yet also diffusely embedded in everyday experience' (2013: 1), meaning that different aspects of human experience may or may not be a reflection of active attempts by Muslims to systematise and articulate Islam (ibid: 14). They urge us to 'reconsider the scales and settings in which Islam is invoked and embodied' (Coleman 2013: 250), advancing an approach that examines 'how, where and why connections and disconnections might be made in relation to – but also in constituting – an Islam that can be characterised as "immanent"' (ibid: 248).

Concluding this theoretical exposition, the common challenge that scholars have faced when conceptualising Islam is the fact of its sheer diversity. Muslims engaging with and deriving meaning from Islam in various ways and locales did not prevent the endeavour for a coherent definition of Islam. In his highly erudite and comprehensive *What is Islam? The Importance of Being Islamic* (2016), Shahab Ahmed contended that, if Muslims engaged with and interpreted sources related to what is abstractly thought of as an Islam that is presumably impossible to define, and more so articulate meaningful ways of being Islamic, then they certainly would have a shared notion of what constitutes Islam. Recognising that 'at the centre of the historical articulation of Islam have been processes of inter-Muslim debate and disputation' (Ahmed 2016: 146), Ahmed sought to re-orient the debate from 'unity in diversity' towards a recognition of the phenomenon of outright, internal contradiction in the claims that Muslims make about Islam. More than discursive traditions that become authoritative through favourable power dynamics, he highlighted the co-existence of contradictory interpretations of the divine Revelation. Ahmed placed Islamic philosophy, Sufism and the literary and visual arts as equally central to the polyvocal tradition of Islam as the established legal schools of the ulama.

The coherent definition of Islam that Ahmed proposes reconciles not only multiplicity, but more importantly, as he demonstrates, internal contradiction. He starts with the definition of Islam as hermeneutical engagement (2016: 345), drawing attention to the processes of interpretation and understanding that arise from human commitment to the divine Revelation. The hermeneutical engagement happens at the level of *Text* (Qur'an), *Pre-text* (the prior traditions of thought in which the Revelation takes place) and *Con-text* (the body of meaning already derived from previous hermeneutical engagements, which provides the semiotic space for further interpretations) (ibid: 345–66). Although an abstract definition, Ahmed's discussion of the Balkans-to-Bengal complex is instructive for grasping such a proposition of Islam. Several anti-essentialist moves can be identified here: first, he shifts the attention from the classical period of early Islam to what he calls the post-formative paradigm of the Balkans-to-Bengal complex that flourished from the fourteenth to nineteenth century from Southern Europe across the Middle East, Anatolia and Iran, all the way to Central and South Asia. Second, he posited this as one of the major historical paradigms – if not *the* historical paradigm – of Islam (ibid: 82). Third, he identified in the poetry of Hafiz, Islamic philosophy, Sufism and the proliferation of such discourses in the pervasive institution of the madrasah a central conceptual register through which Muslims derive meaning and value that is no less Islamic than other hermeneutical engagements, legal or otherwise. In doing so, Ahmed instructs us that 'not everything that Muslims do is Islamic, but we should take seriously all Muslim expressions of meaning as Islam' (Pregill 2017: 159).

Thematic Parallels in the Politics of Muslim Identities in Asia

The above discussion aimed to demonstrate that, in studying Islam, the focus remains on Muslim actors who engage with historical traditions of thought and practice as well as with their contemporary empirical conditions. *The Politics of Muslim Identities in Asia* comprises nine case-studies that historicise and contextualise – in other words, *situate* – such Muslim expressions in their contingent social and political dynamics. In order to avoid super-Islamising Muslims, it needs to be acknowledged that religion does not necessarily condition a believer's entire existence. While we should not overdetermine the role of religion in the formation of identities and acknowledge the multiple sites of affiliation available to the modern subject, we can observe the significance of religion in the formation of collective forms of belonging, as well as a marker of difference between and within communities. The intent of the book is to survey the ways in which religious affiliation sparks a politics of difference in contexts where Islamic practices, beliefs and aspirations are contested, as well as where Muslims are framed as the Other.

The book does not offer a new conceptual approach to Asia but illustrates the diversity of historical and political contexts that sustain Muslim identities across the geographical locales of South and Southeast Asia, including China. While the multidisciplinary chapters focus on specific nation-states and national histories, intersecting themes draw attention to larger – transnational, regional and global – processes that influence the politics of Muslim identities. The first three chapters explore aspects of Muslim identity construction that are often marginalised, addressing Islamic thought and religious freedom in the domains of literature, feminism and secular law in Singapore, Malaysia and Pakistan.

The book opens with Nazry Bahrawi's 'Speculative Verses of Islam in Singapore Malay Literature'. Much like Ahmed's legitimisation of literature as a medium through which Muslims debate and derive Islamic meaning and interpretation, Bahrawi approaches 'literature as a mode of critical inquiry into Islamic thoughts and practices'. Arguing that the discourse of Islamic thought should not be confined to the normative fields of *fiqh*, *usuluddin*, shari'ah laws and *tafsir*, he makes the case for 'literary Islam' and analyses the sensibilities that inform the fiction of Malay/Muslim writers from Singapore in their treatment of Islamic themes. The chapter offers an overview of Singapore's Islamic landscape, problematising the Malay/Muslim label and the complexities surrounding Malayness as a racial identity. The racialist approach to governance based on the CMIO model (Chinese, Malay, Indian and Others) resulted in the strongly institutionalised nature of Islam in Singapore, where Muslims are governed on personal matters under the Administration of Muslim Law Act (AMLA), introduced the year after the Republic's independence and implemented in 1968. Against this backdrop of institutional Islam, Bahrawi sketches the trajectory of Islamic thought in the regional literary movements of *Sastera Islam* and *Sastera Profetik* and identifies a departure from the earlier traditionalist resurgent orientation of the 1980s and 1990s towards a speculative and critical appraisal of religiosity.

Another strand of critical appraisal is explored by Syed Imad Alatas in his study on 'Women and Islamisation in Malaysia', which draws attention to the fact that women are often seen as the cultural bearers of ideal Muslim societies. The Islamisation of the 1970s and 1980s in Malaysia placed a salient emphasis on the moral project of the family, together with a disproportionate concern with how women ought to practise their faith. The chapter traces the various strands of Islamic thought in Malaysian socio-political life, from the Kaum Muda reformist movement at the beginning of the twentieth century to the formation of the nationalist United Malay National Organisation (UMNO) in 1946 and the breakaway of conservative ulama who formed the Pan-Malaysian Islamic Party (PAS) in 1951 with the intent of creating an Islamic state. As Malaysia is often lauded as a moderate Muslim country, Alatas turns to the efforts of civil society groups that challenge Islamist discourses. He traces women's mobilisation from its inception in the anti-colonial and nationalist movements to some recent responses among female Muslim NGOs and activists to discourses on Islam and religiosity in Malaysia. The chapter shows that women's contestations of the practice of

Islam, ranging from conservative to progressive, often challenge the state-sanctioned version and so are integral and emblematic of national attempts to define what it means to be an ideal Muslim.

Also reflecting on state-sanctioned forms of Islam, Matthew J. Nelson brings into focus the mechanisms of 'Securing Muslim Boundaries' through the political instrumentalisation of religious difference in Pakistan and Malaysia. Looking at the intersection between constitutional law and allegations of heresy, Nelson argues that the political and often formal legal exclusion of heretics as a source of public disorder facilitates the consolidation of Muslim community boundaries and identities. The chapter's comparative approach illustrates the different historical circumstances and political dynamics that lead to the limitation of religious freedom following allegations of heresy and religious deviance. In Malaysia, political competition over the delineation of the Malay-Muslim identity facilitates cycles of mutual recrimination between the main parties, the United Malay National Organisation (UMNO) and the Pan-Malaysian Islamic Party (PAS), and other formations focused on *dakwah* or Muslim religious revitalisation such as the Malaysian Islamic Youth Movement (Angkatan Belia Islam Malaysia or ABIM) and Darul Arqam or al-Arqam (now also known as Global Ikhwan). Nonetheless, heretics are rarely addressed through blasphemy laws, but rather detained under provisions outlined in Malaysia's Internal Security Act (ISA) or Malaysia's Security Offences (Special Measures) Act, accusations of 'sedition' or state-level laws targeting offences against the precepts of Islam. In Pakistan, intra-Muslim allegations of heresy revolve around securitising the Ahmadiyya minority to protect the orthodoxy of the Sunni majority. Even though nationalist elites defended the fundamental rights of the Ahmadiyya, waves of legal reform and Islamist demands ultimately defined the Ahmadiyya as non-Muslim, 'an existential threat from within' and thus a threat to public order. Nelson argues that, far from securing the state, the securitisation of the Ahmadiyya fuelled a torrent of *takfiri* politics and demonstrates that the delegitimisation and exclusion of 'heretics' is not pursued on the grounds of shari'ah law or jurisprudence, but rather through the power to define public order.

This is in contrast to Indonesia, where Islam has more recently been used as a political tool to draw a distinction between the country's Muslim and non-Muslim population. While religious freedom is inscribed in the state philosophy of the Pancasila, Syafiq Hasyim explains this conservative turn in terms of the strategic repositioning of the MUI (Majelis Ulama Indonesia, Council of Indonesian Ulama) from *khadim al-hukuma* (the guardian of the government) to *khadim al-ummah* (the guardian of the Muslim community). He argues that the MUI plays a central role in the emergence of Islamic populism and identity politics in Indonesia and illustrates how its 'agenda of shariatisation' has influenced Indonesian politics, especially the blasphemy case of Basuki Tjahaja Purnama, the Chinese Christian candidate in the Jakarta gubernatorial elections in 2017. Hasyim argues that the MUI produces fatwas and religious advice that cherish illiberal attitudes towards religious freedom and hence threaten the democratic principle of the Pancasila state.

The idea of the ummah as a sense of common belonging has been a historical constant in the Muslim imagination (Ahmed 2016: 143). Scholars have recognised its importance in uniting Muslims acrosse the entire diversity of practice. Sayyid reminds us that the key to the expansion of the Muslim empire is precisely this ideological sense of belonging, which led to 'the construction of a Muslim political identity that could not be reduced to an Arab ethnicity or nomadic positionality' (2012: 7). This he contrasts with the racialised ideologies of European empires, which denied the colonial subjects being citizens of Western empires.[4] While in Indonesia the discourse of ummah is used as populist rhetoric, Nazneen Mohsina analyses how the Bangladeshi diaspora turns to the global ummah as a renewed source of political identity based on a militant Islamism. Her chapter positions the contemporary Islamist discourse in Bangladesh within the country's larger relationship with the Middle East. First, she highlights the geopolitical context in which Bangladesh became an independent nation-state, when the dependence on Middle Eastern petrodollars led to the endorsement of an Islamic element to nationalism. She then turns to the uneven process of globalisation that sustains the international migration of Bangladeshi blue-collar workers to more developed countries. Examining the instrumental role that migration has played in shaping Islamist movements in Bangladesh, Mohsina cautions that Islamism is impossible to understand without situating it in the context of different global developments. The movement of ideas, symbols and people demonstrates how Islam has been (and still is being) used to mobilise political support from the masses and legitimise revolt in Muslim countries. Bangladeshi diasporas have not only returned with ideas to change the system in their homeland, but they have also travelled to foreign lands to participate in violent conflict and serve the Muslim ummah. Mohsina argues that the unevenness of globalisation and international migration have strengthened Islamist movements in Bangladesh and the appeal to transnational identities.

Rejecting the presumed division between religion and politics, Islamism refers to a movement that began in the 1930s in Egypt and India, initiated by figures such as Hassan al-Banna and Abdul A'la Maududi who founded the Muslim Brotherhood and Jama'at-i Islami respectively. Their founders were not traditional fundamentalist religious figures, but modern professionals who sought alternatives to Western ideologies. Central to Islamist movements is an articulation between politics and religious norms under the guidance of Islamic law. Therefore, Islamism can be defined as 'a religious ideology that seeks to retrieve a moral-political order either by establishing

[4] Cemil Aydin (2017) makes a distinction between the concept of ummah and the idea of the Muslim world, the latter having started as a call for political unity of Muslims as subjects of European empires.

an Islamic state or by creating an ideological umma' (Cevik 2016: 15).[5] The ways in which Islam is elevated to political ideology is heavily contextual. The conflict in Mindanao, Southern Philippines, is an eloquent example of how liberation struggles can often steer towards a religious rhetoric and identity. When the Moros of Mindanao and adjacent islands in the Southern Philippines launched their armed separatist movement in the early 1970s under the leadership of the Moro National Liberation Front (MNLF), their struggle was mainly a nationalist one that aimed to establish an independent Bangsamoro (Moro nation) with its own state. Nathan Gilbert Quimpo argues that international developments – such as the circulation of radical Islamist ideas, the Soviet–Afghan War and its aftermath – as well as breakdowns in the Mindanao peace process were the main factors behind the rise of Islamism in the Moro struggle and, more recently, for the major inroads of its violent extremist form, jihadism. Quimpo traces how Islamists emerged as a major force in the Mindanao conflict, a war that has become one of the bloodiest and most protracted ethnic conflicts in Asia. Following the establishment of the Moro Islamic Liberation Front (MILF) in the 1980s, intra-Islamist competition not only supplanted Moro nationalism as the dominant ideology in the Moro struggle; Islamism also became the ideological point of reference for the Moro people. Quimpo examines the ideological spectrum of Islamism in Mindanao, including its radical and extremist variants seen in groups such as Abu Sayyaf and the jihadists affiliated with the Islamic State of Iraq and Syria (ISIS), as well as the deradicalisation of the MILF. In light of the 2019 inauguration of the Bangsamoro Autonomous Region in Muslim Mindanao (BARMM), he argues that the peace prospects in Mindanao are dependent on the Philippines government negotiations with both the Islamist MILF and the MNLF, which, in turn, face a major challenge in dealing with traditional Muslim politicians steeped in patronage politics and warlordism.

The final three chapters analyse the mechanisms through which Muslim minorities are framed as the Other in India, Myanmar and China. Within the context of intensified ethno-nationalism, the predatory identities (Appadurai 2006) of the majority Hindu, Burmese and Han populations mobilise political violence against their Muslim minorities. The tension builds on colonial legacies of racial and religious categorisations, which often led to a perception of Muslims as foreign and 'reminders of the betrayal of the classical national project' (ibid: 43). The British introduced representative politics in colonial India by differentiating between different religious groups and encouraged migration from British India to supply the colonial administration in Myanmar, which caused the disenfranchisement of the Buddhist Burman

---

[5] Recognising that not all Islamic perspectives on religion and politics can be captured under the term 'Islamism', Cevik proposes Muslimism as a new orthodoxy that intersects both liberal and fundamentalist Islam, which she illustrates among the Turkish Muslim bourgeoisie.

majority. The narrative of indigeneity plays a further role in marginalising Muslims. While in India Muslims are contrasted to the presumed indigenous Hindu population, in multi-ethnic Myanmar historical amnesia prevents the Rohingya from being recognised as one of its 135 ethnic communities. The Turkic Uyghur minority in China are not only considered unpatriotic for speaking a different language and professing a different religion but have also been increasingly targeted by the state as a national threat. Following 9/11, Muslims have been increasingly portrayed as uniquely susceptible to violence and purveyors of Islamic terrorism. Many governments have instrumentalised the global 'war on terror' discourse to justify not only religious repression but outright genocide against their Muslim populations.

Analysing how Muslims are represented in literature and political discourse, Irfan Ahmad identifies a process of Re-Orientalism in the deployment of Orientalist tropes that marginalise Muslims in India. He puts the novel *White Tiger* by Aravind Adiga (2008) and the Sachar Committee Report (SCR) (2006) in conversation with each other, in order to illustrate strategies of what he calls Hindu Orientalism. The way in which Muslims are stigmatised and erased from the story of rising India in Adiga's novel echoes the justifications from Hindutva formations to suppress the implementation of policy recommendations that address the poor socio-economic conditions of Muslims in India. Ahmad contends that the SCR was a landmark event in the modern history of India for bringing the marginalisation of Muslims in political economy and democratic life to the forefront of political debate. Nonetheless, the responses from the Bharatiya Janata Party (BJP) government and the right-wing Hindu nationalist Rashtriya Swayamsevak Sangh (RSS) subverted the issues identified by the report by superficially linking them to terrorism, separatism and anti-Indianness. Ahmad argues that the SCR was dismissed because of the triumph of Re-Orientalism against the empirically and literally demonstrated deprivation and marginality of Muslims. He closes the chapter with a reflection on the interrelationships between democracy, minorities and 'inclusive development', arguing that militarised and ceremonial democracy in India effectively undermined 'democratic sensibility as an ethos'.

In 'The Making and Unmaking of the Rohingya', Imrul Islam shows how the transmutation of Muslim identity not only led to genocide in the state of Rakhine, but also retroactively allowed the Myanmar state to justify it. Islam traces the rise of antipathy against the Rohingya from the first ethnic schisms during British colonial rule to the rise of Bamar-Buddhist nationalism, the restrictions on religious freedom of non-Buddhist minorities under military rule and the subsequent process of Burmanisation that promoted Buddhism as the official state religion. By the time the most insular country in Asia held its first democratic elections in 1990, the Rohingya had already been denied citizenship and barred from voting. As Buddhism became a political tool, with monks partaking in anti-regime protests, Buddhist far right organisations such as MaBaTha played a central role in mobilising anti-Muslim sentiment and violence. Islam describes the eruption of violence in 2012 as a precursor to genocide, with various international human rights organisations denouncing the genocidal tendencies of what was downplayed as an incident of inter-communal violence. He underlines that the Arakan Rohingya Salvation Army (ARSA), a group of Muslims who have taken up arms against police and military outposts in Rakhine, is described by the Myanmar state as a terrorist organisation and used as a justification for genocide. In her 2019 hearing at the International Court of Justice, democratic leader Aung San Suu Kyi described the clearance operations of the military – during which entire villages were razed and unthinkable atrocities committed against the Rohingya – as counter-terrorism operations. Today, there are more Rohingya living in refugee camps in Bangladesh than in Rakhine, and those who remain in Myanmar are registered as Internally Displaced Persons (IDPs). Islam argues that the framing of the Rohingya as particularly prone to violence and radicalisation is mediated by epistemic Islamophobia, which ultimately leads to the justification of violence and denial of genocide by the Myanmar state.

In the final chapter, Joanne Smith Finley examines another human rights crisis happening in Xinjiang, Northwest China, where up to one million Uyghur Muslims are extra-judicially detained in internment camps for purposes of 'political re-education'. Smith Finley draws on a series of sources, including human rights research and her fieldwork in Xinjiang, and takes a historical approach to present how the Chinese state came to this policy juncture. In contrast to the 1980s, when Deng Xiaoping's conciliatory practices allowed religious, linguistic, educational and cultural freedoms for ethnic minorities, a series of protests in the 1990s led to heavy religious restrictions and were met with disproportionate force by the Chinese authorities. The ferment of the 1990s, following the Tian'anmen Square protests and the collapse of the Soviet Union inspired Uyghurs to conceive of organised political opposition to central rule. At the same time, the Open-Door policy of the 1980s increased Uyghurs' mobility and contact with the wider Islamic world. This period of Islamic revival has been a peaceful one, during which Uyghurs not only shared a feeling of victimhood at the hands of Chinese oppression, but also found in Islam a vehicle for personal and national reform. Smith Finley argues that 'Islam was not the root cause of dissatisfaction, but rather a response', a symbol of resistance against oppression. Following the US-led 'global war on terror', the Chinese state justified the introduction of counter-terror measures in Xinjiang, which included the detention of Uyghurs on separatism charges, migration of Han settlers to Xinjiang and pre-emptive policing. Moreover, peaceful demonstrations were recast as terrorist incidents, while Uyghur Islam and the Uyghur language were perceived as national security threats. Further reforms were introduced, which led to the systematic securitisation of Uyghurs. Smith Finley argues that, while the Chinese state's ultimate goal is to protect the territorial integrity of China and to secure its northwestern border for the Belt and Road Initiative, its

securitisation policy has had the opposite effect of heightening societal insecurity in Uyghur communities and strengthening Islamic revival.

Understanding Difference

The brief exposition above shows that the chapters situate the politics of
Muslim identities in their complex histories and current social and political
dynamics. They draw on colonial legacies and political debates that defined
national trajectories, as well as regional and global developments that facilitate the exchange of ideas and people. They demonstrate that the ways in
which people draw meaning from Islam are contingent on larger social and
political dynamics at any given moment. In most cases, identity politics is
part of the colonial inheritance and becomes a hindrance to the realisation of
democratic societies. Different forms of ethno-nationalism are mirrored by
struggles for autonomy and secession. In Muslim-majority countries where
Islam is often embedded in the state structure, there exist intra-Muslim
contestation around orthodox Islam and often the persecution of minorities, while in pluralist societies living in relative peace inter-ethnic tensions
surface in conjunction with other social issues or global developments. This
deeply embedded politics of difference can engender tragic outcomes, as
some of the chapters show. Superficial, essentialist accounts of difference
have to be criticised, confronted and dismissed to promote a thorough
understanding of our human and historical contexts.

In this sense, we need to reflect on a few key questions. How is alterity
produced and further perpetuated in scholarly discourse? What are the
consequences of such an awareness of alterity in everyday life, in the way in
which one perceives the world and interacts with others? Namely, how are
Islam and Muslims theorised and perceived as different? How are boundaries
drawn between Muslims and non-Muslims, among Muslims themselves?
What are the contingent politics and ideologies that sustain and promote such
divisions? In the rising climates of populism, xenophobia and Islamophobia,
it is imperative that we reflect on how identity boundaries and alterity are
politicised and ideologised towards divisive ends. By *situating the politics of
Muslim identities*, I hope that we can move away from essentialising, understand Islam and Muslim identities in their diversity and reflect on the contingent politics within which discrete forms of being and belonging unfold.

*Some chapters in this volume were presented as part of the Seminar Series
on Muslim Societies in Asia that the editor organised at the S. Rajaratnam
School of International Studies (RSIS), Nanyang Technological University (NTU),
Singapore, from 2016 to 2018. My sincerest gratitude goes to my colleagues and
friends at RSIS, Saleena Saleem, Chan Xin Ying, Rashaad Ali and Najwa Abdullah
Sungkar, as well as Dr Farish Noor and Dr Leon Moosavi for their support and guidance. I am very fortunate to have worked with and learnt from them and stay hopeful
for the generations they continue to inspire.*

References

Ahmad, I. (2017), *Religion as Critique: Islamic Critical Thinking from Mecca to the Marketplace*. Chapel Hill: University of North Carolina Press.

Ahmed, S. (2016), *What is Islam? The Importance of Being Islamic*. Princeton: Princeton University Press.

Alatas, S. F. and Sinha, V. (2017), *Sociological Theory Beyond the Canon*. London: Palgrave Macmillan.

Al-Azmeh, A. (1996), *Islams and Modernities*. London: Verso.

Al-Azmeh, A. (2003), 'Postmodern Obscurantism and the Muslim Question', *Journal for the Study of Religions and Ideologies* 2(5): 21–47.

Appadurai, A. (2006), *Fear of Small Numbers: An Essay on the Geography of Anger*. Durham: Duke University Press.

Asad, T. (1986), *The Idea of an Anthropology of Islam* (Occasional Paper Series, Center for Contemporary Arab Studies). Washington, DC: Georgetown University.

Asad, T. (1993), 'The Construction of Religion as an Anthropological Category', in Talal Asad, *Genealogies of Religion: Discipline and Reasons of Power in Christianity and Islam*, 22–27. Baltimore: Johns Hopkins University Press.

Aydin, C. (2017), *The Idea of the Muslim World: A Global Intellectual History*. Cambridge, MA: Harvard University Press.

Bowen, J. (2012), *A New Anthropology of Islam*. Cambridge: Cambridge University Press.

Cevik, N. (2016). *Muslimism in Turkey and Beyond: Religion in the Modern World*. New York: Palgrave Macmillan US.

Coleman, S. (2013), 'Afterword: De-Exceptionalising Islam', in M. Marsden and K. Retsikas (eds), *Articulating Islam: Anthropological Approaches to Muslim Worlds*. Dordrecht: Springer.

Eickelman, D. F. and Piscatori, J. (2004), *Muslim Politics*. Princeton: Princeton University Press.

El-Zein, A. (1977), 'Beyond Ideology and Theology: The Search for the Anthropology of Islam', *Annual Review of Anthropology* 6: 227–54.

Fitzgerald, T. (2008), *Discourse on Civility and Barbarity: A Critical History of Religion and Related Concepts*. Oxford: Oxford University Press.

Geertz, C. (1971), *Islam Observed: Religious Development in Morocco and Indonesia*. Chicago: University of Chicago Press.

Gellner, E. (1981), *Muslim Society* (Cambridge Studies in Social Anthropology, 32). Cambridge: Cambridge University Press.

Gellner, E. (1990), 'The Civil and the Sacred', *The Tanner Lectures on Human Values*.

Hefner, Robert W. and Horvatich, P. (1997), *Islam in an Era of Nation-States: Politics and Religious Renewal in Muslim Southeast Asia*. Honolulu: University of Hawaii Press.

Hodgson, M. (1993), *Rethinking World History: Essays on Europe, Islam and World History*. Cambridge: Cambridge University Press.

Hughes, A. (2013), *Muslim Identities: An Introduction*. New York: Columbia University Press.

Huntington, S. P. (1993), 'The Clash of Civilisations?', *Foreign Affairs* 72(3): 22–49.

Mamdani, M. (2002), 'Good Muslim, Bad Muslim: A Political Perspective on Culture and Terrorism', *American Anthropologist* 104(3): 766–75.

Marsden, M. and Retsikas, K. (2013). *Articulating Islam: Anthropological Approaches to Muslim Worlds*. Dordrecht: Springer.

Mirsepassi, A. and Graham, T. (2015), *Islam, Democracy and Cosmopolitanism: At Home and in the World*. Cambridge: Cambridge University Press.

Salvatore, A. (2009), 'Tradition and Modernity within Islamic Civilization and the West', in Muhammad Khalid Masud, Armando Salvatore and Martin Bruinessen (eds), *Islam and Modernity: Key Issues and Debates*. Edinburgh: Edinburgh University Press.

Pregill, M. E. (2017), 'I Hear Islam Singing: Shahab Ahmed's *What is Islam? The Importance of Being Islamic*', *Harvard Theological Review* 101(1): 149–65.

Salvatore, A. (2013), 'The Sociology of Islam: Precedents and Perspectives', *Sociology of Islam* 1(1): 7–13.

Sayyid, S. (2012), 'Empire, Islam and the Postcolonial', *MnM Working Paper No 9*, International Centre for Muslim and Non-Muslim Understanding, University of South Australia.

Soares, B. and Osella, F. (2009), 'Islam, Politics, Anthropology', *The Journal of the Royal Anthropological Institute* 15: 1–23.

Varisco, D. (2005), *Islam Obscured: The Rhetoric of Anthropological Representation*. New York: Palgrave Macmillan US.

Zubaida, S. (1995), 'Is There a Muslim Society? Ernest Gellner's Sociology of Islam', *Economy and Society* 24(2): 151–88.

SPECULATIVE VERSES OF ISLAM IN SINGAPORE MALAY LITERATURE

Nazry Bahrawi

The discourse of Islamic thought should not be confined to the normative fields of *fiqh, usuluddin,* shari'ah laws and *tafsir.* It can also be seen in literature, even though this discipline has been marginal to Islamic studies. This article aims to address this gap. It begins from the acknowledgment that literary fiction channels and shapes Islamic thought if we consider the well-known cases of Salman Rushdie's *The Satanic Verses* and Naguib Mahfouz's *Awlad Haritna.* Like their peers in Muslim cultures elsewhere, Malay / Muslim writers in Singapore, too, have engaged deeply with Islamic thought in their works. What are their sensibilities? This chapter will explore their works as aspiration and critique of the state of Islamic practices in the Republic. It considers Malay literature produced in both Bahasa and English. First, it will situate Singapore Malay literature within the region of Muslim Southeast Asia by tracing its responses to ideas such as Sastera Islam in Malaysia and Sastera Profetik in Indonesia. Then, it will consider selected contemporary works from Malay writers in Singapore in order to arrive at a sense of the evolution and trajectory of Islamic thought in contemporary literature.

Sometime in the early twelfth century, the Andalusian Muslim polymath Ibn Tufayl released unto the world *Hayy Ibn Yaqzan,* one of the medieval world's most renowned works of philosophical fiction (Goodman 2003). The text recounts the allegorical tale of the titular feral child raised in the wild, who came to discover that the abstract truth about the cosmos is congruent with the teachings of Islam. His awakening was entirely the product of his own observation of the natural world, with Hayy only officially professing Islam at the mature age of thirty, when he first encountered another human being, Salaman. Scholars have written about the text's influence on European philosophy, particularly the British empiricism peddled by John Locke (Aravamudan 2014), as well as for inspiring imaginative works about feral children and undiscovered worlds, such as Daniel Defoe's *Robinson Crusoe* (1719) (Lamont 2002). Little has been written about its impact on and links to

Islamic thought. This is unfortunate considering that the treatise was penned in the hope of speaking to the Islamic practices of its day. For instance, it can be read as propagating the idea that theology and rational thought had developed in tandem rather than in opposition. The academic afterlife of *Hayy Ibn Yaqzan* is a fitting example of a lacuna that exists in the field of contemporary Islamic studies. To put it simply, there has been little emphasis on investigating the ebb and flow of Islamic thought from the perspective of literary studies. It is a gap that this chapter hopes to modestly plug. Focusing on Singapore, it aims to depict a bird's-eye view of the evolution of the city-state's Islamic intellectual landscape by way of literary texts produced by its minority Muslims. In doing so, it hopes to introduce readers to the complex articulations of Muslim identities in a multi-religious state sandwiched between two bigger majority-Muslim nations, Malaysia and Indonesia. This chapter has the objective of demonstrating that a literary study of Islam can be generative. To begin on this odyssey is to first unpack the concept of literary Islam.

The Case for Literary Islam

The intersections between literature and Islam that punctuate Ibn Tufayl's philosophical fiction continues well into the twentieth century, in the form of two novels by Muslim authors. These are *Awlad Haritna* (*Children of Gebelawi*) by the Nobel Prize winner Naguib Mahfouz of Egypt and *The Satanic Verses* by Salman Rushdie, a Pakistani-British author. To qualify, these novels are not commensurable with the way in which *Hayy Ibn Yaqzan* directly intervenes in the practice of Islamic theology to champion the use of reason for the worship of God. Rather, the two allegorise aspects of Islamic history to represent non-religious themes such as dictatorship and repression in Egypt in the case of Mahfouz, as well as migration and alienation of Indians in England in the case of Rushdie. Yet, the authors' respective recourses to Islamic history have resulted in the issuance of a fatwa calling for their deaths by Islamic clerics. These have had some life-threatening consequences. For instance, the Japanese translator of Rushdie's book, Hitoshi Igarashi, was murdered in 1991, while Mahfouz was stabbed (but fortunately survived) in 1994. Their examples strengthen the case for the study of literature as a mode of critical inquiry into Islamic thought and practices, which is the method that I will adopt in this essay. A good start is to consider the varied ways in which this has been done. To this end, I will touch on three works, focusing on the parts relevant to this study. Two of them relate to the Malay Archipelago where Singapore is situated.

The first is Ziad Elmarsafy's *Sufism in the Contemporary Arabic Novel* (2012), which explores the use of Sufi aesthetics in the works of six Arab novelists, including Naguib Mahfouz. Qualifying that his study is meant to be illustrative and not exhaustive, Elmarsafy theoretically grounds his book primarily in Western discourses of aesthetics. He begins with Derek Attridge's argument that literature is the 'creation of the other' where otherness in Attridge's words refers to 'that which is, at a given moment, outside the horizon provided by the culture for thinking, understanding, imagining, feeling, perceiving' (Elmarsafy 2012). Elmarsafy modifies Attridge's position to argue that this otherness can be articulated as 'divine and human variants' when one is considering the appropriation of Sufi symbols in the contemporary Arabic novel, even if Attridge insists that it should not include 'the mystical belief in an exterior agent' (ibid: 2). With this premise, Elmarsafy goes on to show in his chosen works the manners in which Sufi images and idioms in the contemporary Arabic novel should not be simply seen as responding to political events or historical phases. Rather, they delve deep into the universal themes of 'love, desire, hospitality and survival' (ibid: 11). I echo Elmarsafy's penchant for hybridity. That is to say, the works that I have chosen here will not just be taken as indicative of specific political events or historic phases in Singapore. They may touch on these, but they also deal with themes concerning the constitution of the self, which are psychological and philosophical in nature.

A second pertinent work is Ronit Ricci's *Islam Translated* (2011) which trains its critical eye on a single text, *The Book of One Thousand Questions*. Originally penned in Arabic sometime in the tenth century, this text fictionalises a dialogue between the Prophet and a Jewish interlocutor named Ibnu Salam. Ricci analyses its Malay, Javanese and Tamil translations to theorise the existence of an Arabic cosmopolis which is built on an extensive literary network spanning parts of South and Southeast Asia and whose members had localised and vernacularised Arabic and Islamic texts. For instance, the Javanese version of the book repositioned Ibnu Salam as a Javanese guru rather than as a Jewish scholar, as pointed out by Muhammad Ali in his review of the book (2013: 879). The value of Ricci's work to this research pertains to the intricate ways in which a literary text mobilises Islamic motifs to speak to its immediate context. The works that I have chosen perform the same function.

Finally, I would like to refer to my own 2016 essay 'Textual Desires', published in the magazine *Critical Muslim* (Bahrawi 2016). There, I argue that literariness is a principal feature of Southeast Asian Islam, by pointing to several premodern and modern examples. Two are instructive here. First, I point to a poem written in the sixteenth century by the mystic-poet Hamzah Fansuri from Aceh. Translated as *Poem XXII* by Peter Riddell, this work employs the use of metaphorical language to lend credence to the Sufi doctrine of *wahdatul wujud*. This doctrine proposes that Godliness is inherent in human beings and encourages a 'unity of being' between creator and creation by way of worship and meditation. In essence, *wahdatul wujud* runs counter the legalistic bent of the shari'ah-minded Islamic clerics of Fansuri's day. It does so by appealing to *ijtihad* (independent reasoning) in the way in which Fansuri had written against the grain that God is unattainable to the ordinary Muslims. A second example is the 1995 novella *TIVI* by Malaysia's National

Laureate Shahnon Ahmad. The work utilises what Shahnon describes as the literary technique of *juzuk azab* or 'divine retribution' to emulate the fire and brimstone parts of the Qur'an. The novel features a sexually decadent family whose members are eventually struck down by lightning. *TIVI* can be considered one of several examples of works from Malaysia that uphold the concept of Sastera Islam, which sees literature as a form of worship (*ibadah*), channelling the Qur'anic injunction to enjoin the good and forbid the evil that can be found in verses 3:110, 3:114 and 7:157 (ibid:74). Other examples abound in my essay, but suffice it here to say that that the two examples I have furnished demonstrate literariness as a feature common to Southeast Asian Islam, regardless of their leanings. Situated at the heart of Southeast Asia, Singapore is not exempt from the impact of these larger regional trends.

Singapore's Islamic Landscape

One of the most widely used terms that one will encounter while researching about Islam in Singapore is the label 'Malay/Muslim' or 'Malay-Muslim'. Its use is widespread by Singaporeans of all ilk. It can be said that the term has been seared into the local lingo through the media, political speeches and everyday conversations. Indeed, the term surmises the Republic's approach and practice of Islam. Linguistically, an absence of the slash or dash would produce the term 'Malay Muslim' or 'Muslim Malay' where the second word in the pair constitutes the noun and the first its adjective. The implication of the slash's absence would be that there are Muslims who are Malays in the case of the first pair, or that there are Malays who are Muslims in the case of the second. However, the presence of the slash or dash between the two words suggests that we are encountering two nouns which are related and possibly equivalent. In other words, it signals that Malays are synonymous to Muslims. Is there some truth to this? If we consider Singapore's demographic patterns, the equivalence between the two identities is backed by statistical evidence. The 2010 census records that 98.7 percent of the Malays are Muslims, a slight decrease from 2000 when this was recorded at 99.6 percent (Singapore Census of Population 2010). Culturally, this has led to the phenomenon articulated as *masuk Islam, masuk Melayu* or 'to become a Muslim is to become Malay', referring to the idea that embracing Islam also means taking on Malayness as an ethnic identity marker.

This intermingling of religion and race means that mapping Singapore's Islamic landscape requires some understanding of its ethnic landscape, too. Here, Malays count as a minority group in Singapore. The 2010 census has it that they form 13.4 percent of Singapore residents, which is not too far from the 13.9 percent recorded in 2000 (ibid). Yet, the censuses do not capture the complexities surrounding Malayness as a racial identity. To begin, Article 152(2) of the Singapore constitution defines the Malays as 'the indigenous people of Singapore', while Article 5 of the same constitution upholds a member of the Malay community as anyone who considers himself or herself to be a member and is accepted as such, regardless of whether that person is 'of the Malay race or otherwise' (Constitution of the Republic of Singapore). Speaking at a forum, Singapore constitutional law expert Kevin Tan points out that this later definition suggests that the Malay race is a social construct because it is 'next to impossible to define who is or is not a Malay' (Chan 2017).

Tan's commentary channels critiques of Singapore's racialist approach to governance often articulated as the CMIO model – an abbreviation for Chinese, Malay, Indian and Others. These very categories structure the census. They also inform other policies dealing with social issues, public housing and political representation. For instance, Singapore dispenses social aid by way of ethnic-based self-help groups such as the Singapore Indian Development Association (SINDA) for the Indians, the Chinese Development Assistance Council (CDAC) for the Chinese and the Council for the Development of Singapore Malay/Muslim Community (*Yayasan Mendaki*) for the Malays. In a seminal study focused on policies relating to Singapore Malays in the 1990s, Lily Zubaidah Rahim points out that Singapore's ethnic-based self-help groups have led to 'unequal engines of support' for Singapore's underachievers (Zubaidah Rahim 1998). For instance, she points to generous financial incentives that the CDAC dispensed to Chinese unskilled labourers in 1992 to upgrade themselves, which members of the Indian and Malay communities did not receive. This had put the former in a position where he or she 'is more likely to attain higher qualifications and greater possibilities of social mobility compared to the non-Chinese worker' (ibid: 238–9).

Complications are also evident within the Malay community itself. The master category of 'Malay' encompasses various ethnic groups from the region of maritime Southeast Asia, such as Javanese, Boyanese, Bugis, Sundanese and Banjarese, to name a few. Then, there are Arab, Pakistani and Indian Muslims who do not come from outside the region but can be considered culturally Malay by way of intermarriage or their practice of Malay culture, which includes the use of the Malay language as a lingua franca. This nuance is best embodied in the personage of the nineteenth-century literary figure Abdullah Abdul Kadir, popularly known as Munshi Abdullah. Given his motley ancestry of Arab, Tamil and Malay, Abdullah is often described as a Jawi Peranakan, which refers to a Muslim person of Indian and Malay heritage who was born in the Malay Archipelago. Despite his complicated ethnic mix, Abdullah has also been hailed as the 'father of modern Malay literature' on the back cover of some of his innovative creative works in the Malay language, the most famous being *The Hikayat Abdullah*. I will revisit some of these later.

Moving on to Islam proper, it is important to consider the history of its administration given Singapore's penchant for institutional governance. Muslims in Singapore are predominantly Sunnis who practises the Shafi'i jurisprudence school of thought (*madhab*). They are governed on personal matters relating to marriage and divorce, property, financial provision and the like by the Administration of Muslim Law Act (AMLA), introduced the year after the Republic's independence in 1966 and implemented in 1968. The legislation is supported by Article 153 of the constitution, which states that 'legislature shall by law make provisions for regulating Muslim religious affairs and for constituting a Council to advise the President in matters relating to the Muslim religion' (Administration of Muslim Law Act). The implementation of AMLA has led to the creation of several state institutions whose mandate is the administration of Islam in different spheres. Foremost among these is the Islamic Religious Council of Singapore (MUIS). The statutory board is in charge of several functions concerning the religious lives of Muslims. These include the administration of mosques, the formal and informal education of Islamic religious knowledge which includes the training of Islamic clerics (*asatizah*), the management of *wakf* properties and *zakat* (tithe), as well as matters pertaining to halal certification and the Muslim pilgrimage to Mecca (hajj). MUIS is also home to the office of the Mufti, the highest seat of Islamic authority who is appointed by the president. This unit looks after the affairs of religious life of Singapore Muslims by dispensing fatwas (Islamic religious rulings) and *irsyad* (religious advisory) on issues concerning the contemporary practice of Islam in Singapore. It has, for instance, issued a fatwa recommending the performance of more than one round of Friday prayers and the bringing forward of the Friday prayers in light of the COVID-19 outbreak. The Mufti's office is also responsible for crafting sermons that are read across mosques during Friday prayers, as well as the morning prayers for Eid. Another important institution that is enabled by AMLA is the Syariah Court, which looks after cases of Muslim marriage, divorce, annulment and related matters arising from divorce such as the custody of children. According to Noor Aisha and Azhar, the purview of the court in cases of divorce is to 'salvage a broken marriage as far as possible', to the point of recommending counselling as the first course of action (Noor Aisha and Ibrahim 2017). The AMLA also stipulates that Muslims donate a portion of their monthly salary ranging between S$3 and S$26 according to the specified tiers to the Mosque Building and Mendaki Fund (MBMF). The fund's earnings are meant to fulfil three functions: to finance educational and social programmes for Malay/Muslim families through the self-help group Mendaki; to build, upgrade and develop mosques; and to support future and existing needs concerning Islamic religious education. This is not compulsory, as AMLA also allows for Muslims to opt out from contributing to the MBMF fund.

The strongly institutionalised nature of Islam in Singapore is supported by the presence of non-state actors collectively known as Malay/Muslim Organisations (MMOs). Two of them are worth mentioning here. The first is Persatuan Ulama dan Guru-Guru Agama Islam Singapura (Pergas) or Singapore Islamic Scholars and Religious Teachers Association. Established in 1957, the organisation has the objective of looking after the development of *asatizah* in Singapore. To this end, it runs a weekly madrasah that offers certification such as Arabic Language and Certification in Islamic studies and a bachelor's degree in Islamic Revealed Knowledge and Heritage, in collaboration with the International Islamic University Malaysia. Pergas also offers scholarships and financial assistance to students pursuing Islamic studies at different levels of education. An MMO institution that fulfils a unique function in Singapore's Islamic landscape is the Muslim Converts' Association of Singapore, or Darul Arqam. It was established in 1980 by a group of Muslims, including converts, who felt the need 'to explain and discuss Islam in English and other languages' (Green and Tahir 2016: 523). They did so with the objective of staving off the pressure of *masuk Islam, masuk Melayu*. Since their founding, the group has run several programmes, including the administration of Muslim converts, which includes pre-conversion and post-conversion education courses, as well as a legal clinic by volunteer lawyers offering legal advice to those who cannot afford it. Other MMOs deliver a range of religious and social programmes such as managing madrasahs, welfare homes and childcare centres.

Singapore's Islamic landscape is not without its challenges. For the purpose of this essay, I will be focusing on the issue of non-violent religious resurgence among the Malays, as it appears as a predominant theme in literary works produced by Singapore's Malay/Muslims. While this essay will adhere to the term religious resurgence, it is important to note that the same religious orientation has been described as traditionalist-revivalists by Azhar Ibrahim to mean the proponents of an exclusivist form of Islam that views themselves as 'the true custodians and interpreters of Islam' (Azhar Ibrahim 2019a: 24). According to Noor Aisha, this had become 'so dominant that it negates, marginalises and silences competing Malay thought and perspectives that are vital to the development and well-being of the community and the larger society' (Noor Aisha 2019: 33). She outlines several features: first, its proponents believe in the Islamisation of knowledge as an ideological chastisement of what they deem to be Westernised, secular knowledge that is taught in Singapore's public schools. Enrolment has increased in Singapore's six full-time madrasahs, where students are required to learn Islamic and non-Islamic subjects, to the point that the government had to cap it at 400 places (Channel Newsasia 2015). Noor Aisha also pointed out that the madrasah's religious education and pedagogy have not been critically appraised to ensure its compatibility with 'the demands of Singapore society and the modern world' (ibid: 44). Its students, for instance, have little knowledge of prominent Muslim thinkers from the region. Second, Muslim resurgents have essentialised the shari'ah by defining it as an unchanging set of rules and regulations. This is problematic because it ignores the historical and societal context of Singapore. Noor Aisha points to several examples, but one is worth mentioning here as it demonstrates their begrudging resignation as a minority group. The first is the support of *hudud*, or punishments derived from the Qur'an and hadith, which is allegedly mandated by the shari'ah. Here, they recommend that apostates are subjected to 'a discretion-ary form of punishment to be determined by an "Islamic authority"' (ibid: 48), which ignores the scholarship of Muslim scholars who reject such pun-ishments on the premise that it counters the principles of freedom, compas-sion, justice and mercy which are congruent with Islamic teachings. While the resurgents are supportive of *hudud*, they accept their exemption for it on account of being 'political emasculated as a minority' (ibid).

Pan-Nusantara Literary Affinities

Singapore literature is often described as works produced in its four 'mother tongue' languages – English, Malay, Mandarin and Tamil. Compared to English works, those produced in Malay reveal a close connection to their literary counterparts in Singapore's immediate neighbouring countries of Malaysia, Indonesia and Brunei, all of which are home to a Malay-majority population. This is not to say that literary works in other languages show no such bearings. For instance, Brian Bernards' study of Sinophone literature in *Writing the South Seas* (2015) draws comparison between Chinese-language works in Singapore and Malaysia. Yet, the degree to which Malay literary writings actively refer to each other suggests intense trans-national influ-ences and confluences. In no small part, this has to do with the historic ties between Singapore and Malaysia. Following their independence from Britain, Singapore merged with the Federation of Malaya to form Malaysia in 1963. Nearly three years later, in 1965, the two parted ways when Singapore became a sovereign republic following disagreements between the state and federal governments on race relations and economic matters.

An instance of this interconnectedness can be seen in the development of the Malay literary arts organisation Angkatan Sasterawan '50, or Asas '50. Established in 1950, this Singapore-based Malay literary arts organisation pledges to pursue the ideals of 'art for society's sake' (*seni untuk masyarakat*) to distance itself from the literary practice of 'art for art's sake' (*seni untuk seni*). Disagreeing with the left-leaning orientation of the former, founding member Hamzah Hussin left Asas '50 in 1954 to form Angkatan Persuratan Melayu Baru to champion the latter. Following separation, other found-ing members such as Keris Mas and Usman Awang left Singapore for Malaysia. As a result of this brain drain, activities slowed down, but Asas '50 continued its operation. Continuing its pursuit as a Singapore institution into the twenty-first century, its members included prominent Singapore Malay writers such as the Cultural Medallion winners Mohamed Latiff Mohamed and Suratman Markasan. This movement resonates with the ideals of another literary organisation in neighbouring Indonesia. This is Lembaga Kebudayaan Rakyat (Lekra), or Institute for the People's Culture, also founded in 1950. Affiliated with the Indonesian Communist Party (PKI), Lekra championed socialist realism as an art form. With famous figures such as Pramoedya Ananta Toer and Affandi as members, they believed

that art must reflect 'realities' on the ground and take on the activist function of changing things for the better. So zealous was their belief in this
cause that they engaged in a cultural boycott of signatories to the Manifesto
Kebudayaan, or Cultural Manifesto, which upheld an expansive view of
the arts as not needing to be realist or political. Lekra was disbanded in
1965, as result of the anti-communist purge following a failed coup that
was blamed on the PKI, although the scholarship on this event points to a
divide concerning the veracity of this claim. The regionwide movement for
socialist realism suggests that the evolution of Malay literature in Singapore
cannot be divorced from what is happening in the region, also known as the
Nusantara.

An Islam-oriented pan-Nusantara ideology that had some bearing
on Malay literature in Singapore is the above-mentioned Sastera Islam.
Translated directly as 'Islamic literature', this was the result of the *dakwah*
(propagation) movement calling for Malays in Malaysia to embrace Islam
as a complete way of life (*deen*) during the 1970s and the 1980s, as observed
by the literary scholar Ungku Maimunah (1989). Sastera Islam is a reaction
against the 'art for society' movement embraced by Lekra and Asas '50.
According to its main ideologue Shahnon Ahmad, the latter is materialistic
and lacks spirituality. As a counter-point, Sastera Islam is instead better seen
as the pursuit of 'art for Allah's sake'. As I have argued in my essay, the
ideology of Sastera Islam upholds a view of Islam as fixed and Muslims as a
monolithic whole, which in turn supports the practice of *taqlid* or the uncritical acceptance of traditional Islamic teachings (Bahrawi 2016: 75).

However, Sastera Islam is not the only articulation of Islam in modern
Nusantara literature. Another literary reflection has been expressed as
Sastera Profetik, or Prophetic Literature, which is tracecable primarily to the
Indonesian author Kuntowijoyo and, to a lesser extent, Abdul Hadi W. M.
and Emha Ainun Nadjib. According to Kuntowijoyo, Sastera Profetik has
three elements: humanisation, liberation and transcendence. Channelling the
work of Jabrohim of Universitas Ahmad Dahlan (2015) who has interpreted
Kuntowijoyo's concept, each of these means a specific thing in literary works
related to Indonesia. Humanisation is the act of countering dehumanisa-
tion in the way in which the public has behaved like a mass of uncritical
automatons, leading to a state of spiritual alienation. Liberation refers to the
resistance against external and internal instances of hegemony. An instance
of external hegemony is one exercised by a powerful state over a weaker
one, as is happening between Israel and Palestine, while an instance of
internal hegemony can be seen during the reign of Indonesia's New Order
government. Finally, transcendence refers to an awareness of Godliness that
could also be described as sufistic. However, the essence of transcendence
in Sastera Profetik is not specific to Islam but can refer to a general acknowledgment of divinity beyond the human. When it is expressed as sufistic by
Kuntowijoyo, this essence includes the invocation of qualities such as *khauf*
(fear), *raja'* (hope), *tawakkal* (submission), *qana'ah* (acceptance of God's gifts)

and others. In this sense, Sastera Profetik is not too different from Sastera Islam. Both movements stem from the premise that literature is an act that enjoins the good and forbids the evil, as sanctioned by the Qur'an. However, it is important to note that Sastera Profetik is not concerned with legalistic practices of Islam. Rather, it privileges the spiritual, like Hamzah Fansuri's precept of *wahdatul wujud* in his premodern literary poems.

Speculating Islam in Singapore Malay Literature

Two qualifications need to be made about my analysis of Malay literature in Singapore. First, I am taking an expansive view of what qualifies as 'Malay literature'. While Singapore is prone to categorising its literatures by way of language, I include as Malay literature English-language works produced by Malays on issues relating to Malay lives, themes and issues. This stems from the argument that culture is not a static phenomenon and intersects with other spheres, such as language and religion. It is also a refusal to endorse the above-mentioned racialist practice of *masuk Islam, masuk Melayu*. To this end, I am recognising the view that Malayness is not traceable to one's skin colour or heritage, but a life-style choice and a worldview. In this section, I will consider the evolution of Singapore Malay literature and its intersections with Islam in three periods – colonial, post-independence and contemporary. A case can be made to consider pre-colonial literary works such as *Sejarah Melayu*, or the *Malay Annals*, but I am choosing to focus on these three periods as they are the immediate precursor and consequences of the nation-state. A briefer second qualification has to do with the fact that this study cannot be taken as an instructive quantitative analysis of the entirety of Malay literature in Singapore. Taking a leaf from Elmarsafy's study, this analysis is meant to be illustrative. I will outline a select group of writers to draw attention to trends, or patterns, that are related to Islamic thought in Singapore. As far as possible, it will consider works by male and female writers in pursuit of gender diversity. This is why it will refer to lesser-known writers such as Helmilina Muhamad Som, as opposed to Isa Kamari who is more prolific.

We begin with Munshi Abdullah, the father of modern Malay literature, who produced works in the nineteenth century, during the period of British colonisation. Writing at a time when the nation-state was not yet conceptualised, Abdullah cannot be comfortably called a Singapore or Malaysian writer. Rather, he was a Malayan writer who lived and traversed between Melaka and Singapore, and eventually passed in Jeddah while on the hajj. Given the interconnectedness of Malay literature in the region, Abdullah arguably is part of the tradition that makes up Singapore Malay literature. His views on the Islamic practices of his day can be found in his magnum opus *The Hikayat Abdullah* written between 1840 and 1843. In an interesting section complete with illustrations, Abdullah describes a bevy of Malay supernatural beings such as the *polong* and the *penanggalan* (1970: 116). Even as he demonstrates a deep knowledge of the mythologies and legends surrounding these beings, Abdullah stresses that the belief in and fear of them will cause *shirk* or the attribution of divinity to someone other than Allah. In this sense, Abdullah was an unflinching believer in the principle of *tawhid*, the principle of one indivisible God. This instance reveals that Abdullah privileges the use of reason over the belief in *adat*, which is the Malay word for customs or traditions. By way of Islamic orientation, Abdullah can be considered a reformist whose theological ideals were unencumbered by superstition and borne from the process of logic.

Traces of Abdullah's orientation can also be seen in the post-independence works of the Singapore author Mohamed Latiff Mohamed. Here, we can consider his short story 'Creepy Crawlies' composed in the 1980s. The story features an unnamed protagonist narrating his experience of insects taking over his body and stealing his rice. The young man begins the story by generously allowing the insects to explore his body because he acknowledges that they are God's creatures, just like him. However, the insects then launch an intense attack on his mortal coil so unbearable that he begins vomiting worms. The protagonist also begins to wonder if his experience is real or a hallucination. In desperation, the young man begins reciting the *shahadah* and *Fatiha*. The last paragraph reads:

> I decide to recite the *kalimah syahadah*. I utter the *Fatiha* repeatedly. I realise I have become the symbol of a Muslim repeled by his own image. I continue to swim in the illusion of His Oneness. I surrender myself to nature. (2017: 38).

Read symbolically, the story thematises human hubris. It addresses the Islamic view that assigns humans the custodianship of the planet as its *khalifah*, or vicegerent, as advised in the Qur'anic verse 2:30. The story suggests that humanity has, in fact, shunned this responsibility and exploited nature to the point that we can no longer avoid the repercussion.

Another story written in 2003 seems to echo this sentiment. Titled 'Virus X', the story is written as a piece of science fiction by female author Helmilina Muhamad Som. It takes the perspective of the leader of a pathogen who goes by the moniker 'Ketua X' or 'X Chief' as he embarks on an all-out war with the human race. The story was composed in the same year as the SARS outbreak in Singapore, signalling its inspiration in real life. Like 'Creepy Crawlies', the story can also be read as a critique of human hubris. One paragraph reads:

> Humans have labeled themselves brilliant. Their creations are not original but had long been articulated in the Holy Book. They are too arrogant to admit that these ideas were not theirs. They will not surrender to destiny and will try all means to change their fate. Without a care for halal and haram. To them, anything goes. Humans have forgotten that intentions are not equatable to the halal way. (2003: 138–39, translation mine)

Both stories employ the *juzuk azab* technique outlined by Shahnon Ahmad, in the sense that characters are subjected to excruciating pain at an unexpected time. Yet, it is also notable that neither story settles neatly into the category of Sastera Islam. 'Virus X' seems to tick all the boxes as a normative Sastera Islam story, especially in the way in which it privileges the jurisprudence element of Islam when it references 'the halal way'. The story also seems to uphold Islamic supremacy in its claim of how the Qur'an has already specified all the inventions that humanity upholds as 'original'. On the other hand, 'Creepy Crawlies' does neither. The story trains its critique on the abuse of nature. Its recourse to Islam is meant to soothe, not to punish. Between the two, 'Creepy Crawlies' lends credence to Abdullah's reformist bent, continuing on his call to employ reason in the practice of Islam. 'Virus X', however, appears to propagate the notion of Islam as *deen*, as a source of not just ethics, but also human creation.

Yet another religious orientation can be gleaned from Singapore's Malay literary works. I would describe them as *tasawuf* literature or works that thematise Sufi doctrines or some form of spirituality. A contemporary work that embodies this is *Iftitah*, a collection of poems by Muhammad Khairool Haque. The 2019 poetry collection is marked by a clear absence of the *juzuk azab* technique. In fact, they can be described as non-didactic. There is some recourse to *dakwah*, or Islamic propagation, but it is not done through the invocation of a vengeful, punitive God who rules by might and spite. Instead, readers will encounter sublime verses that prod deeper reflection. Take, for instance, the short poem titled 'Esok Hari Raya', translatable to 'Tomorrow's Hari Raya':

> Tomorrow's Hari Raya
> but we haven't
> even started
> truly fasting. (2019: 98, translation mine)

The same sense of sublimity can also be seen in Fairoz Ahmad's contemporary short story 'The Day the Music Died', which approaches religiosity from a philosophical lens. The 2019 story narrates the fantastical tale of one fateful Thursday when melody and rhythm disappear from Earth, to the point that the muezzin bungles the daily call for prayers at the mosque. He is tied up and outcast to the edge of town by the public who cannot take his monotonous call. They interpret the event to be a sign that *qiyamat*, the end of the world, is near. Strangely, things return to normal the next day. The muezzin manages to escape his shackles. His voice is once again harmonious. The public has seemingly forgotten the extraordinary event, and no one ever brings it up again.

While Fairoz's story was written in a style just as subliminal as Khairool's poem, the difference between them is that Islamic theology does not appear front and centre in the former. The story does not have a clear agenda. It begs a variety of non-exhaustive questions. Is the draw of religion reliant primarily on its aesthetics? Or are humans really interested in a deep engagement with religiosity beyond its formal qualities? The lack of a clear message to the story adds to its appeal. More importantly, the story is a departure from the realist narrative bent of Munshi Abdullah. Rather, it is penned in the form of a fable and introduces its readership to the idea of enchantment, which upholds that not everything in the world has a rational explanation or clear conclusion. Mysteries are part of life, and in fact inform the way we live. To this end, there is sufficient cause to speculate that Abdullah would not have been too pleased with the magical elements of Fairoz's story. Both Khairool and Fairoz's short stories seem closer in orientation to Kuntowijoyo's concept of Sastera Profetik, particularly in regard to its recourse to the third theme of transcendence.

Yet another fantastical piece of contemporary Malay literary work worth mentioning is *The Gatekeeper*, a 2017 novel by Nuraliah Norasid. Clinching the Epigram Books Fiction Prize a year before its release, the book imagines a city named Manticurra, much like Singapore, where humans live along-side mythical creatures. The protagonist is Ria, a female medusa who has been outcast to the underground settlement Nelroote after she unleashes her power and turns several policemen into stone for attempting to take her sisters away from her home in the name of land redevelopment. The story is an allegory of modern Singapore and feeds into the Malays' sentiments of dispossession; many of them had to relocate from their villages (*kampong*) to public housing in the years following the Republic's independence. In an interesting hybrid of Malay and Greek cultures, Ria dons the Islamic head-scarf to hide her hair of snakes. Read as an allegory, this suggests a cultural impetus to the *hijab*, indicating that theology is not the only reason why Muslim women wear it. Religious symbols are employed for social better-ment, fitting into the reformist agenda traceable to Abdullah's works.

Moving away from the genre of fantasy, I would like to turn my attention to science fiction by considering the short story 'Kesumat Sang Avatar', trans-latable as 'The Avatar's Wrath', written by Farihan Bahron in 2016. Although there is no outward mention of Islam in the story, it can be read as a com-mentary on Islamic belief. It does so by referencing the theme of creation. Can humans play God? This question is not uncommon in global science fiction. Mary Shelley's Frankenstein is a case in point. Yet, Farihan's story asks this within the confines of Islamic theology, a rarity in itself. Zahid, a program-mer, invents an artificial intelligence named Katie based on his former girl-friend. Playing out the cliché, Katie the AI rebels against her creator and takes control of his programmes. At one point in the story, the question of human life turns philosophical in a conversation between Katie and her creator.

'Zahid, what are humans made of?'
'From a religious perspective, we come from the soil. But, if we take the scien-tific approach, then ninety-nine percent of the human body is comprised of six elements: oxygen, carbon, hydrogen, nitrogen, calcium and phosphorus. These

elements can also be found in the crevices of the planet, which we can call the earth. In this sense, the religious perspective is congruent with the scientific perspective'. (2017: 45, translation mine)

Once again, the propensity to employ the use of reason in the practice of Islam is evident. However, unlike Helmilina's 'Virus X' which can also be described as science fiction, Farihan's story does not uphold the primacy of Islam over science.

To conclude is to revisit some of the astute observations made by the Singapore-based Malay studies scholar Azhar Ibrahim in a recent essay titled 'The Trials of the Progressive' (2019b). In it, he observes that Malay literature in Singapore has been privy to progressive ideals that he defines as 'reformist ideas against religious traditionalism and obscurantism' (2017: 70), especially in the early to mid-twentieth century, through authors such as Syed Sheikh al-Hadi and Sheikh Tahir Jalaluddin. The latter two had started the journal *Al-Imam* in 1906, modelled after the reformist-minded Egyptian journal *Al-Manar* published by Rashid Rida. However, Azhar also concludes that the Singapore Malay literary scene is not as 'distinctively and consistently progressive' (ibid: 84) in the post-independence period. This brief but focused study suggests that this situation may be changing, or perhaps has already transformed, towards the path of Islamic reformism. How to understand the incongruency? It is important to note the difference in the basic premise between this study and Azhar's – namely, that this study expands the definition of Malay literature to include writings in English and not just Bahasa. Another noteworthy observation is the fact that contemporary Malay literature does not settle neatly into the dichotomies of yesteryear's movements in the Nusantara. The stories of Nuraliah, Fairoz and Farihan may have possessed Abdullah's reformist zeal, but they do not chastise or devalue myths and fables in the way in which he did. In this sense, they have managed to unshackle themselves from the dogmatic reigns of the creed of *seni untuk masyarakat* championed by Asas' 50. On the other end, Helmilina's 'Virus X' takes on the form of science fiction while still maintaining the traditionalism of Shahnon Ahmad's techniques of *juzuk azab* in his realist fictions. If categories of yore no longer hold true, then one might consider coining a new moniker for this phenomenon. Such works might be better called Sastera Spekulatif, or Speculative Literature, given their inclination to fables, mythologies and other fantastical forms in the pursuit of progressive religious ideals. Read as an indication of the larger religious landscape in Singapore, this trend of Sastera Spekulatif suggests that a number of contemporary Malay authors could possibly be lending voice to a heightened sense of critical self-reflexivity in their generation's Islamic practices and beliefs. If the trend continues, then this would signal a notable evolution of Islam in Singapore, from the traditionalist-resurgent orientation of the 1980s and 1990s to what is better described as a circumspective interpretation of Islam that is at times spiritual, at times critical.

References

Abdullah bin Abdul Kadir (1970), *The Hikayat Abdullah*, trans. A. H. Hill. London and New York: Oxford University Press.

Administration of Muslim Law Act, Singapore Statues Online, <https://sso.agc.gov.sg/Act/AMLA1966> (accessed 2 February 2021).

Aravamudan, S. (2014), 'East-West Fiction as World Literature: The Hayy Problem Reconfigured', *Eighteenth-Century Studies* 47(2): 195–231.

Azhar Ibrahim (2019a), 'Inhibited Reformist Voices: The Challenge of Developing Critical Islamic Discourse in Singapore', in Norshahril Saat and Azhar Ibrahim (eds), *Alternative Voices in Muslim Southeast Asia: Discourse and Struggles*, 22–30. Singapore: ISEAS-Yusof Ishak Institute.

Azhar Ibrahim (2019b), 'The Trials of the Progressive: Malay Literary and Cultural Expressions in Singapore', in Norshahril Saat and Azhar Ibrahim (eds), *Alternative Voices in Muslim Southeast Asia: Discourse and Struggles*, 67–88. Singapore: ISEAS-Yusof Ishak Institute.

Bahrawi, N. (2016), 'Textual Desires', *Critical Muslim* 7: 69–80.

Bahron, F. (2017), 'Kesumat Sang Avatar', in F. Bahron, *Kesumat Sang Avatar: Kumpulan Cerpen*. Singapore: Unggun Creative.

Bernards, B. (2015), *Writing the South Seas: Imagining the Nanyang in Chinese and Southeast Asian Postcolonial Literature*. Seattle: University of Washington Press.

Chan, Cheow P. (2017), 'Law Expert Kevin Tan Says the S'pore Constitution's Definition of "Malay" Is Anomalous', *Mothership* (9 September 2017), <https://mothership.sg/2017/09/law-expert-kevin-tan-says-the-spore-constitutions-definition-of-malay-is-anomalous/> (accessed 1 February 2021), para.10.

Channel Newsasia (2015), 'Up to 400 Primary 1 Places Available Each Year in Singapore's Madrasahs', 21 January 2015, <http://eresources.nlb.gov.sg/> (accessed 2 February 2021).

Constitution of the Republic of Singapore, Singapore Statutes Online, <https://sso.agc.gov.sg/Act/CONS1963#legis> (accessed 1 February 2021).

Elmarsafy, Z. (2012), *Sufism in the Contemporary Arabic Novel*. Edinburgh: Edinburgh University Press.

Fairoz Ahmad (2019), 'The Day the Music Died', in F. Ahmed, *Interpreter of Winds*. Singapore: Ethos Books.

Goodman, L. E. (trans. and ed.) (2003), *Ibn Tufayl's Hayy ibn Yaqzan: A Philosophical Tale*. Chicago: The University of Chicago Press.

Green, A. and Ibrahim Tahir (2016), *Hand to Heart: The Collective Spirit of Malay/Muslim Organisations in Singapore*. Singapore: OPUS Editorial Private Limited.

Helmilina Muhamad Som (2003), 'Virus X', in Helmilina Muhamad Som, *Millenia: Kumpulan Cerpen*. Singapore: Asas 50.

Lamont, T. (2002), 'Mutual Abuse: The Meeting of Robinson Crusoe and Hayy Ibn Yaqzan', *Eedibiyat* 13(2): 169–76.

Lily Zubaidah Rahim (1998), *The Singapore Dilemma: The Political and Educational Marginality of the Malay Community*. Kuala Lumpur: Oxford University Press.

Mohamed Latiff Mohamed (2017), 'Creepy Crawlies', in Nazry Bahrawi (trans.), *Lost Nostalgia: Stories*. Singapore: Ethos Books.

Muhammad Ali (2013), 'Review of Islam Translated: Literature, Conversion, and the Arabic Cosmopolis of South and Southeast Asia by Rinit Ricci', *Journal of World History* 24(4): 877–80.

Muhammad Khairool Haque (2019), 'Esok Hari Raya', in Muhammad Khairool Haque, *Iftitah: Sebuah Karya Sastera Kerohanian*. Pulau Pinang: Baytul Hikma.

M. M. Jabrohim (2015), *Nilai-Nilai Profetik Dalam Karya Sastra Indonesia: Sastra yang Memperhalus Akhlak, Mencerdaskan Akal, dan Menajamkan Nurani*. Yogyakarta: Universitas Ahmad Dahlan, <http://eprints.uad.ac.id/7927/1/Nilai-Nilai%20 Profetik%20dlm%20Sastra%20%20Indonesia.pdf> (accessed 2 February 2021).

Noor Aisha Abdul Rahman and Azhar Ibrahim (2017), *Singapore Chronicles: Malays*. Singapore: Straits Times Press.

Noor Aisha Abdul Rahman (2019), 'Religious Resurgence Amongst Malays and its Impact: The Case of Singapore', in Norshahril Saat and Azhar Ibrahim (eds), *Alternative Voices in Muslim Southeast Asia: Discourse and Struggles*, 33–66. Singapore: ISEAS-Yusof Ishak Institute.

Ricci, R. (2011), *Islam Translated: Literature, Conversion, and the Arabic Cosmopolis of South and Southeast Asia*. Chicago: University of Chicago Press.

Singapore Census of Population 2010, Department of Statistics Singapore, <https:// www.singstat.gov.sg/publications/cop2010/census10_stat_release3> (accessed 1 February 2021).

Ungku Maimunah Mohd. Tahir (1989), 'The Notion of "Dakwah" and its Perceptions in Malaysia's Islamic Literature of the 1970s and '80s', *Journal of Southeast Asian Studies* 20(2): 288–89.

2

WOMEN AND ISLAMISATION IN MALAYSIA: CONTESTATIONS ON THE PRACTICE OF ISLAM

Syed Imad Alatas

Although Islam is the religion of the federation according to the Malaysian constitution, non-Muslims are allowed to practise their religion freely. Malaysia has been celebrated as a model moderate Muslim country by observers and analysts alike. While Islam has been practised in the Malay world from as early as the thirteenth century, the Islamisation of the 1970s and 1980s demonstrated the salient visibility of Islam in socio-political life. The presence of more hardline Islamic elements in the government and society at large has also posed a challenge to the image of moderate Islam. Integral to the contestations on the practice of Islam was the status of Muslim women and how they were being treated, from the legal recourse available to them, to their everyday experiences. Female Muslim activists began to debate about Malaysian society and the role of women in Islam. These groups differed from each other in their approaches to religion in modern society. This chapter looks at some responses among female Muslim NGOs and activists to state discourses on Islam and religiosity. Their views exist in a social milieu where state interpretations of Islam hold authority, albeit not an unchallenged one. This chapter demonstrates that such contestations on what it means to be Islamic are emblematic of national attempts to define what being an ideal Muslim means.

Islam in Malaysian Socio-political Life

Malaysia is lauded as a moderate Muslim country worthy of emulation by the rest of the Muslim world, due to its ability to synthesise Islam and modernity (Ahmad Fauzi 2018: 381). However, the emergence of hardline Islamist elements in Malaysian society has turned this image on its head. Notwithstanding the absence of a major racial/religious conflict since 1969, the image of moderate Islam is constantly being challenged. In 2016, there were reports of Malaysian youths being sympathetic to the international terrorist group ISIS (Islamic State in Iraq and Syria). At least 150 people were arrested due to alleged links with ISIS (Mohd Azizuddin 2016). Malaysian scholars and civil society members remain pessimistic about whether Malaysia will ever be conducive to open discussions on Islam without fear of reprisal. Furthermore, the new ruling government, Perikatan Nasional (National Alliance), consists of conservative Muslim personalities from Malay nationalist and Islamist parties. Despite this gloomy picture, one should not ignore the efforts of civil society groups in Malaysia to challenge Islamist and exclusivist discourse. In a country where Islam is used to garner political mileage, questions of governance are necessarily tied to debates about religiosity and the ideal Muslim society. In most, if not all Muslim countries, women are seen as the cultural bearers of this ideal from the perspective of national efforts in re-establishing a cultural identity in the post-colonial period (Ahmed 1992: 164). The realities of women in the Malay world have changed throughout history. In the pre-colonial period, women in traditional Malay society enjoyed a certain degree of economic independence. In inheritance, they were entitled to a share of land equal to that of their brothers. Generally, they were not restricted to domestic roles of housewife or caregiver. Both Islam and *adat* (traditional Malay culture) played a role in Malay society so that women enjoyed privileges equal to men. It is in the post-independence period where the twin forces of economic development and an Islamic resurgent movement undermined the emphasis on *adat*, while increasing male control over economic and cultural resources, with Islam used as a justification (Ong 1990: 260). The phenomenon of Islamisation in the 1970s and 1980s brought to the fore the issue of how Muslim women were being treated. The emergence of female Muslim NGOs constitutes a response to this phenomenon whereby these groups sought to argue for their interpretation of Islam, which they felt was more progressive. This chapter argues that contestations among female Muslim NGOs on what it means to be Islamic are emblematic of contestations at the national level on what being an ideal Muslim means. A brief history on Islam in Malaysia will be provided before focusing on Islamisation as a turning point in this history that saw Islam being championed by various groups as a total way of life. The gendered aspect of Islamisation will receive some elaboration, before explaining how Muslim women, through several examples of female Muslim NGOs, have responded to the assertion of Islam in Malaysian society. Finally, this chapter will conclude with a way forward in terms of understanding the different religious orientations of these female Muslim NGOs.

Malaysia consists of a federation of thirteen states and three federal territories. Muslims form about 60 percent of the population, with non-Muslims accounting for a significant minority. The Bumiputera ('sons of the soil') account for about 70 percent of the Malaysian population (Department of Statistics Malaysia 2020). The Bumiputera consist of both Malays and non-Malay indigenous groups in the East Malaysian states of Sabah and Sarawak.

Constitutionally, Malaysia is a secular state with Islam being the 'religion of the Federation' (Federal Constitution of Malaysia 2010). Malays are automatically defined as Muslims in the federal constitution. While non-Muslims are allowed to practise their religion, Islam has left an indelible mark on the political governance of the country. It has influenced discussions and debates on socio-cultural life, an example being the controversy over the usage of the word *Allah* (Arabic for God) by non-Muslims (Tariq 2013). The meaning ascribed to Islam as the official religion of the country remains debatable. To understand how Islam came to occupy such an important place in Malaysian socio-political life, one needs to understand the relationship that the people have had with Islam.

Islam can be said to have arrived in Island Southeast Asia as early as the thirteenth century, with Muslim traders and mystics playing a key role (Daniels 2017: 19). Although it is difficult to quantifiably attribute the spread of Islam to any one group, the direct relationship between trade and the spread of Islam in the Malay world is a strong one (Andaya and Andaya 2017: 57). The port of Malacca (one of the thirteen current states of Malaysia) was a key centre for the acceptance of Islam in the Malay world. The rulers' embrace of Islam translated into the religion being used as a logic of governance in the Malay kingdoms. The Malay rulers' adoption of Islam in turn 'influenced large numbers of Malays to embrace Islam' (Muhammad Haniff 2007: 289). In this process, Islam came to embody a core aspect of identity on the Malay Peninsula. However, British rule in the eighteenth century had a significant impact on the legal position of Islam in Malaya (now Malaysia). While it was British policy to not interfere in religious matters, this did not prevent them from limiting Islamic practices, especially where the implementation of Islamic law was concerned. The British sought to limit the influence of Islam on family law while introducing their own 'secular legal system' (Hooker 1983: 16). The independence of *qadis*, or Islamic judges, was also restricted; they were not allowed to arrest and sentence offenders. Islamic education also faced restrictions during colonialism. Prior to the arrival of the British, Islamic education provided a means for continuing the spread of Islam among the Malays. The creation of Islamic schools, or madrasahs, in the nineteenth century provided education not just in theological but also vocational subjects (Azmi and Shamsul 2004: 349). Students learnt the religious subjects of Islamic jurisprudence, tradition and mysticism, while being taught mathematics, English and business. While the British did establish Malay medium and Islamic religious schools in rural areas, it concentrated more of its efforts on the English medium schools. It was British policy that Malay and Islamic education did not enjoy the same priority as English education.

The beginning of the twentieth century witnessed a reformation movement led by religious figures such as Syed Sheikh Al-Hadi, who founded the Kaum Muda (reformist) movement. These figures were strongly influenced by the modernist ideas of Jamal al-Din al-Afghani and Rashid Rida. The spirit of the movement lay in a call upon Muslims to 'return to the true teachings of Islam based on the Qur'an and Sunnah (Prophet's tradition) in order for them to make progress' (Muhammad Haniff 2007: 290). The movement was a response to what its pioneers viewed as the influence of Western imperialism. It had a strong influence on the Muslim community, founding prominent madrasahs such as the Sekolah Al-Hadi and the Madrasah Al-Mashor. It was during this period that the identity politics within the anti-British movement began to emerge. The Kaum Muda deemed the Kaum Tua (traditionalists) as the real reason why Malaya was not progressing. The traditionalists were rendered the 'destroyers of Islam' (Azmi and Shamsul 2004: 349). In response to these accusations, the traditionalists labelled the reformists as deviants and accused them of being Wahhabis, a term referring to the puritanical interpretation of Islam developed by Muhammad ibn Abd al-Wahhab (Ahmad Fauzi 2020: 189). However, even amidst these differences there was a tolerance of alternative views; states with more progressive traditionalist scholars allowed the Kaum Muda to engage in debate (Roff 1983: 323–38). Eventually, the Kaum Tua gained control of the religious bureaucracies of most states. Another significant response to British rule was the formation of the UMNO (United Malays National Organisation) in 1946, symbolic of an urgent need for Pan-Malaysian unity and opposition against the Malayan Union. The Malayan Union was viewed negatively by Malay-Muslim nationalists and the ulama (Islamic religious elites), as it extended citizenship to immigrant communities and curtailed the political rights of the Malay royalty. The ulama were instrumental in the formation of the UMNO. Yet, the UMNO did not receive full support from many of the Muslim clerics within the party who felt that Islam was not given priority as a form of governance. The UMNO was seen as a secular party that was not Islamic enough (Liow and Pasuni 2015: 51). As result, these clerics broke away from the UMNO and formed the Pan-Malaysian Islamic Party (PAS) in 1951. Their manifesto was the creation of an Islamic state.

The racial riots of 13 May 1969 marked yet another development that strengthened the role of Islam in Malaysian governance. The riots were a reaction to the Chinese-majority opposition Democratic Action Party (DAP) gaining significant ground during the 1969 general elections in the state of Selangor. The government introduced the New Economic Policy (NEP) to uplift the status of the Malays and 'bridge the gap with the Chinese' (Muhammad Haniff 2007: 296). Many promising Malay students were sent to educational institutions abroad in efforts to produce a Malay professional class. During their stints abroad, these students were exposed to Islamic movements and the thought of Muslim activists from countries such as Egypt. This exposure led to the creation of an Islamic resurgent sentiment within these students (Verma 2002: 101). Many students returned and joined organisations sympathetic to PAS, such as the Muslim Youth Movement of Malaysia (ABIM). The presence of both the UMNO and PAS resulted in a rivalry over who was more Islamic. The Islamisation race in the 1970s and 1980s could be seen as the epicentre of this rivalry, when former prime minister Mahathir Mohamad set up religious institutions within the government to ensure that state Islam could be 'systematically disseminated to the Malay population' (Olivier 2016: 270). Many clerics who studied in countries such as Egypt and Saudi Arabia were recruited into these government institutions. It was this institutionalisation of religion that ironically led to accusations by PAS that the UMNO was not promoting Islam to the fullest extent possible (Liow 2003: 3). While Islamisation in Malaysia affected various aspects of the country, such as the economy, culture and education, this chapter will focus on the impact that Islamisation has had on the articulation of women's issues in Malaysia. Before that, the women's movement in Malaysia needs to be historically contextualised.

The Women's Movement in Malaysia

The women's movement in Malaysia has undoubtedly had to navigate the complexities of its historical circumstances, in particular, its colonial past. The earliest signs of a feminist consciousness in Malaysia point to the 1920s, when Malay Muslim male reformers such as Syed Syeikh Al-Hadi and Zainal Abidin Ahmad championed education as a means for women to emancipate themselves from patriarchal family structures that sought to restrict them to domestic household roles. The years after World War II and British colonialism saw the feminist struggle assume a nationalist character. As has been noted, 'the most successful mobilisation of women in Malaysian history has been in the anti-colonial and nationalist movements' (Suat Yan 2003: 50). These movements consisted of both left-wing and right-wing groups, although the former was quickly banned when the British imposed emergency rule in 1948. The UMNO was an example of the right-wing tradition. From it came Kaum Ibu (KI, Women's Association), which was the UMNO's women's branch. KI's main objective was to oppose the Malayan Union. The issues of women's rights, marriage reform and education for girls were subsumed under the objectives of achieving independence. It was only after colonialism that women's concerns could be discussed specifically in relation to their everyday experiences. Such a fight was motivated by internal and external factors, such as Islamisation and a global economic downturn, respectively. The former sought to relegate women to more subservient roles in society, while the latter exposed the vulnerabilities of women who became unemployed in the electronics sector. In the short term, the most important factor enabling the institutionalisation of the women's movement in Malaysia was the end of colonialism. Violence against women was a hot-button issue around which Malaysian women of all backgrounds could unite.

There were several local groups that started to mobilise against different forms of violence against women in the post-independence period. In 1963,

KI and the Women's Council, an advisory body set up in 1961, combined to form the National Council of Women's Organisations (NCWO) to spearhead the struggle for women's emancipation. The NCWO was comprised mainly of welfare, religious and service-oriented women's organisations. They were instrumental in lobbying for maternity leave for women, the outlawing of polygamy for non-Muslims, raising the age of marriage to eighteen years and instituting civil family laws for all non-Muslims. Not much later, Malaysia experienced very slow economic growth in the 1970s, followed by a depression in the mid-1980s. Many women who were employed in the electronics industry were retrenched in the 1970s. Unemployment deprived them of a sense of independence elusive in a patriarchal household. In this same period, Malay youth who were disillusioned with western-influenced consumerism championed a total insertion of Islam into Malaysian life. The NCWO itself engaged with Muslim family laws during this period of Islamic resurgence. For example, they requested that these laws be standardised in each state so that a Muslim man would not be able to circumvent the family law of a particular state in order to contract a second marriage in secrecy. Until then, violence against women was not given a discursive space. In the 1980s, women's rights activism in Malaysia slowly became professionalised. Not only was there a marked increase in the number of local women's groups, but these organisations also started to offer full-time paid positions. Women's interests were no longer seen as merely *ad hoc* volunteer work that people do as a hobby; it became a type of formal waged work and was understood as a form of collective organising. Of these women's groups and NGOs, some were grounded in religious beliefs, while others were more secular-based.

The 1980s constituted a period where these women's NGOs cooperated on the issue of Violence Against Women (VAW) and joined the Joint Action Group against Violence Against Women (JAG-VAW). The JAG-VAW was formally established in 1984 and is today known just as the Joint Action Group for Gender Equality (JAG). The NCWO joined forces with the JAG when meetings were held to discuss lobbying for a Domestic Violence Act in Malaysia in the 1990s. The Association of Women Lawyers, another NGO, initiated a discussion between women's NGOs and the Malaysian Royal Police on the topic of domestic violence. The struggle was met with a lot of resistance, particularly by male legislators, politicians, as well as religious authorities. This is because domestic violence, as a matter pertaining to the family, came under the purview of shari'ah law for Muslims rather than civil law for non-Muslims. This legal structure was all the more worrying for Muslim victims of domestic violence. JAG-VAW held discussions with various Islamic bodies to earn their support (Suat Yan 2003: 46). It was not until 1995 that the Domestic Violence Act was passed. This milestone signalled a turning point in the amount of attention paid specifically to women's rights and violence against women. Women were more open in talking about their experiences with rape and domestic violence because now there existed NGOs who would lobby on their behalf, legally or otherwise. In fact, the number of domestic violence cases reported by women increased from 532 in 1994 to 1,413 in 1996 and 5,799 in 1997 (Suat Yan 2000: 136).

The state itself also grew concerned with the status of women in Malaysia. Women's NGOs during this period were instrumental in necessitating the formation of the Department of Women's Affairs in 1992. Female officers in the government were more vocal on women's issues, including unwed mothers and the unequal treatment and status of foreign husbands. They attended conferences overseas related to the improvement of women's opportunities, including the Beijing Conference in 1995. The female officers in the government were also concerned with improving the relationship between NGOs and the government. State-led Islamisation in the early 1980s brought into focus the status of Muslim women and how they were being treated, from legal structures available to them to the everyday experiences of these women.

Islamisation and Muslim Women

Islamisation in Malaysia may be likened to a phenomenon called 'Islamic resurgence' where there was a re-awakening of Islamic sentiment. The resurgence started as a proselytisation (*dakwah*) movement 'aimed as Islamizing society from the bottom by promoting Islam as a comprehensive way of life – to make Muslims become better Muslims' (Norani, Zainah and Zaitun 2005: 80). There were calls by conservative religious elites for a return to Islamic life-styles as perceived to exist at the time of Islamic conquest (Stark 2003). One of the more prominent Muslim organisations that came out of this period was ABIM, who gained popularity among the Muslim-educated youths. ABIM was critical of the government for not (sufficiently) incorporating Islamic values in social and economic policies. The Islamisation of Malaysian society touched on the life-styles and values of Malay-Muslims. Muslim women in particular demonstrated a greater public concern with morality. Many of them began to don the *tudung* (scarf) and the Arab-style long loose *jubah* (robe). The return of Malaysian students from the West, who were exposed to political Islam, transformed the local *da'wah* movement into a radical political movement. It criticised secular, Westernised governments in Muslim-dominated countries and sought to fight for an Islamic state. PAS became the party choice of Malaysian youths in their struggle for an Islamic state and the comprehensive institutionalisation of shari'ah law. By the 1980s, when laws for Muslims were instituted to create a single set of 'personal laws', the 'Muslim family' became the central focus in Islamic elite discourse in Malaysia. Tied to this focus was an agenda for setting behavioural norms for the Muslim community amidst the phenomenon of cultural cosmopolitanism where Malaysians were being exposed to Western ways of life. Stivens' (2006) essay on state moral projects in Malaysia is useful in explaining how the moral projects of family values assumed a central place in the Islamisation of Malaysian society. Within the trope of Islamisation, a main response to the alleged decline of the family was an emphasis on the need for 'Asian values', which was seen to encompass values such as a strong attachment to the family. The state propagated an apocalyptic discourse of the family in crisis, rocked by marital troubles and juvenile delinquency. Hence, there was a need to 'save' the family. The character of Muslim family life has been a particular issue within the 'Asian values' discourse in Malaysia (Stivens 2006: 356). The inclusion of the moral project of family values has implications for family, gender relations and women's rights within families. The family is presented as a 'critical site for producing new versions of purer Islam, and parents, especially women, within it carry a large responsibility for securing an Islamic future through the rearing of children' (ibid: 358). The family became the means by which the Islamisation movement had to succeed since Islamisation could only begin from within. The approach to the family was gendered, whereby there was a concern about the responsibilities of both husband and wife within a Muslim family. The expectations placed on men and women were markedly different. In fact, 'the control of women, their social roles, movements and sexuality form the core of the Islamic fundamentalists' view of gender roles and relations in the "pristine Islamic society and state" which they seek to establish' (Norani, Zainah and Zaitun 2005: 86). Generally, Islamisation in Malaysia stressed the secondary status of Muslim women as wives and mothers. A good Muslim woman was also expected to educate others on Islam (Sleboda 2001: 111). Muslim women were a symbol of Malaysian efforts in delineating gender roles according to the conservatives' interpretation of Islam.

Female Muslim NGOs and the State: Differing Approaches to Islam

The gendered aspect of Islamisation in Malaysia entailed a focus into the public and private lives of Muslim men and women. However, the attention seemed to be more rigorous in the case of women. Seen as a symbol of Malaysia's Islamisation, there was a disproportionate concern with how women ought to practise their faith. While Muslim women's concerns were relatively sidelined during colonialism, '[f]amily Law within Shari'a was initially codified [. . .] during the British colonial era, and reflected, as well as the Qur'an, both Malay custom and Western law' (Olivier 2020: 170). This codification retained relative freedoms for Malay women. The evolution of family laws after colonialism soon began to reflect a male bias. In the 1970s, these laws were still 'women-friendly'. By the 1980s, women's legal status was ambivalent at best before it became an exclusive domain of male privilege in the 2000s (Maznah 2014: 177). For example, while polygamy was legally permissible in the 1980s, the government put in place difficult conditions that had to be met. The living standards of a man's first wife and children could not be jeopardised. He also had to prove that his new marriage was just; his first wife had to give consent. By the year 2000, a man could marry another woman with minimal hurdles, even if he did not have the financial means to do so. In a similar vein, men could pronounce divorces out of court, as long as they paid a fine or served a short jail term. They were not required to settle any marital claims brought by their wife. On the contrary, it was more difficult for women to obtain divorce, even by judicial means, as this meant having to go through the burdensome process of 'ineffective counselling and reconciliation exercises, besides maintaining that they have been obedient wives' (Nik Noriani 2003: 36). The minimal condition a Muslim woman had to meet to have any chance of obtaining a divorce was that she had to be obedient, or not be guilty of committing *nusyuz* (a term often understood as a wife's disobedience to her husband).

It is against the backdrop of these discourses during Islamisation that female Muslim activists began to debate Malaysian society and the role of women in Islam. These groups differed from each other in their approach to religion in modern society. Female Muslim NGOs in Malaysia do not merely produce discourses on women's issues on their own. This discursive pro-duction is always done in relation to both state and non-state actors. Labels used for these NGOs – such as 'conservative' and 'liberal' – point to a wider discourse in Malaysia on what is the 'right' way to practise Islam and what is seen as deviant. These differences in approaches to women in Islam further underlie the religious orientations, not just of these NGOs, but of Malaysian Muslim society in general. As in most Muslim-majority countries, the politi-cisation of Islam in Malaysia means that religious orientations cannot avoid being studied in terms of how much they conform to or challenge state interpretations of Islam. Female Muslim NGOs respond to and are affected by these interpretations. They may agree that Islam must pervade every aspect of life as much as possible, without room for debate. These NGOs can be exclusivist in nature, excluding Muslims they deem 'not Islamic enough'. Yet, some NGOs may advocate for an Islamic way of life while allowing for alternative interpretations of Islam. Islamisation and conservative elements within the official ulama have made these discussions more contentious. Additionally, the phenomenon of Islamic resurgence in Malaysia is symbolic of and masks the wider divisions between the dominant religious orienta-tions of traditionalism and modernism.

Religious Orientations and the State

While the religious orientations of female Muslim NGOs in Malaysia have not been studied in detail, if at all, much has been written on the religious orientations present in the Malay world in general. In Indonesia, tradi-tionalism, modernism and neo-modernism have been studied extensively by various scholars (Barton 1997; Woodward 2001; Pradana Boy 2015). Traditionalism refers to an orientation that 'cherishes the tradition which it has received' (Towler 1984: 82). While the embrace of tradition may be appreciative or defensive in nature, there is an unquestionable acceptance of tradition from the past. If any element of this tradition is called into question, the traditionalist will be 'unable to conceive of doubt or contradiction' (ibid: 83). Furthermore, there is an emphasis on the hereafter; worldly concerns are a form of irreligiosity. In Indonesia, groups such as Nahdlatul Ulama embody the orientation of traditionalism. Responding to traditionalism is the religious orientation of modernism. Modernists denounce various aspects of traditionalism such as mysticism and the practice of pilgrimage to the tombs of Sufi saints (Woodward 2001: 33). Only the Qu'ran and the prophetic tradition is authentic. Unlike traditionalists, modernists claim that 'they are not bound by *taqlid* (blind imitation of traditional authorities), by a dependence on the *madzab* (school of jurisprudence), and are free to make up their minds for themselves on issues through the practice of *ijtihad*' (Barton 1997: 324). Muhammadiyah in Indonesia is an example of a modernist organisation. They would also argue that any modern scientific discovery can trace its origins within the Qu'ran. Islamic modernists look to the Qu'ran and the traditions of the Prophet (hadith) 'to seek a fresh interpretation and synthesis for modern times' (Shepard 1987: 311). At best, the modernist has an ambiguous relationship with the 'West', appreciating Western sciences while castigating Western culture. Modernist organisations can also be explicitly political in that they want to establish an Islamic state, albeit through participation in the democratic process.

Neo-modernism as an orientation may be attributed to the thinking of the Muslim intellectual Fazlur Rahman. During the twentieth century, Muslim intellectuals such as Rahman interpreted Islam's lack of cultural progress (as compared to the West) as the result of an absence of a 'critical-rationalist interpretation of the religion' (Bektovic 2016: 1). Islamic tradition had to be re-interpreted. Neo-modernists are 'concerned more with Muslim values and ethics than with law' (Woodward 2001: 35). They argue that Islamic law is an open-ended tradition that must be interpreted according to changing historical and cultural contexts. They resemble the early modernists in their commitment to rational inquiry, *ijtihad*, and progress, 'particularly in the area of education' (Barton 1997: 342). However, neo-modernists seek to combine the early modernist concern for *ijtihad* with the rich intellectual heritage of classical Islamic scholarship. As compared to other religious orientations, neo-modernism can be thought of as progressive. Rather than yearn nostalgically for a 'golden image of Islam', there is an optimism for the future in terms of the progress and development of Islam. It adopts a positive attitude towards modernity and progress. With regards to 'Western' ideals such as democracy and human rights, neo-modernists argue that 'in these ideals Islam shares a common heritage with the West' (Barton 1997: 344). While it is critical of certain aspects of Western culture, it does not view Western and Islamic culture as profoundly irreconcilable (unlike some modernists). As a result, neo-modernists argue against the notion that there can or should be an Islamic state. Rahman himself criticised modernists for being too concerned with a reconciliation between the Qu'ran and modern rationality while making 'little attempt to treat the Qu'ran as a whole and to formulate first its worldview, then systematise its ethics and finally derive particular doctrines and laws from it' (Rahman 1980: 244). Lastly, neo-modernists strive for an open and inclusivist understanding of Islam, which includes an atmosphere where people of different faiths live together and respect one another.

In Malaysia, Nagata (1984) and Muzaffar (1986) have looked at the phenomenon of Islamic revivalism, taking as their departure point the Dakwah Movement in Malaysia in the 1970s and 1980s. The latter argues that Islamic identity has become a vital factor in the Islamic resurgence due to modernisation and the influx of Western culture. The former provides a more comprehensive overview of the manifestations of the Dakwah movement, stressing that one cannot view it in the singular. Instead, the 1970s saw several organisations espousing Dakwah's ideas from different points of view. Nagata also touches on identity, arguing that the Islamic resurgence was also a response to a need to reassert Malay identity. More recently, a study of ideas of prominent religious personalities in Malaysia focused on various issues as discussed by the religious elite, such as the role of women and the idea of an Islamic state (Norshahril 2010). It concluded that traditionalism is a major orientation subscribed to, as reflected in the selection and discussion of issues raised by the religious elite. Likewise, female Muslim NGOs subscribe to a religious orientation. If an NGO has views that are traditionalist, this stance will be reflected in how it deals with women's issues and questions of what constitutes an ideal Muslimah. There will be an unquestionable acceptance of tradition from generations of the past. They will seek recourse to history, citing how women were treated and viewed during the early years of Islam. There will be a reluctance to deal with (changes in) contemporary society. However, a modernist NGO would have a more critical approach to tradition. It will be weary of or do away with the four schools of jurisprudence in Islam in relation to discussions on women. There will be a steadfast adherence to the Qur'an and Prophetic tradition as guidelines for women's role in society.

In the Malaysian case, both the traditionalist and the modernist may 'agree on the need for the public dominance of Islam'; what they disagree on is how an Islamic state and society will look like (Norshahril 2020: 4). Most Malay-Muslim women in the 1980s were not affiliated with the feminist project. Instead, many of them, especially the youths, were drawn to Islamic movements such as ABIM. They sought to either counter or confirm male-biased Islamic movements that flourished during the Islamisation period. Malay Islamist women were strongly opposed to the influence of 'Westernisation' and the objectification of women's bodies. They believed that the scarf would protect them from everyday sexual harassment. The assertion of a post-colonial cultural identity only reinforced the idea that the West was markedly different from and hostile to the Islamic way of life. However, women's groups still had to engage with religious authorities and elites within an 'Islamically' acceptable social framework (Foley 2004: 58). Among these activists, the Muslim NGO Sisters in Islam (SIS, formed in 1993) can be said

to be the most prominent group of activists, as they attempt to revise patriarchal interpretations of Muslim laws and educate the public on women's
rights in Islam. They have consistently adopted a multi-pronged approach
when trying to challenge the monopoly of the ulama through public education, networking and advocacy. Yet, SIS's efforts have not come without
backlash from both Islamist groups and the government. Their credentials
on speaking on religion are routinely questioned because they are not educated in religious schools, nor do they have a degree in Islamic studies from a
recognised university in the Arab world. Hence, their message about gender
equality in the household is deemed to be inspired by 'alien Western values'.
The announcement of an edict (fatwa) against SIS by the Selangor government in 2014 symbolises the ideological contestations of Islam in Malaysia.
SIS was deemed to be holding on to 'liberalism' and 'religious pluralism'
and, as a result, labelled as deviating from Islamic teachings (Lim 2019). SIS
is still challenging this fatwa.

Other NGOs differ from SIS in terms of their approach to women's issues
in Malaysia. For example, groups such as Wanita IKRAM Malaysia and
Helwa ABIM (the women's wing of ABIM) disagree with SIS over the shun-
ning of polygamy altogether. When SIS launched a campaign against polygamy in 2003, Helwa ABIM and the women's wing of PAS opposed the idea
of the campaign (Ng, Maznah and Tan 2006: 101). They argued that such a
campaign challenging a male entitlement would cast Islam in a bad light.
They are also more particular about how a Muslim woman dresses; one of
the first priorities of Helwa ABIM was to get Muslim women to don the veil
(Maznah 2004: 141). It further attributes to Muslim wives the responsibility
of being obedient to her husband and serving as caregiver for the children.
Her purity is also emphasised more than the husband's. Hence, ideological clashes between conservative and more progressive groups do exist.
On the more extreme end of the ideological spectrum is Ikatan Muslimin
Malaysia (Isma, Alliance of Malaysian Muslims). Originally, their aim was
to develop 'total Islamic living and culture' among 'middle-class Muslims'
(Maznah 2020: 144). Founded in 1997, their focus shifted to fighting against
an alleged surge of liberalism and secularism in Muslim society. Its women's
wing, Wanita Isma, tried to exclude the more progressive Muslim women's
NGO from the civil society space. They have gone to the extent of associating Muslim feminists with the LBGT movement in a derogatory manner.
Wanita Isma positions Islam and liberalism as polar opposites. For them,
Islam provides a bastion against the threat of liberalism, whereby religious
knowledge can guide Muslim women and protect them from being influenced by forces of deception and ways of thinking that can damage their
character (*Ilmu agama mampu memandu wanita muslimah daripada terpengaruh
dengan tipu daya dan pemikiran yang boleh merosakkan keperibadian Muslimah*)
(Norsaleha 2015: 13).

The above-mentioned groups all agree that Islam needs to be interpreted
and practised in such a way that Malaysian society is able to function. The

disagreement lies in what the practice of Islam will look like at the societal and the individual level. Yet, it is ultimately the state that decides on the 'correct' interpretation of Islam. Those seen to be feminist and liberal are a threat to an Islam that is bureaucratic. The labelling of SIS as deviant illustrates the point that an interpretation of Islam is seen to be inaccurate in relation to bureaucratic authority. The female Muslim NGOs in Malaysia then exist on a continuum of how much they differ from the religious bureaucracy in terms of their mode of thinking.

Conclusion

Through a focus on women's issues, this chapter has attempted to argue that the contestations of religious interpretation represent a wider debate over what is Islamic and what is deviant from Islam. Gender is just one of many aspects of social life whereby various players have sought to assert their own interpretations of Islam. Gender also provides an example of how the image of 'moderate Islam' in Malaysia is tenuous at best. While the presence of various female Muslim NGOs across an ideological spectrum show that state definitions of Islam do not go unchallenged, the challenges come at a cost: even more conservative groups such as Wanita IKRAM have been labelled as 'liberal' by ordinary Malaysians and other activists. However, the spectrum of religious orientations among female Muslim NGOs in Malaysia has not been explored at length. More research should be conducted on the religious orientations to which these NGOs subscribe, in relation to each other and to the state. While the NGOs are not the sole representatives of how Malaysians think, they do serve as a useful empirical field for how activists who argue for their version of Islam interpret religion in modern society.

References

Ahmad Fauzi Abdul Hamid (2018), 'Shifting Trends of Islamism and Islamist Practices in Malaysia, 1957–2017', *Southeast Asian Studies* 7(3): 363–90.

Ahmad Fauzi Abdul Hamid (2020), 'Regaining the Islamic Centre? A Malaysian Chronicle of Moderation and Its Discontents', in M. N. Mohamed Osman (ed.), *Pathways to Contemporary Islam: New Trends in Critical Engagement*, 181–212. Amsterdam: Amsterdam University Press.

Ahmed, L. (1992), *Women and Gender in Islam*. New Haven, CT: Yale University Press.

Andaya, B. W. and Andaya, L. Y. (2017), *A History of Malaysia* (3rd ed.). London: Palgrave Macmillan.

Azmi Aziz and Shamsul A. B. (2004), 'The Religious, the Plural, the Secular and the Modern: A Brief Critical Survey on Islam in Malaysia', *Inter-Asia Cultural Studies* 5(3): 341–56.

Barton, G. (1997), 'Indonesia's Nurcholish Madjid and Abdurrahman Wahid as Intellectual Ulama: The Meeting of Islamic Traditionalism and Modernism in Neo-Modernist Thought', *Islam and Christian-Muslim Relations* 8(3): 323–50.

Bektovic, S. (2016), 'Towards a Neo-Modernist Islam: Fazlur Rahman and the Rethinking Islamic Tradition and Modernity', *Studia Theologica* 70(2): 1–19.

Daniels, T. (2017), *Living Sharia: Law and Practice in Malaysia*. Washington, DC: Washington University Press.

Department of Statistics Malaysia (2020), *Current Population Estimates, Malaysia, 2020*, <https://www.dosm.gov.my/v1/index.php?r=column/cthemeByCat&cat=155& bul_id=OVByWjg5YkQ3MWFZRTN5bDJiaEVhZz09&menu_id=L0pheU43NWJw RWVSZklWdzQ4TlhUUT09> (accessed 22 July 2020).

Federal Constitution of Malaysia (2010), <http://www.agc.gov.my/agcportal/up loads/files/Publications/FC/Federal%20Consti%20(BI%20text).pdf> (accessed 22 July 2020).

Foley, R. (2004), 'Muslim Women's Challenges to Islamic Law: The Case of Malaysia', *International Feminist Journal of Politics* 6(1): 53–84.

Hooker, M. B. (ed.) (1983), *Islam in Southeast Asia*. Leiden: Brill.

Liow, J. C. (2003), 'Deconstructing Political Islam in Malaysia: UMNO's Response to PAS' Religio-Political Dialectic', *RSIS Working Papers 45*. Singapore: Institute of Defence and Strategic Studies.

Liow, J. C. and Pasuni, A. (2015), 'Islam: The State and Politics in Malaysia', in Meredith L. Weiss (ed.), *Routledge Handbook of Contemporary Malaysia*, 50–59. London and New York: Routledge.

Lim, I. (2019), 'SIS: Court's Fatwa Challenge Refusal Dark Moment for Malaysia, Women's Rights', *Malay Mail*, 27 August 2019, <https://www.malaymail.com/ news/malaysia/2019/08/27/sis-courts-fatwa-challenge-refusal-dark-moment- for-malaysia-womens-rights/1784769> (accessed 1 May 2021).

Maznah Mohamad (2004), 'Women's Engagement with Political Islam in Malaysia', *Global Change, Peace and Security* 16(2): 133–49.

Maznah Mohamad (2014), 'Women, Family and Syariah in Malaysia', in Sophie Lemiere (ed.), *Misplaced Democracy: Malaysian Politics and People*, 175–92. Selangor: Strategic Information and Research Development Centre.

Maznah Mohamad (2020), *The Divine Bureaucracy and Disenchantment of Social Life: A Study of Bureaucratic Islam in Malaysia*. Singapore: Palgrave Macmillan.

Mohd Azizuddin Mohd Sani (2016), 'ISIS Recruitment of Malaysian Youth: Challenge and Response', *Middle East Institute*, 3 May 2016, <https://www.mei.edu/content/map/ isis-recruitment-malaysian-youth-challengeand-response> (accessed 1 May 2021).

Muhammad Haniff Bin Hassan (2007), 'Explaining Islam's Special Position and the Politic of Islam in Malaysia', *The Muslim World* 97(2): 287–316.

Muzaffar, C. (1986), 'Malaysia: Islamic Resurgence and the Question of Development', *Sojourn: Journal of Social Issues in Southeast Asia* 1(1): 57–75.

Nagata, J. (1984), *The Reflowering of Malaysian Islam: Modern Religious Radicals and their Roots*. Vancouver: University of British Columbia Press.

Ng, Cecilia, Maznah Mohamad and Tan Beng Hui (2006), *Feminism and the Women's Movement in Malaysia: An Unsung (R)evolution*. New York: Routledge.

Nik Noriani Nik BadliShah (ed.) (2003), *Islamic Family Law and Justice for Muslim Women*. Kuala Lumpur: Sisters in Islam.

Norsaleha Mohd Salleh (2015), 'Penolakan Terhadap Agenda Feminisme dan Liberalisme Di Malaysia', <https://www.researchgate.net/profile/Norsaleha_ Salleh/publication/287232617_PENOLAKAN_TERHADAP_AGENDA_FEMIN ISME_DAN_LIBERALISME_DI_MALAYSIA/links/5674c2a108ae502c99c788a4 .pdf> (accessed 27 July 2020).

Olivier, B. (2016), 'The Malaysian Islamization Phenomenon: The Underlying Dynamics and Their Impact on Muslim Women', *Islam and Christian-Muslim Relations* 27(3): 267–82.

Olivier, B. (2020), *Islamic Revivalism and Politics in Malaysia: Problems in Nation Building*. Singapore: Springer Nature.

Ong, A. (1990), 'State versus Islam: Malay Families, Women's Bodies, and the Body Politic in Malaysia', *American Ethnologist* 17(2): 258–76.

Norani Othman, Zainah Anwar and Zaitun Mohamed Kasim (2005), 'Malaysia: Islamisation, Muslim Politics and State Authoritarianism', in Norani Othman (ed.), *Muslim Women and the Challenge of Islamic Extremism*, 78–108. Selangor: Sisters in Islam.

Norshahril Saat (2010), 'The Muslim Religious Elite in Contemporary Malaysia: A Study of Dominant Ideas and Orientation of Prominent Religious Personalities and their Impact', unpubl. MA thesis, National University of Singapore.

Norshahril Saat (2020), 'The Politics of Islamic Discourse in Malaysia', in Norshahril Saat and Azhar Ibrahim (eds), *Alternative Voices in Muslim Southeast Asia: Discourses and Struggles*, 3–8. Singapore: ISEAS Publishing.

Pradana Boy Zulian (2015), 'Fatwā in Indonesia: An Analysis of Dominant Legal Ideas and Modes of Thought of Fatwā-Making Agencies and their Implications in the Post-New Order Period', unpubl. PhD diss., National University of Singapore.

Rahman, F. (1980), 'Islam: Legacy and Contemporary Challenge', *Islamic Studies* 19(4): 235–46.

Roff, William R. (1983), 'Whence Cometh the Law? Dog Saliva in Kelantan, 1937', *Comparative Studies in Society and History* 25(2): 323–38.

Sleboda, J. (2001), 'Islam and Women's Rights Advocacy in Malaysia', *Asian Journal of Women's Studies* 7(2): 94–136.

Stark, Jan (2003), 'The Islamic Debate in Malaysia: The Unfinished Project', *Southeast Asia Research* 11(2): 173–201.

Stivens, M. (2006), '"Family Values" and Islamic Revival: Gender, Rights and State Moral Projects in Malaysia', *Women's Studies International Forum* 29(4): 354–67.

Suat Yan, L. (2000), 'The Domestic Violence Act: Current Challenges to Malaysian Women', *Journal of Asian Women's Studies* 8: 135–38.

Suat Yan, L. (2003), 'The Women's Movement in Peninsular Malaysia, 1900–99', in Meredith L. Weiss and Saliha Hassan (eds), *Social Movements in Malaysia: From Moral Communities to NGOs*, 45–74. London: Routledge.

Tariq, Q. (2013), 'Govt Wins Appeal, Herald Banned from Using Word "Allah" over Public Safety', *The Star*, 14 October 2013, https://www.thestar.com.my/news/nation/2013/10/14/allah-the-herald-catholic-muslim/ (accessed 1 May 2021).

Towler, R. (1984), *The Need for Certainty: A Sociological Study of Conventional Religion*. London: Routledge and Keagan Paul.

Verma, V. (2002), *Malaysia: State and Civil Society in Transition*. Boulder: Lynne Rienner Publishers.

Woodward, M. (2001), 'Indonesia, Islam, and the Prospect for Democracy', *SAIS Review* 21(2): 29–37.

SECURING MUSLIM BOUNDARIES: RELIGIOUS FREEDOM AND PUBLIC ORDER IN PAKISTAN AND MALAYSIA

Matthew J. Nelson

This chapter examines the construction of religious identity boundaries via the identification of outsiders (here, so-called 'heretics') in Muslim-majority Pakistan and Malaysia. Specifically, I show how constitutional formulations concerning religious freedom are politically operationalised in a boundary-defining description of heretics as 'a source of public disorder'.[1] As a source of 'disorder', heretics are relegated to the margins of each country's constitutional community: situated on the *margins* of the community, they help to define those who remain *inside*.

Constitutional provisions concerning religious freedom typically allow elected, executive and judicial officials to set aside otherwise obligatory patterns of fundamental-rights enforcement whenever they succeed in asserting (politically) that 'public order' is threatened. Historically, this approach to religious freedom emerged in France's 'Declaration of the Rights of Man' (1789), which noted that '[n]o one shall be disquieted [. . .] on account of his religious views [. . .] provided their manifestation does not disturb the public order' (Article 10). This privileging of 'order' over 'rights' reappeared in several subsequent constitutions, including the Ottoman constitution of 1876 (Article 11).[2] It also figures prominently in the International Covenant on Civil and Political Rights (1966, Article 18) and, for present purposes, in the constitutions of Pakistan (Article 20) and Malaysia (Article 11).[3] I focus

---

[1] On the entanglement of religion, law, and the politics of identity in debates regarding religious freedom, see Sullivan et al. (2015).

[2] Article 11 of the *Constitution of the Ottoman Empire* (1876) stated that 'the state will protect the free exercise of faiths [. . .] on condition of public order and morality not being interfered with'.

[3] Article 18 of the *International Covenant on Civil and Political Rights* (ICCPR 1966) states that 'everyone shall have the right to freedom of thought, conscience and religion', including the 'freedom, either individually or in community with others and in

on the ways in which this peripatetic legal formulation relates to politically motivated claims that the *provocations* of so-called 'heretics' threaten
public order and, therein, the religious and constitutional boundaries of two
Muslim-majority states.

I make three points. First, I note that, when it comes to religious freedom,
Pakistan and Malaysia behave like other states: they treat religious freedom
as a constitutional right 'subject to' politically contingent claims regarding
public order. Second, I note that, in both states, the sources of politically contingent concerns regarding public disorder are not set apart from those who
self-identify with the religious majority. (Those defined as dangerous and
destabilising heretics *also* self-identify as 'Muslim'.) Finally, I note that efforts
to shore up the boundaries of each country's Muslim identity frequently rely
on a three-step reading of constitutional clauses regarding religious freedom:
first, so-called heretics are framed as religious provocateurs; second, their
religious provocation is said to pose a risk to public order; and, finally, the
rights of these so-called provocateurs are (lawfully) limited, placing otherwise peaceful religious practitioners beyond the normal protections of each
country's constitutional laws.[4]

In Pakistan and Malaysia, I argue that Muslim community boundaries are
partially defined by *limiting* the constitutional rights of so-called heretics.
However peaceful they may be, those cast as heretics are placed outside the
boundaries of the majority community in three ways: religiously (as 'heretics'), politically (as 'provocateurs') and legally (as a threat to 'public order').

Religious Provocation, Public Disorder, Constitutional Exclusion and Identity

In their work on boundary-formation and identity, Rogers Brubaker and
Frederick Cooper (2000: 15) note that 'preserving cultural distinctiveness',
or identity, is often tied to an active process of 'maintaining bounded
groupness', with periodic criticism of those seen as 'passing' (here, otherwise invisible heretics) serving as an effective form of discipline. Similar

public or private, to manifest his religion or belief [. . . however, this freedom . . .]
may be subject [. . .] to such limitations as are prescribed by law and are necessary
to protect public safety, order, [and so on]'. Pakistan accepted the ICCPR in 2010
with reservations regarding Article 18; those reservations were dropped in 2011.
Malaysia has not signed the ICCPR. In the *Constitution of Pakistan*, Article 20-A
states that 'subject to law, public order, and morality, every citizen shall have
the right to profess, practice, and propagate his religion'. In the *Constitution of
Malaysia*, Article 11-1 states that 'every person has the right to profess and practice
his religion', with Article 11-5 adding that 'this article does not authorize any act
contrary to any general law relating to public order [. . .]'.

[4] Balzacq (2011: 9) makes a similar point, noting that 'law defines [. . .] the normal and
the deviant, the inside and the outside, [. . .] and [. . .] the scope of application for
fundamental [constitutional or human] rights'.

efforts to construct notions of bounded groupness by policing those cast
as internal 'others' have been highlighted by Fredrick Barth (1969) and
Andreas Wimmer (2013). With specific reference to religion, this process has
appeared in the work of Talal Asad (1986), Mary Douglas (1996) and Tony
Marx (2003).

Focusing on group boundaries and constitutional law (with specific reference to public order), the work of Carl Schmitt (1985) is essential. Schmitt
notes that, when fundamental rights are set aside in a bid to defend ostensibly existential group boundaries, they are often *legally* set aside via provisions subordinating constitutional rights to the preservation of community
order. Giorgio Agamben (2005) treats these patterns of 'exception' as spaces
without law. But, in his book *Political Theology*, Schmitt treats them, more
accurately, as exceptional spaces *within* the law.[5] In effect, Schmitt reads
constitutional laws regarding religious freedom 'subject to public order' as
spaces of boundary-policing discretion – zones of discretion incorporating
hints of despotic power within the constitution itself.

Group boundaries, in Schmitt's formulation, are never simply given. They
are actively produced by political actors who, turning to constitutional law,
read certain actions or ways of being as a form of 'provocation' threatening 'public order'. Taking issue with disorder, they then treat their targets
as boundary-defining *exceptions* to the enforcement of otherwise applicable
rights.

Beyond Brubaker and Cooper, Agamben and Schmitt, I examine the
process whereby otherwise peaceful but ostensibly heretical forms of religious
'passing' are placed beyond the normal application of existing constitutional
rights. Specifically, turning to recent trends in international relations, I show
how heretics are cast as threats to public order and therein national security.
Within what is known as the international-relations literature on 'securitisation', group identities are actively constructed via political processes within
which others are cast as 'threats' (Buzan et al. 1997; Weldes et al. 1999).

Securitisation theorists have devoted relatively little attention to religion.
And even when they have touched on religion, they have rarely examined
the political instrumentalisation of *internal* religious differences (that is,
heresy) (Laustsen and Waever 2000; Vuori 2011; Sheikh 2014). With reference
to Islam, for instance, their work has generally focused on non-Muslims who
'securitise' Islam (or Muslims) as a whole – for example, via Islamophobic
security policies (Cesari 2012; Croft 2012; Mavelli 2013). This differs from
my focus on the ways in which *intra*-religious others are cast as threats to
doctrinal and state security in a bid to shore up the boundaries of this or that
religious identity.

[5] In the *Constitution of Pakistan* (Article 233) and the *Constitution of Malaysia* (Article
150–6A), constitutional 'emergency' powers cannot be used to limit a fundamental
right to religious freedom; this limit is baked straight into provisions that enshrine
religious freedom itself.

Conventionally, religious freedom is construed as a fundamental right with three dimensions. The first dimension, typically regarded as inviolable, is an internal dimension (the domain of religious 'faith'). The second is external (religious 'manifestation'). This second dimension is often seen as subject to legal regulations: broadly, regulations that treat the essential features of each person's faith as inviolable while, at the same time, subjecting ostensibly non-essential manifestations (for example, specific ritual practices) to periodic legislative supervision (Scolnicov 2011).

Even apart from this bifurcated approach to religious freedom as a fundamental individual right, however, religious freedom is also seen as having a third (collective) dimension – one in which each religious community is seen as being entitled to manage its own religious affairs. In Pakistan and Malaysia, religious communities are seen as having a fundamental right to frame their own religious doctrines, rituals and institutions in ways that remain at least partially removed from the formal legal directives of the state (Pakistan: Article 20-B; Malaysia: Article 11-3).[6]

Unfortunately, it is not uncommon to find an *individual's* right to peaceful manifestations of his or her religious freedom unsettling a *community's* sense of its own religious boundaries. This is particularly true in cases of heresy – typically, cases in which otherwise constitutionally protected individual beliefs or practices depart from what others see as 'collective' religious norms. In these cases, otherwise protected forms of religious deviance are often reframed as an 'exceptional' threat to community boundaries and, in some cases, an 'existential' threat to community identity and security.

In Pakistan and Malaysia, the beliefs and practices of so-called Muslim heretics are often said to present a risk of doctrinal confusion within the Muslim community as a whole. (In effect, heretics are said to spur forms of religious confusion that provoke destabilising forms of public disorder.) As such, those accused of heresy are recast as religious-*cum*-political subversives who actively increase the Muslim community's vulnerability to various external threats. Their otherwise peaceful and ostensibly protected religious beliefs and practices are simply reframed as a constitutionally unprotected – indeed, actively proscribed – security threat.

In what follows I highlight the ways in which politically situated concerns about doctrinal disunity shape (1) politically motivated claims regarding public disorder, (2) the limitation of constitutional provisions regarding religious freedom, and, ultimately, (3) the ongoing construction of identity

---

[6] In the *Constitution of Pakistan*, Article 20-B states that 'subject to law, public order, and morality, every religious denomination and every sect thereof have the right to establish, maintain, and manage its [own] religious institutions'. In the *Constitution of Malaysia*, Article 11-3 states that 'every religious group has the right to manage its own affairs' and 'establish and maintain institutions for religious [. . .] purposes', adding in Article 11-5 that 'this article does not authorize any act contrary to any general law relating to public order [. . .]'.

Matthew J. Nelson

boundaries in Muslim-majority Pakistan and Malaysia, placing those accused of Muslim 'heresy' beyond the limits of each country's 'Muslim' community.

Background: Muslim Heresy, Public Disorder and the Law in Pakistan and Malaysia

Both Pakistan and Malaysia share a post-colonial attachment to British common law as well as a set of constitutional commitments balancing explicit protections for religious freedom with Islam as the state religion.[7] (Crucially, the enumeration of fundamental rights in the constitutions of both countries marked a clear departure from British constitutional principles regarding the unfettered sovereignty of parliament.) Matters of Muslim heresy, however, are not confined to constitutional questions. In both countries, ordinary criminal laws also figure prominently.

In Pakistan, heretics are engaged via several amendments to colonial criminal laws concerning blasphemy. (Exactly the *same* laws were inherited, in Malaysia, from the Indian Penal Code of 1860.) Between 1860 and 1927, §295–8 of the Indian Penal Code, focusing on blasphemy, did not refer to 'public order'. In 1927, however, this Code was revised (adding §295-A) to address intentional insults resulting in public 'outrage' and, thus, public disorder (Ahmed 2009: 179–81). After 1980, Pakistan's General Zia-ul-Haq further amended Pakistan's (derivative) penal code to protect Islam in particular (ibid.: 183). Since then, the Pakistani Penal Code has criminalised certain beliefs or pratices that 'outrage' the feelings of Pakistani Muslims (§298-C).[8]

In Malaysia, heretics are only rarely addressed via the country's (similarly derivative) blasphemy law. Instead, they are typically addressed in one of three ways. Some are confronted with draconian detention provisions outlined in Malaysia's Internal Security Act (ISA) and, since 2012, in Malaysia's Security Offences (Special Measures) Act. Some are accused of 'sedition'.[9] But, given the federalised structure of laws governing Muslim religious affairs in Malaysia – specifically, the fact that binding rules regarding Islamic matters are generally reserved for regional sultans and the state-

---

[7] In the *Constitution of Pakistan*, Article 2 states that 'Islam shall be the state religion of Pakistan'. In the *Constitution of Malaysia*, Article 3-1 states that 'Islam is the religion of the Federation'.

[8] Like Pakistan, Malaysia tried to revise its colonial blasphemy laws. But, in 1988, amendments seeking to criminalise any act causing or intending to cause religious disunity (§298A) were struck down when Malaysia's Federal Court decided in *Mamat Daud* v. *PP* (1 MLJ 119) that, insofar as these amendments concerned 'religion', they should be introduced by individual states (Faruqi 2005: 3).

[9] Malaysia's *Sedition (Amendment) Act* (2015) also guards against any hostility 'on the ground of religion'.

level bureaucrats or elected officials who work under them – most are not accused of federal crimes at all. Instead, and particularly since the mid-1980s, they are accused of crimes within each Malaysian *state* (Fernando 2006).[10] These state-level laws target 'offences by persons professing Islam against [the] precepts of that religion' (for example, 'false doctrine', 'deviationist' teachings and 'wrongful worship').

Many states around the world are constitutionally empowered to set aside the enforcement of a fundamental right to religious freedom whenever they perceive a threat to public order. In Pakistan and Malaysia – regimes that occasionally describe themselves as 'Islamic' states – this pattern is *not* rooted in the application of shari'ah or *fiqh* (that is, Islamic jurisprudence). Instead, this pattern lies in the invocation of constitutional and common-law provisions pertaining to fundamental rights – specifically, fundamental-rights clauses concerning public order. It is in fact the identification of 'a threat to public order' and, therein, the limitation of a fundamental right to religious freedom, that allows for the clarification of Muslim community boundaries.

Religious Freedom, Public Order and the Construction of a 'Muslim' Identity in Malaysia

In peninsular Malaya, Islam emerged as the religion of the majority sometime after the fifteenth century. However, owing to an influx of Chinese (mostly Buddhist or Taoist) traders and tin miners, then South Indian (mostly Hindu) colonial clerks and agricultural labourers during the nineteenth and early twentieth century – that is, during the course of British colonial rule – Malay Muslims now make up just over half of the country's total population. During the anti-colonial nationalist struggle, frictions between Malay Muslims and non-Malay Chinese and Indians persisted, with some Malay nationalists insisting that Chinese and Indian residents should not be recognised as full citizens. Subsequent negotiations ensured that the country's independence in 1957 was built on a more expansive understanding of citizenship. Yet, in 1969, race riots showed that some Malays still resented forms of economic and political marginalisation.

Since 1969, successive governments have done more to privilege the interests of Malaysia's 'indigenous' Malays. In fact two Malay-oriented political parties have battled each other to define – and defend – the country's Malay Muslim majority. Each has sought to clarify who is, and who is not, a 'Malay', noting that, strictly speaking, the country's constitution defines a Malay as *inter alia* 'a person who professes Islam'.

The first of these two parties is the United Malays National Organisation or UMNO (established 1949), which held a super-majority in Malaysia's national parliament almost continuously between 1957 and 2008. (This

---

[10] In the *Constitution of Malaysia*, Article 11-4 notes that Malaysia's *states* are empowered to control the propagation of doctrine amongst Muslims.

majority was briefly absent in 1969.) The second party is the (Islamist) Parti Islam se-Malaysia or PAS (established 1951), with particular regional strength in the northern states of Kelantan and, occasionally, Terengganu. Alongside these two parties, non-party groups focused on *dakwah* or Muslim religious revitalisation have also figured prominently in ongoing efforts to define the parameters of Malaysia's Muslim identity. These include the Malaysian Islamic Youth Movement (Angkatan Belia Islam Malaysia or ABIM, established 1971) and groups like Darul Arqam or al-Arqam (now also known as Global Ikhwan, established 1968).

Across these different groups, competing efforts to control the delineation of Malay-Muslim identity are easy to discern. During the country's first national election in 1959, for instance, an UMNO-led alliance emerged with a powerful majority, but the precursor of PAS, known as the Pan-Malaya Islamic Party (PMIP), made a strong showing in Kelantan and Terengganu along the country's northern border with Thailand. Perceiving a split in the Malay-Muslim vote, UMNO accused Malaya's Islamists of dividing the community 'from within' and, in doing so, threatening the country's national security. But, during Malaysia's second election in 1964, PMIP responded in kind, describing meat prepared by UMNO supporters, marriages with UMNO supporters and prayers said alongside UMNO supporters as religiously forbidden or *haram*. One member of PMIP's Ulema Council even described UMNO members as *kafirs* (infidels), setting off a tit-for-tat pattern of mutual recrimination in which each group sought to place the other outside the pale of Islam (Abdullah 1999: 268). In the end, UMNO accused the leader of PMIP, Barhanuddin al-Helmy, of sedition. Specifically, they accused him of collaborating with radical Muslim nationalists in Indonesia to overthrow UMNO's government. Moving beyond questions of heresy to questions of public order, Al-Helmy was detained (without trial) under Malaysia's Internal Security Act.

UMNO went on to lead a ruling coalition known as 'Barisan Nasional' (BN) in 1973. This coalition, citing concerns regarding public disorder, dissolved Kelantan's PAS-led state-level government in 1977, imposing emergency rule (Kessler 1978: 35). In fact, shortly thereafter, previously quiescent groups such as ABIM became more politicised, with PAS's 'old guard' finding itself increasingly pushed aside by 'young Turks' like ABIM's Anwar Ibrahim and Abdul Hadi Awang. After visiting Tehran in early 1979, Ibrahim organised a 'Day of Solidarity' to express ABIM's support for Iran's Islamic revolution. Judith Nagata notes that there was no 'official [...] UMNO position on ABIM', but throughout this period UMNO officials made 'frequent verbal attacks' on what they called 'deviant' groups'. According to Nagata, UMNO was obsessed with Malay-Muslim 'disunity' and the ability of parties like PAS and groups like ABIM to 'split [...] the Muslim vote' (Nagata 1980: 427).

By 1981, close political observers like Mohamad Abu Bakar were reporting numerous UMNO-led scare-mongering campaigns in which ABIM activists were described as '*dakwah songsang*' or heretics. These campaigns also cited concerns regarding internal and external security – concerns in which UMNO claimed that Malay-Muslim students were being 'used' by 'anti-national' elements (including Shi'i clerics). When one of UMNO's own youth initiatives, Nasrul Haq, grew too quickly and appeared to threaten its patrons, even this initiative was banned in several states for 'its "dubious" use of religion' (ibid: 433).

In 1981, Dr Mahathir Mohamad became Malaysia's Prime Minister. After coopting his erstwhile opponent, ABIM leader Anwar Ibrahim, Mahathir launched an even more intensive effort to define and defend Malaysia's Muslim community.[11] Specifically, he unveiled a programme known as 'The Inculcation of Islamic Values' with a resolution urging both federal and state-level Islamic Councils to collaborate in defending the 'purity' of Malaysian Islam (Noor 2003: 206). The country's federal Islamic Council, relocated within the Office of the Prime Minister was charged with recommending new ways to identify those who might be purveyors of 'deviationist' or provocative teachings and punished for 'offences against the precepts of Islam' (ibid).

In the meantime, seeking to consolidate its electoral position in Kelantan after 1990, PAS introduced a set of policies seeking to assert its own understanding of Muslim boundaries by 'cleansing' the state of so-called heresies within the performing arts – threatening to ban UNESCO-recognised *mak yong* performances, for instance, unless a character from the Indian epic *Ramayana* (namely, 'Ramachandra') was replaced with a Muslim character aptly re-named 'Rahman' (Hoffstaedter 2011: 124–5). PAS's attack on otherwise peaceful forms of Kelantanese art, however, initiated a chain reaction, with UMNO describing PAS as a 'threat' to Malay-Muslim culture, even as PAS described UMNO as a threat to Islam itself. Minor skirmishes merely seemed to justify the public-order claims underpinning each group's 'securitisation' of the other.

Not long before this cycle of mutual recrimination in Kelantan, Mahathir's UMNO-led government published a White Paper entitled 'Threat to Muslim Unity and National Security' implicating PAS along with several other ostensibly 'deviant' groups in a range of 'subversive' activities (Barroclough 1986: 196).[12] Turning to matters of national security to address its concerns about division 'from within', several PAS leaders were arrested under Malaysia's Internal Security Act, complaining that their fatwas and speeches caused 'enmity and conflict amongst Muslims' in ways that directly threatened public security (Noor 2003: 206). As Kamarulnizam Abdullah explains,

---

[11] ABIM activists who refused to follow Anwar Ibrahim to the UMNO took over as junior leaders under PAS's President Yusuf Rawa (1983–9): Hadi Awang, for instance, became PAS Vice President (Noor 2003: 208).

[12] In 1994, the leader of Darul Arqam, Ustaaz Asha'ari, was detained for ten years under Malaysia's ISA.

quoting a separate White Paper commissioned to review the government's use of internal-security measures to suppress 'deviant' PAS supporters in a deadly crackdown known as the 'Memali' incident, the state refused to suffer any group that might 'create [. . .] chaos' by 'splitting the solidarity of Muslims' (Abdullah 1999: 272).[13] Division, if you will, was seen as *prima facie* evidence of religious provocation and public disorder meriting extraordinary security measures.

By the late 1990s, UMNO saw itself as the undisputed czar of Malaysia's Muslim identity. But, in 1999, national and state-level elections brought together a new opposition coalition known as the Barisan Alternatif (BA), including PAS and a new party known as the National Justice Party led by the wife of (imprisoned) ABIM leader Anwar Ibrahim. Once again, this coalition split the Malay-Muslim vote; in fact for the first time ever UMNO was supported by a minority of Malay-Muslim voters (Noor 2003: 201). Perhaps not suprisingly, Prime Minister Mahathir threatened to invoke §298-A of the Malaysian Penal Code (punishing acts 'causing disharmony, disunity, or feelings of enmity [. . .] on grounds of religion') the following year, targeting anyone who sought to 'disunite' the country's Muslim majority (Martinez 2001: 480).

Finally, the exclusive power of each Malaysian *state* to punish so-called Islamic deviation was reinforced by Malaysia's Court of Appeal in 2002.[14] In Terengganu, a peaceful religious-reform movement known as the Sky Kingdom led by Ariffin Mohammad (also known as Ayah Pin), who saw himself as a reincarnation of Mohammad as well as Jesus, Shiva and the Buddha, fell prey to protracted attacks. Already, Ayah Pin had been jailed on the pretext of failing to obey a state-level fatwa banning his movement as 'deviant'. But, in 2005, his followers were physically assaulted. The vigilantes were not arrested. Instead, fifty-eight Sky Kingdom followers were detained for violating Terengganu's (state-level) Shari'ah Criminal Offences Act. Described as doctrinal provocateurs, these peaceful religious practitioners were arrested to *preempt* any possibility of future public disorder (Human Rights Watch 2005).

Already, UMNO was involved in a similar assault on Malaysian Shi'a, beginning with a 1996 National Fatwa Council decree stating that, within Malaysia, only Sunni Islam was permitted – effectively reversing a 1984 fatwa in which the Jafari and Zaidi branches of Shi'ism were legally recog-

---

[13] In the Memali Incident, PAS member Ibrahim Mahmood battled government forces seeking to detain him and his supporters under the ISA for *'kafir-mengafir'* (*takfiri*) activities.

[14] *Kamariah bte Ali* v. *Kerajaan Negeri Kelantan* (2002) 3 MLJ 657 (Faruqi: 10). This endorsement of state-level power was further reinforced in *Sulaiman Takrib* v. *Kerajaan Negeri Terengganu and Kerajaan Malaysia* (2008) 3 MLRA 257 and *ZI Publications Sdn Bhd* v. *Kerajaan Negeri Selangor and Kerajaan Malaysia* (2015) 5 MLRA 697.

nised as 'Muslim'. Given the federalisation of Muslim doctrinal affairs, this 1996 fatwa could only be operationalised by individual states. But, in due course, ten out of fourteen states adopted it. In 1997, ten Shi'a were detained, and in 2000 six more (Shah and Sani 2011: 671). In 2010, more than 200 Shi'a peacefully commemorating the martyrdom of Hussein were detained under the (state-level) Selangor Shari'ah Criminal Offences Enactment (1995) and accused of threating 'national security' (Gooch 2011). Shi'ism, argued the Director-General of Malaysia's federal Islamic Council, was 'a cancer that [had] to be prevented' before it became 'a threat to Muslim unity' (*Malay Mail* 2013). In 2013, Malaysia's Home Ministry formally banned The Malaysian Shi'a Association under the pretext of 'national security'.

According to Kamirulnizam Abdullah, turning to what Carl Schmitt saw as each state's sovereign power to define its own legal exceptions, 'any deviation from [the government's] official line' must be placed under sanction, often as a matter of internal 'security' or, indeed, criminal 'sedition' (Abdullah 1999: 277). When fundamental rights are ignored, they are often *legally* ignored. They are legally ignored in what is often described as an 'emergency' push to define and shore up the boundaries of each country's core identity.

Religious Freedom, Public Order and the Construction of 'Muslim' Identity in Pakistan

In Pakistan, allegations regarding religious deviance as a source of disorder leading to a limitation of fundamental rights are equally familiar. The historical circumstances and political dynamics, however, are different, beginning with a series of battles surrounding the drafting of Pakistan's constitution and then continuing with a set of allegations targeting the 'heresy' of one specific group: the Ahmadiyya. Constituting less than one percent of Pakistan's total population, the Ahmadiyya see themselves as 'Muslim', but they are often described as heretical, owing to claims made by the group's late-nineteenth-century Punjabi founder, Mirza Ghulam Ahmad (d. 1908), that he was not merely a religious reformer but a prophet – indeed, a prophet who received revelations *after* the Prophet Mohammad (Friedman 1989). (Typically, Muslims see the Prophet Mohammad as the 'seal' of prophecy itself: Qur'an 33:40.) In light of these claims, the Ahmadiyya are often seen as demarcating the external boundary of Pakistan's 'Muslim' community.

Following the independence and partition of British India, Pakistan emerged in 1947. Located in the Muslim-majority areas of British India – Punjab, Sindh, Balochistan and the Northwest Frontier Province or NWFP in 'West' Pakistan, as well as East Bengal in 'East' Pakistan (later refashioned as Bangladesh following a brutal civil war in 1971) – Pakistan was the world's first state explicitly created on the basis of a religious identity. Despite a Muslim majority of 90–95 percent, however, considerable disagreement surrounded the specific nature of Pakistan's 'Muslim' identity. Those affiliated with Pakistan's leading anti-colonial nationalist party, the All-India (later Pakistan) Muslim League, felt that Pakistan should be a Muslim-majority state in which a largely secular constitution permitted elected legislators to define and, then, re-define the legal relevance of religious values over time. Ostensibly religious parties – particularly, lay Muslim activists associated with the Jama'at-e-Islami or JI (Party of Islam) and the madrasah-based leaders of a party known as the Jamiat-e-Ulema-e-Islam or JUI (Party of the Clerics of Islam) – felt that Pakistan should be a more explicitly 'Islamic' state in which their own ostensibly expert interpretation of the Qur'an and sunnah would check the work of Pakistan's legislature and judiciary. All of these groups felt that Pakistan should be an 'Islamic democracy' with a 'Muslim' head of state. They simply disagreed about (1) the relative weight of 'Islam' and 'democracy' and (2) who might qualify as a 'Muslim'.

Those who led Pakistan's nationalist Muslim League resembled the lay Muslim leaders of UMNO insofar as they opposed conservative religious activists associated with the ulama and Islamist parties like PAS or the JI. In Malaysia, ulama working under regional sultans as the *de jure* 'heads of Islam' in each Malaysian state were empowered to define the terms of Muslim doctrine (largely owing to the federalisation of Muslim religious affairs and, within this, the promulgation of state-level laws concerning Muslim deviance). But in Pakistan, the constitution was drafted by mainstream Muslim elites who insisted that, even as references to Islam might be incorporated within the country's legal apparatus, the ulama would have *no* special right to define the meaning of those references.

Precisely insofar as this was the case, however, Pakistan's ulama and Islamist activists searched for new ways to assert their religious-*cum*-political views. In Malaysia, this competition involved tit-for-tat allegations of heretical provocation (and, therein, public disorder) targeting a rather wide range of groups – from UMNO to PAS, ABIM, Darul Arqam, the Sky Kingdom and local Shi'a. But in Pakistan, this competition brought politically marginalised groups such as the JI and the JUI together in a focused campaign targeting just one group in particular: the Ahmadiyya. Initially, Pakistan's nationalist elite sought to define a constitution in which the Ahmadiyya were protected as peaceful religious practitioners, steering clear of any formal judgement regarding their religious self-identification (Qasmi 2010). But, again, conservative activists opposed this approach. They insisted that the Ahmadiyya should be relegated – together with Hindus, Sikhs, Christians and Parsis – to a separate 'non-Muslim' electorate while being denied any access to constitutionally defined Muslim rights (for instance, access to an explicitly 'Muslim' presidency).

Even before Pakistan's first constitution was unveiled in 1956, this right-wing amalgamation resorted to anti-Ahmadi pogroms that led to Pakistan's first martial law (1952). This spate of martial law was followed by a judicial inquiry culminating in a report known as the 'Munir Report'. Returning to the link between constitutional notions of religious freedom, allegations of deviance and public order, this report blamed Pakistan's first stretch of martial law on religious activists seeking to bolster their own religious and political credentials by implicating state institutions and security forces in intra-Muslim allegations of heresy. Reflecting on the disagreement between conservative activists and the Ahmadiyya, for instance, the report explained that the greatest danger facing Pakistan lay in expressions of intra-Muslim 'bitterness'. When 'viewed in [an] international context', the report explained, stretching beyond the issue of public order to questions of national security, 'any movement which [might] arouse sectarian bitterness was fraught with [very] grave consequences'. Protests targeting the doctrinal deviance of the Ahmadiyya, they noted, with a nod to India, were most 'inopportune' in a country facing powerful external threats (*Report of the Court of Inquiry* 1954: 290).

During the 1940s, 1950s and 1960s, nationalist elites articulated an approach to the Ahmadiyya that differed dramatically from the approach adopted by Pakistan's ulama and Islamists, with nationalists *defending* the rights of the Ahmadiyya even as their opponents used violence in a vigilante effort to *deny* them. By 1973–4, however, nationalist opinion had slowly shifted, seeing vigilante action as, in many ways, a predictable response to Ahmadi 'provocations'.

This shift emerged via two waves of legal reform. The first wave, prompted by Prime Minister Zulfiqar Ali Bhutto in response to yet another stretch of protests by conservative religious activists, introduced Pakistan's second constitutional amendment officially clarifying the boundaries of Pakistan's 'Muslim' identity by defining the Ahmadiyya as 'non-Muslims'.[15] Passed unanimously by the country's National Assembly in 1974, this amendment leapt over any consideration of individual religious self-identification to subject an entire group of citizens to a 'constitutionalised' form of *takfir*. In effect, the Assembly seized on claims emanating from the Ahmadiyya themselves – that they constituted 'a separate community' (of devoted 'Muslims') – to suggest that the Ahmadiyya posed an existential threat to the unity of Pakistani Muslims and, indeed, Pakistan itself 'from within' (Qasmi 2014: 204).

As Asad Ahmed explains, the ulama saw the Ahmadiyya as 'dangerous and harmful [both] to the Muslim community and to the state'. They were harmful to the community as 'their heterodox beliefs destabilised the fundamentals of faith and created [doctrinal] uncertainty'. And, turning to Pakistan's Penal Code, their beliefs *also* figured as 'an offence' for they '"outraged" the feel-ings of the [. . .] community'. Above all, however, Ahmed notes that state officials sought to ban Ahmadi events and practices as 'a threat to public

---

[15] Within Pakistan's second constitutional amendment, Article 260 was revised to define a 'Muslim' as one who 'does not believe in, or recognise as a prophet or religious reformer, any person who [. . .] claims to be a prophet [. . .] after Muhammad'.

order' (Ahmed 2010: 287). Indeed, as Ali Usman Qasmi (2014: 204) points out, drawing on a painstaking review of the National Assembly's proceedings that produced Pakistan's second constitutional amendment, allegations regarding the possibility of public disorder provided a clear legal platform for 'denying some of the rights [. . .] guaranteed by the constitution' itself.

Ultimately, the attorney-general who chaired the National Assembly proceedings leading to Pakistan's second constitutional amendment did not believe that government was required to prioritise an 'individual' right to religious freedom (Article 20A). Instead, he argued that Pakistan's parliament was fully empowered to introduce constitutional amendments even to the point of subjecting fundamental rights to 'limitations' (Kazi 2015: 91). Specifically, he noted that Pakistan's parliament was empowered to guard against any 'encroachment' on Muslim legal prerogatives – particularly, encroachments associated with some form of 'tangible material damage' (for example, diluting access to a Muslims-only presidency) (Qasmi 2014: 192). In effect, he suggested that any such damage would only increase the possibility of public disorder. And, to preempt this disorder, he noted that parliament was entitled, by way of amendments targeting the constitutional 'definition' of a Muslim (Article 260), to regulate any infraction growing out of what he called 'false belonging' (ibid: 193).

Accommodating long-standing Islamist demands, Pakistan's National Assembly sought to clarify who was a Muslim by specifying more clearly who was not. In fact, even apart from the Assembly's *political* logic, stressing Muslim identity, its *legal* logic was firmly tied to an account of religious identity bound up with an account of doctrinal encroachments and religious provocations threatening public order. After the mid-1970s, those guilty of 'false belonging' were not merely heretics or imposters. In keeping with existing clauses limiting the application of fundamental rights, their presence was read as religiously disturbing, even offensive, in ways that posed a risk to public order. Cutting straight to the link between community identity, public order and national security, Sadia Saeed (2007: 145) notes that the Ahmadiyya were constructed, not merely as divisive 'heretics', but also as 'disloyal and traitorous'. Underpinning the Assembly's evisceration of their constitutional rights, she explains, even peaceful Ahmadi citizens were cast as the country's new 'enemy within'.

Moving beyond the constitution, Pakistan's second wave of legal reform was led by General Zia-ul-Haq during the 1980s. Responding to yet another round of protests by the same configuration of conservative religious activists, General Zia moved beyond the constitution to amend Pakistan's blasphemy law. In 1984, §298 of the Pakistan Penal Code was amended, adding §298-C to prevent the ('non-Muslim') Ahmadiyya from 'posing' as Muslims or referring to their faith as 'Islam' and, in doing so, 'outraging' other Muslims in ways that might lead to public disorder.

Zia's penal-code amendments were challenged in Pakistan's Supreme Court as a violation of the Ahmadis' fundamental right to religious freedom.

But, in 1993, the Court upheld these amendments on grounds explicitly stressing public order.[16] In the landmark case of *Zaheeruddin* v. *The State*, a group of Ahmadiyya appealed to overturn their prior conviction for wearing badges bearing the Muslim profession of faith (*kalima*) and celebrating the Ahmadi centenary in Jhang – a celebration the local district magistrate sought to ban as 'a risk to public order' (Lau 1995; Mahmud 1995). In its judgment, however, the Court doubled down on a securitisation of Ahmadi beliefs and peaceful religious practices as a 'a threat to the integrity of [the] Ummah' and, beyond this, the 'tranquility of the [Muslim] nation', indeed, an 'organised attack' on the 'ideological frontiers' of Islam (*Zaheeruddin*: 1765). As Amjad Mahmood Khan explains, the Court held that 'Ahmadi religious practices, however peaceful, angered and offended the Sunni majority; [. . . so] to maintain law and order, Pakistan would [. . .] need to control [them]' (Khan 2003: 228).

According to Pakistan's Supreme Court, even peaceful Ahmadi beliefs and practices had the effect of 'infuriating' and 'instigating' Pakistani Muslims, creating 'serious cause for [a] disturbance of the public peace' (*Zaheeruddin*: 1777). In fact they went even further, associating peaceful Ahmadi beliefs and practices with provoking a religious 'civil war' (ibid; Khan 2015: 18). As such, the Court held that it was necessary to restrict the peaceful practices of the Ahmadiyya (as 'provocative') in a *preemptive* bid to avoid any future outburst by Pakistan's religious majority.

Of course, this 'securitisation' of peaceful Ahmadi beliefs and practices did not secure the state. It merely fuelled a torrent of *takfiri* politics, with numerous groups accusing one another of intra-Muslim heresies that 'provoked' vigilante action and, therein, public disorder. Within just a few years, prevailing trends had shifted beyond the Ahmadiyya to new targets – including, as in Malaysia, local Shi'a (Zaman 1998: 699).

Conclusion

Focusing on South and Southeast Asia (Pakistan and Malaysia), this chapter examines the ways in which state-society interactions and, more specifically, constitutional politics concerning the meaning of religious freedom 'subject to public order' open up spaces for Muslim identity formation rooted in patterns of (intra-Muslim) religious-*cum*-legal exclusion. Moving beyond the ways in which *religion* as a marker of difference plays a role in identity construction, this chapter focuses on the ways in which allegations of doctrinal 'deviation' construed as a form of intra-religious provocation threatening 'public order' underpin the *legal* delineation of 'Muslim' community boundaries.

Here, formal legal processes of constitutional governance targeting intra-religious forms of religious plurality are filtered through a process wherein

---

[16] *Zaheeruddin* v. *The State* 26 SCMR (SC) 1718.

individuals and groups identified as doctrinal provocateurs are recast as an exception to the enforcement of otherwise applicable rights – in this case, an individual right to peaceful religious practice and religious self-identification. In Pakistan and Malaysia – states with constitutional provisions clearly identifying Islam as the state religion – the treatment of heretics is not rooted in the terms of Islamic law. Instead, it is closely tied to internationally recognised legal provisions concerning religious freedom.

But Pakistan and Malaysia are not alone. In China, we see peaceful Falun Gong practitioners being securitised as an internal threat to the *qigong* spiritual exercises accepted by China's communist regime, with the Chinese government linking its own constitutional understanding of 'religious freedom' and 'public order' (Constitution of the People's Republic of China, Article 36) to familiar tropes regarding the threat posed by 'heretical' conspiracies hatching subversive plots in league with foreign powers (Vuori 2011: 195).[17] In fact, as in Pakistan and Malaysia, these tropes take shape *via* intervening references to public order, with the Chinese government revising its own Criminal Code in 1997 to prohibit 'heretical cults' that 'disturb [...] social order'. And, yet, even as the government portrays Falun Gong as (heretically) '[opposed] to Marxist science', Falun Gong members appear to recapitulate the *takfiri* trends of Pakistan and Malaysia, claiming that the Communist Party itself 'undermine[s] the cohesiveness of the [... nation]'. Each is engaged in a tit-for-tat game of securitisation, stressing the possibility of public disorder in ways that – unfortunately for Falun Gong – lead to a limitation of rights.

Even within the European Union, ostensibly deviant Jehovah's Witnesses have battled Greek Orthodox Christians, with the European Court of Human Rights accepting a formal legal restriction on the fundamental rights of the former. Refusing to strike down a Greek law limiting 'improper' proselytisation, the European Court of Human Rights held that, given the presence of a familiar 'public order' limitation on religious freedom in the Greek constitution (Article 13-2), laws seeking to restrict the construction of a Jehovah's Witness hall of worship could be justified alongside a history of religious tension in Greece. Specifically, Greek laws restricting the rights of otherwise peaceful Jehovah's Witnesses were seen as having 'a legitimate aim' in 'protecting public order'.[18]

Again, the links are familiar: doctrinal deviance equals religious provocation; provocation generates disorder; disorder points to existential threats requiring emergency security measures – up to and including formal limitations on the enforcement of fundamental rights. Every regime is equipped

---

[17] Article 36 (*Constitution of China*, 1982) states that 'citizens of the PRC enjoy freedom of religious belief' and 'the state protects normal religious activities', even though 'no one may use religion to disrupt public order'.

[18] See *Kokkinakas* v. *Greece* 260 ECHR (ser. A), (1993), p. 21 (para 48); *Manoussakis* v. *Greece* 23 ECHR (ser. A) (1996), p. 15 (para 40).

with discretionary powers allowing it to restrict the freedoms of those defined as deviants. Typically, the power to define *public order* is all that is necessary to define – and defend – the boundaries of a given *religious* community.

References

Abdullah, K. (1999), 'National Security and Malay Unity: The Issue of Radical Religious Elements in Malaysia', *Contemporary Southeast Asia* 21(2): 261–82.

Agamben, G. (2005), *State of Exception*. Chicago: University of Chicago Press.

Ahmed, A. (2009), 'Specters of Macaulay: Blasphemy, the Indian Penal Code, and Pakistan's Postcolonial Predicament', in R. Kaur and W. Mazzarella (eds), *Censorship in South Asia: From Sedition to Seduction*, 172–205. Bloomington: University of Indiana Press.

Ahmed, A. (2010), 'The Paradoxes of Ahmadiyya Identity: Legal Appropriation of Muslim-ness and the Construction of Ahmadiyya Difference', in N. Khan (ed.), *Beyond Crisis: Re-Evaluating Pakistan*, 273–314. London: Routledge.

Asad, T. (1986), *The Idea of an Anthropology of Islam*. Washington, DC: Georgetown University.

Balzacq, T. (2011), *Securitization Theory: How Security Problems Emerge and Dissolve*. London: Routledge.

Barraclough, S. (1986), 'Malaysia in 1985: A Question of Management', *Southeast Asian Affairs* [n. v.]: 185–207.

Barth, F. (1969), *Ethnic Groups and Boundaries*. London: Little, Brown and Co.

Brubaker, R. and Cooper, F. (2000), 'Beyond "Identity"', *Theory and Society* 29(1): 1–47.

Buzan, B., Wæver, O. and de Wilde, J. (1997), *Security: A New Framework for Analysis*. Boulder: Lynne Rienner.

Cesari, J. (2012), 'The Securitisation of Islam in Europe', *Die Welt des Islams* 52(3/4): 430–49.

Constitution of China (1982), https://www.constituteproject.org/constitution/China_2004.pdf?lang=en (accessed 5 August 2019).

Constitution of Malaysia (1957), http://www.agc.gov.my/agcportal/uploads/files/Publications/FC/Federal%20Consti%20(BI%20text).pdf (accessed 5 August 2019).

Constitution of the Ottoman Empire (1876), http://www.anayasa.gen.tr/1876constitution.htm (accessed 5 August 2019).

Constitution of Pakistan (1973), http://www.na.gov.pk/uploads/documents/1333523681_951.pdf (accessed 5 August 2019).

Croft, S. (2012) *Securitizing Islam: Identity and the Search for Security*. Cambridge: Cambridge University Press.

Declaration of the Rights of Man (1789), https://avalon.law.yale.edu/18th_century/rights of.asp (accessed 5 August 2019).

Douglas, M. (1996) *Purity and Danger*. London: Routledge.

Faruqi, S. (24 September 2005), 'Jurisdiction of State Authorities to Punish Offences against the Precepts of Islam: A Constitutional Perspective', *The Malaysian Bar*, www.malaysianbar.org.my/constitutional_law/jurisdiction_of_state_authorities_to_punish_offences_against_the_precepts_of_islam_a_constitutional_perspective.html (accessed 5 August 2019).

Fernando, J. (2006), *The Making of the Malayan Constitution*. Malaysia Branch of the Royal Asiatic Society.

Friedman, Y. (1989), *Prophecy Continuous: Aspects of Ahmadi Religious Thought and Its Medieval Background*. Berkeley: University of California Press.

Gooch, L. (27 January 2011), 'In a Muslim State, Fear Sends Some Worship Underground', *New York Times*.

Hoffstaedter, G. (2011), *Modern Muslim Identities: Negotiating Religion and Ethnicity in Malaysia*. Copenhagen: Nordic Institute of Asian Studies.

Human Rights Watch (21 July 2005), 'Malaysia: Protect Freedom of Belief for Sky Kingdom', https://www.hrw.org/news/2005/07/21/malaysia-protect-freedom-belief-sky-kingdom (accessed 5 August 2019).

International Covenant on Civil and Political Rights (1966), https://treaties.un.org/doc/publication/unts/volume%20999/volume-999-i-14668-english.pdf (accessed 5 August 2019).

Kazi, A. (2015), 'The Politics of Balsphemy: Religion and Public Reasoning in Pakistan', unpubl. PhD diss., Cambridge University.

Kessler, C. (1978), *Islam and Politics in a Malay State: Kelantan 1838–1969*. Ithaca: Cornell University Press.

Khan, A. (2003), 'Persecution of the Ahmadiyya Community in Pakistan: An Analysis Under International Law and International Relations', *Harvard Human Rights Journal* 16: 217–44.

Khan, A. (2015), 'Pakistan's Anti-Blasphemy Laws and the Illegitimate Use of the "Law, Public Order, and Morality" Limitation on Constitutional Rights', *Review of Faith and International Affairs* 131: 13–22.

Lau, M. (1995), 'The Case of *Zaheer-ud-din v The State* and Its Impact on the Fundamental Right to Freedom of Religion', *Centre for Islamic and Middle Eastern Law Yearbook* 1, London: School of Oriental and African Studies, https://www.soas.ac.uk/cimel/materials/intro.html (accessed 5 August 2019).

Laustsen, C. and Waever, O. (2000), 'In Defense of Religion: Sacred Referent Objects for Securitization', *Millenium* 29(3): 705–39.

Mahmud, T. (1995), 'Freedom of Religion and Religious Minorities in Pakistan: A Study of Judicial Practice', *Fordham International Law Journal* 19(1): 40–100.

Malay Mail (13 December 2013), 'Jakim: All branches of Shiah in Malaysia violate Islamic law', https://www.malaymail.com/s/581217/jakim-all-branches-of-shiah-in-malaysia-violate-islamic-law (accessed 5 August 2019).

Martinez, P. (2001), 'The Islamic State or the State of Islam in Malaysia', *Contemporary Southeast Asia* 23(3): 474–503.

Marx, A. (2003), *Faith in Nation, The Exclusionary Origins of Nationalism*. Oxford: Oxford University Press.

Mavelli, L. (2013), 'Between Normalisation and Exception: The Securitisation of Islam and the Construction of the Secular Subject', *Millennium* 41(2): 159–81.

Nagata, J. (1980), 'Religious Ideology and Social Change: The Islamic Revival in Malaysia', *Pacific Affairs* 53(3): 405–39.

Noor, F. (2003), 'Blood, Sweat, and Jihad: The Radicalisation of the Political Discourse of the Pan-Malaysian Islamic Party (PAS) from 1982 Onwards', *Contemporary Southeast Asia* 25(2): 200–32.

Qasmi, A. (2010), 'God's Kingdom on Earth? Politics of Islam in Pakistan 1947–1969', *Modern Asian Studies* 44(6): 1197–253.

Qasmi, A. (2014), *The Ahmadis and the Politics of Religious Exclusion in Pakistan*. London: Anthem.

Report of the Court of Inquiry (Punjab Disturbances of 1953) (1954). Lahore: Government Printing.

Saeed, S. (2007), 'Pakistani Nationalism and the State Marginalisation of the Ahmadiyya Community in Pakistan, *Studies in Ethnicity and Nationalism* 7(3): 132–52.

Schmitt, C. (1985), *Political Theology: Four Chapters on the Concept of Sovereignty.* Cambridge, MA: MIT Press.

Scolnicov, A. (2011), *The Right to Religious Freedom in International Law: Between Group Rights and Individual Rights.* London: Routledge.

Sedition (Amendment) Act (2015), http://www.federalgazette.agc.gov.my/outputak tap/20150604_A1485_BI_Act%20A1485.pdf (accessed 5 August 2019).

Shah, D. and Sani, M. A. M. (2011), 'Freedom of Religion in Malaysia: A Tangled Web of Legal, Political, and Social Issues', *North Carolina Journal of International Law and Commercial Regulation* 36(3): 647–88.

Sheikh, M. (2014), 'How Does Religion Matter? Pathways to Religion in International Relations', *Review of International Studies* 38: 365–92.

Sullivan, W., Hurd, E. S., Mahmood, S. and Danchin, P. G. (2015), *Politics of Religious Freedom.* Chicago: University of Chicago Press.

Vuori, J. (2011), 'Religion Bites: Falungong, Securitization/Desecurization in the People's Republic of China', in Thierry Balzacq (ed.), *Securitization Theory*, 186–211. London: Routledge.

Weldes, J., Laffey, M., Gusterson, H. and Duvall, R. (eds) (1999), *Cultures of Insecurity: States, Communities, and the Production of Danger.* Minneapolis: University of Minnesota Press.

Wimmer, A. (2013). *Ethnic Boundary Making: Institutions, Power, Networks.* Oxford: Oxford University Press.

Zaman, M. (1998), 'Sectarianism in Pakistan: The Radicalisation of Sunni and Shi'i Identities', *Modern Asian Studies* 32(3): 689–716.

4

ISLAMIC POPULISM AND IDENTITY POLITICS OF MUI: ISLAMIC LEADERSHIP, HALAL PROJECT AND THE THREAT TO RELIGIOUS FREEDOM IN INDONESIA

Syafiq Hasyim

This chapter examines the role of MUI (Majelis Ulama Indonesia, Council of Indonesian Ulama) in stimulating the emergence of Islamic populism and identity politics in Indonesia. It focuses on MUI's discourse and activism in using Islam as the main argument for attracting the interest of the Indonesian Muslim community and surveys its effect on recent general elections and society at large. Specifically, it addresses MUI's promotion of Islamic leadership during the 2017 Jakarta gubernatorial elections and the 2014 and 2019 presidential elections, as well as the Islamic lifestyle that MUI has been fostering through halal certification for the past three decades. This chapter argues that MUI produces fatwas and religious advice that cherish illiberal attitudes towards religious freedom. Through its strategic positioning as the guardian of the ummah and its shari'ah agenda, MUI has become the main proponent of Islamic populism and identity politics in the post-reform era of Indonesia. As a result, the democratic principle of the Pancasila state that treats all citizens as equal regardless of their religion is under threat.

MUI and the Landscape of Muslim Organisations in Indonesia

The largest Muslim country in the world, Indonesia is neither an Islamic nor a secular state. The founding fathers of Indonesia made a consensus to build Indonesia on the philosophical foundation of the Pancasila since its independence in 1945 (Ismail 1995; Darmaputera 1988). The Pancasila state means that Indonesia is a country that believes in God and also in democracy, social solidarity and justice. Nonetheless, the post-colonial trajectory of Indonesia as the Pancasila state is fraught with difficulties. Social and political conflicts among ethnic and religious groups gave rise to different models of national leadership. Sukarno, the father of Indonesia's independence, had ruled Indonesia (1957–65) under his *guided democracy* because of his authoritarian tendency in managing the divergent voices of democracy (Maarif 1996: 4; Feith 2006). Suharto took over the national leadership since 1967 and led undemocratically for thirty-two years. In 1988, Suharto was forced to resign upon the demand and protest of various segments of Indonesian society, including student activists, NGOs and mass organisations. The resignation of Suharto has brought a more open space, not only for the emergence of democratic aspirations, but also the revivalism of Islamic ideology. Many Muslim organisations and political parties found an opportunity to reclaim their Islamic ideology, which had been repressed under Suharto. Increasingly, many Muslim organisations and political parties are steering away from the philosophical foundation of the Pancasila, asserting instead Islam as their ideology.

Established in 1975 with the support of Suharto, MUI is an ulama institution with a very strong connection to the state (Adams 2004; Mudzhar 1993; Hasyim 2016). Conceived as an umbrella of different existing Muslim organisations, MUI facilitates communication with the government of Indonesia on the affairs of Muslims (MUI 1982: 19; Mudzhar 1993; Adams 2012). The most obvious assignment since the founding of MUI is the provision of Islamic legal opinion (fatwa)[1] and religious advice (*tawsiyya*) for government officials in particular and the Muslim community in general. Indonesian Muslims can address questions on Islam and related topics to MUI, which then issues answers to them. While ministers and senior government staff have been turning to MUI for fatwas and religious advice since the Suharto era, this relationship has been strengthened over the past two decades. The role of MUI in the field of *fatwa* and religious advice in Indonesia is greater than that of other Muslim organisations such as Nadhlatul Ulama,[2] Muhammadiyah,[3] or Persatuan Islam (Persis).[4]

Historically, MUI is the youngest Islamic organisation among them. Proclaimed as a reformist organisation, the Muhammadiyah was established in 1912, with the mission to purify the concept of faith in Islam (*tawhid*) and to further reform or renew Islam (*tajdid*). This was motivated by a desire to bring Muslims back to the worldview of the Qur'an and the hadith. The organisation has worked much more on the aspect of purification than

---

[1] From the perspective of Islamic legal theory, fatwa is defined as Islamic legal opinion. Unlike a *qada* (court decision), a fatwa is not legally binding (Bin Bayyah 2007; Hallaq 2005; Masud, Messick and Powers 1996).

[2] Nahdlatul Ulama is the largest Muslim organisation in Indonesia, established in 1926. This organisation is traditionalist in term of its Islamic thought (Fealy and Barton 1996).

[3] The Muhammadiyah is the second-largest Muslim organisation in Indonesia, established in 1912. It follows a reformist and purist tradition of Islamic thought (Nakamura 2012).

[4] Persatuan Islam (Persis) is also one of the largest Muslim organisations, established in 1923. It follows a reformist tradition of Islamic thought, like the Muhammadiyah (Federspiel 2009).

on Islamic renewal. In terms of fatwas, the Muhammadiyah has a special body called Majelis Tarjih dan Tajdid (Council of Tarjih and Tajdid), whose responsibility is to issue fatwas or other products of Islamic advice. Although the Majelis is active in issuing fatwas, their following is mainly limited to Muhammadiyah members (Majelis Tarjih dan Tajdid Pimpinan Pusat Muhammadiyah 2018; Qibtiyah 2018). Many Muhammadiyah members tend to support MUI fatwas.

Persatuan Islam was born after the Muhammadiyah in 1923, and its vision was also one of Islamic reformism (Federspiel 2009; Saleh 2001). Although concentrated in West Java, it has branches in other regions of Indonesia. Persis has played an active role in developing education and social welfare for Muslims. Like the Muhammadiyah, it also has a special body for issuing fatwas, called Dewan Hisbah (Hisbah Council), whose task is to issue fatwas aimed at understanding the sources of Islamic doctrine as well as questions of faith and worship and shari'ah perspectives on social and political issues (Shalehuddin 2018: 4). So far, Persis fatwas are mostly famous among the followers of this organisation. In its current development, Persis seems to be turning from its mission of Islamic reformism to Islamic purification.

The mission of the Muhammadiyah and Persis in promoting the purification of Islam was met with resistance from a group of ulama in East Java who felt that the religious model of traditional Muslims was being challenged from such Islamic reformist groups. Many traditional Muslim practices, such as visiting graveyards (*ziarah*) and holding prayer for those who passed away, were considered deviant by Islamic reformists. Nahdlatul Ulama (NU) was created in 1926 in East Java as a response to the Saudi influence of Wahhabism, which aimed to destroy the shrines of Islam such as the tomb of the Prophet Muhammad and his companions. The Saudi regime believes that shrines are misleading Muslims into becoming polytheists. In short, NU advocates the traditionalist way of implementing Islam in the archipelago (Nusantara). From the time of its establishment to the current development, NU has played a significant role in matters of state and society in Indonesia in general. In addition, as a traditionalist organisation, Nahdlatul Ulama has more flexibility than other Muslim organisations to adapt to modern issues such as democracy, human rights, interfaith dialogue and minority issues. As the largest Islamic organisation in Indonesia, it also has a fatwa division called Lembaga Bahsul Masa'il (LBM), which guides its members as well as the general public (LTN 2011).

These Muslim organisations communicate and collaborate closely with MUI, but sometimes there is tension given their different religious stances. However, there is a sort of silent agreement to grant MUI the authority to issue fatwas related to faith (*aqidah*). As a consequence, such fatwas carry the conservative stance of MUI, especially when dealing with issues related to pluralism or diversity. MUI's role in the affairs of the state was strengthened during the presidency of Susilo Bambang Yudoyono (2004–9 and 2009–14) who endorsed MUI on many issues, including the halal project. SBY descried

MUI as the police of *aqidah* (Islamic faith) as well as the police of morality. Being the police of *aqidah* gave MUI the license to promote a monolithic understanding on the Muslim creed in Indonesia. MUI has issued multiple fatwas that prosecute those who have a different stance on *aqidah*. In 2005, it reintroduced fatwas that marginalised Muslim groups considered deviant sects of Islam (MUI 2005a; n. d.). Around fourteen Muslim minorities, such as the Ahmadiyyah, al-Qiyadah and al-Islamiyah (Hasyim 2016; MUI, n. d.) were categorised as deviant. As the police of morality, MUI issue fatwas that supports the enforcement of shari'ah as public morality. In addition, MUI has tried to impose shari'ah in national legislation, with State Law No. 44/2008 on pornography being a result of this enterprise. The ideological orientation of MUI is often regarded as the source of Islamic conservatism and funda-mentalism in Indonesia, not least because of its agenda of shari'atisation (Hasyim 2014; Lindsey 2012).[5] MUI is criticised for using religion as a means for political ends, especially in their attempts to promote shari'ah. Hence, the politics of MUI can be called a politics of the shari'ah.

MUI's relation to the government of Indonesia has so far been mutually beneficial. The government sources Islamic legitimacy from MUI, while MUI receives regular financial support from the central and regional govern-ment. MUI is present not only at the national and provincial level, but also at the district and sub-district level. MUI upholds the Pancasila state, not an Islamic state, as the political ideology of Indonesia since the establishment of the country in 1975 (MUI 2011). However, the acceptance of the Pancasila state system has not held MUI back from striving for the implementation of shari'ah law as the guiding principle in the daily life of Indonesian people and having Islam as the ideology of the organisation. For MUI, the state form of Pancasila is different from the agenda of shari'atisation, although Pancasila and the shari'ah are held to be compatible. The stance of MUI can be problematic because the implementation of shari'ah law can stimulate the change from the Pancasila state to an Islamic state, as the shari'ah also touches on matters related to the state. A change so fundamental to the nature of the state in Indonesia has already found supporters in Islamist groups such as Darul Islam in West Java, Aceh and South Sulawesi (Dijk 1981; Formichi 2012).

While the shari'ah has been used in private matters, the people of Indonesia, especially religious minorities, do not endorse the practice of shari'ah at the level of the legal public sphere. The Indonesian public generally upholds the ideological foundation of the Pancasila. However, MUI believes that the shari'ah can be implemented not only at the level of private, but also public sphere. As Indonesia is a majority-Muslim country, MUI argues that the Muslim community has the right to implement shari'ah in their daily life.

---

[5] Shari'atisation refers to the various attempts of the Muslim community to include the shari'ah into the legal and political public sphere of Indonesia. The state legislation on halal product assurance in Indonesia since 2014 is one such example.

Since the Pancasila includes theological reasoning – *Ketuhanan Yang Maha Esa*, Belief in One God – MUI holds that Muslims should be allowed to practise shari'ah in the public sphere. Moreover, MUI often gives full endorsement to those who strive for the enactment of shari'ah law in Indonesia. MUI tries to push its shari'atisation agenda by fashioning the council as a representative of the ummah (MUI 1982), or the Indonesian Muslim community, and advocates for their right to implement the shari'ah in public life, as is illustrated in the state law on the shari'ah economy through the tool of halal certification.

This chapter examines MUI's discourse on the politics of ummah in light of their fatwas on political leadership and their promotion of an Islamic lifestyle through their pioneering work on the policy of halal certification in Indonesia. Analysing the effects of MUI fatwas on the 2017 Jakarta gubernatorial elections, as well as the 2014 and 2019 presidential elections, it seeks to demonstrate how MUI stimulates the emergence of Islamic populism among Muslims groups, on one hand, and identity politics, on the other. In the fragile era of democratic consolidation in Indonesia, MUI's shari'ah agenda presents a considerable threat to minority rights. Complementing secondary research, the chapter relies on data from online media and fieldwork conducted in 2018–19 in Jakarta, Central Java, West Java, North Sumatera and Yogyakarta on Islamic leadership and MUI's halal project.

MUI's Politics of the Ummah and Islamic Populism

MUI's ideological positioning as the guardian of the Muslim community and as an ulama organisation concerned with the interest of the ummah has led to the emergence of Islamic populism. The term employed by MUI publications is, to be sure, not exactly populism, but rather ummah in Arabic, or *umat* in the Indonesian translation (MUI 1982; 2005; n. d.). However, while MUI publications abound in references to the ummah, historically, the council has not positioned itself as its guardian, resembling more of an oligarchic organisation on the side of the ruling regime rather than on the side of the Muslim community. In the period of 1975–98, MUI sought to become *khadim al-hukumah* (the guardian of the government) and not *khadim al-ummah* (the guardian of the Muslim community). This strategic positioning is characteristic of religious-based organisations under authoritarian regimes (Porter 2004), particularly since MUI was dependent on material support from the government (Mudzhar 1993).

At the same time, the term ummah had been very popular among Muslim activists and scholars, given the influence of political Islam in countries such as Egypt and Iran in the late 1970s. Although Indonesia is not a theocratic state, in the popular imagination the term ummah is linked to the concept of political Islam (Mandaville 2002; Al-Barghouti 2008) and understood as a political entity rather than a religiously-oriented human collective (Mada 1970; Formichi 2012; Mardjono 2001).

The Suharto regime supported MUI in becoming an intermediary ulama organisation that facilitates discussions about the aspirations and interests of the ummah. However, ummah in this context did not refer exclusively to Muslims as it currently figures in the imagination of Islamist groups. In the Suharto era, the term ummah was used to refer to all citizens of Indonesia regardless of their religion, in which the Muslim community was a key group besides other religions and believers. The term *umat* was often subsequently employed together with the term *beragama*, and *umat beragama* became an Indonesian phrase that signified the community of believers. Nonetheless, this inclusive notion of *umat* has slowly disappeared from public discourse in the post-reform era of Indonesia. Amidst the resurgence of political Islam that followed the resignation of Suharto, its meaning reversed to its original to refer exclusively to the community of Islam. A more open space for freedom also signified a more open space for the emergence of identity politics as well as Islamic populism. As the majority group, *umat Islam* of Indonesia began to think of their political interest.

The resignation of Suharto in 1998 was a tremendous loss for MUI, as the council lost its prime political support and had to adjust to the new climate of Indonesian politics. As a consequence, MUI changed its tagline from *khadim al-hukumah* to *khadim al-ummah* (the guardian of the Muslim community). This indicates that the shift in MUI orientation was not merely ideological in revising the importance of the ummah, but also reflects a strategic and pragmatic vision for a political doctrine of Islam and the political realm of the Muslim community. By aligning with the interest of ummah, MUI drew much support from the Indonesian Muslim community and secured an important role as a pressure group organisation, which increases its bargaining power to the point of dictating policy to the Indonesian government. MUI instrumentalises its capacity as a fatwa-giver and religious adviser to influence the government and frame policy in the name of the Indonesian Muslim interest. The council has pressured law-makers in both the executive and legislative bodies of Indonesia to produce legislation that is favourable to shari'ah and has undertaken efforts in the name of *umat Islam*. Apart from fatwas, MUI has deployed mass mobilisation, demonstrations and protests to illustrate the aspirations and interests of *umat Islam*.

MUI's Discourse on Political Leadership and its Effect on General Elections

MUI claims that their concern for political leadership in Indonesia is a priority in guarding the interest of *umat Islam* (MUI, n. d.; 1982: 198). The council insists that political leaders, especially in the majority-Muslim areas, should be Indonesian Muslims. The argument is that an Islamic political leader is guaranteed to follow the interest of *umat Islam*. As political leadership becomes a priority, MUI has also tried to persuade Indonesian Muslims to pay attention to Islamic theological differences when electing their political leaders. The general elections – the presidential and gubernatorial elections – are therefore heavily scrutinised and used by MUI to polarise society and pave the way for Islamic populism and identity politics.

The 2017 Jakarta Gubernatorial Elections

A revealing instance of this kind was the 2017 Jakarta gubernatorial election, which featured Basuki Tjahaja Purnama (also known by the moniker Ahok), an ethnic Chinese and Christian, Anies Baswedan (the former minister of national education) and Agus Harimurti Yudoyono (son of former president Susilo Bambang Yudoyono) in the first round of the election. The final electoral race for the position of Jakarta governor was between Ahok and Anies, a rivalry that was increasingly understood as one between a non-Muslim and a Muslim. Although the Jakarta gubernatorial election is a provincial election, the politics of Jakarta is very influential on national politics. Since the success of Jokowi in the 2014 presidential election, winning the office of Jakarta governor signals a stepping-stone towards becoming the president of Indonesia. As a result, the gubernatorial elections become a prime focus for MUI's promotion of Islamic leadership.

MUI had a mission to block Ahok from being elected as the Jakarta governor in 2017 and issued a special fatwa that disallowed the Jakarta Muslim voters to elect Ahok because he was Christian and allegedly blasphemous to Islam (Peterson 2020).[6] Although MUI formally recognises that all citizens of Indonesia have equal rights to run for political leadership positions, the council has a tendency to discredit non-Muslim leadership. The council uses Sunni theological arguments to justify that political leaders should be Muslim and instrumentalises race and religion (Hosen 2016) to promote Islamic leadership.

Even though Ahok had a successful first mandate, MUI and Islamist groups did not account for his well-off legacy simply by virtue of him not being Muslim and flouted their ability to shape the views and aspirations regarding non-Muslim leadership among the ummah in Indonesia. The instrumentalisation of fatwas by MUI has become an effective way of mobilising the ummah and led to the establishment of the so-called GNPF-MUI (Gerakan Nasional Pengawal Fatwa-MUI, National Guardian Movement for the MUI Fatwa) in 2016. This organisation started off as a community organiser to implement the idea of MUI fatwas at the grassroots level, and it played a pivotal role as an intermediary organisation in the case against Ahok. The mission of the movement, apart from rejecting Ahok as the Jakarta governor, was to strive for Islamic leadership and political Islam in Indonesia. Their harsh position towards Ahok and Jokowi was only an immediate target,

---

[6] For an Indonesian-language account, see https://www.tribunnews.com/metro politan/2016/10/12/politisi-golkar-fatwa-mui-tegaskan-ahok-miliki-cacat-moral (accessed 13 August 2020).

with the long-term goal being the permanent change of the Indonesian state system from the Pancasila to a theocratic state of Islam.

Employing the legitimacy of the MUI fatwa, the GNPF-MUI was highly successful in mobilising the largest Islamist movement in the modern history of Indonesia. This movement was called Aksi Bela Islam (ABI, Action to Defend Islam) or 212 movement. On 4 November 2016, hundreds of thousands of people gathered around the National Monument to pressure Jokowi to speed up the process of Ahok's detention. The public narrative that they tried to develop was that Muslims should defend Islam from the insult of Ahok and that Jokowi should take responsibility, too, since Ahok was his political ally in the capital-city of Jakarta (Peterson 2020). Although the ABI movement benefitted from the legitimacy of the MUI fatwa on Ahok, when MUI discovered that they also targeted Jokowi, the council withdrew from their collaboration with the GNPF-MUI, requesting them to change their name and drop their attachment to MUI. It is notable that, although MUI did not want to be associated with the GNPF-MUI, it did not issue a fatwa to ban the series of their demonstrations.[7] MUI's stance was ambiguous: on one hand, it provided the fatwa as the theological justification for the demonstrations, but, on the other hand, it tried to clear its name by disassociating from the ABI demonstrations.

Ultimately, the MUI fatwa against Ahok[8] targeted the national leadership of Jokowi. When Ahok's legal investigation was triggered by MUI through its fatwa, Jokowi was already in the third year of his presidency. His opponents were still enthusiastic to topple him, using any opportunity at hand, and MUI's fatwa provided a theological justification to push for Islamic leadership in Indonesia. MUI needed a Muslim governor in Jakarta while Islamist and Jokowi-rejectionist groups like the ABI movement needed a simultaneous contention to destabilise the leadership of Jokowi. A perfect combination capitalising on identity politics and Islamic populism arose. The use of identity politics was visible in the use of Islam as the argument for rejecting the leadership of non-Muslims. The use of Islamic populism was visible in the strategic staging of the movement as the aspiration of the ummah. The General Chairman of MUI, Ma'ruf Amin, stated that he received multiple requests to issue a fatwa saying that Ahok was blasphemous to the Qur'an and the ulama.[9]

---

[7] For an Indonesian-language account, see https://www.beritasatu.com/nasional/400585-mui-tegaskan-tidak-ada-hubungan-dengan-gnpf-mui (accessed 7 August 2020).

[8] This fatwa is called Pendapat dan Sikap Keagamaan Majelis Ulama Indonesia (Religious Opinion and Position of Council of Indonesian Ulama). See https://news.detik.com/berita/d-3318150/mui-nyatakan-sikap-soal-ucapan-ahok-terkait-al-maidah-51-ini-isinya (accessed 6 August 2020).

[9] For an Indonesian-language account, see https://www.liputan6.com/news/read/2842030/sidang-ahok-ketua-mui-sebut-keluarkan-fatwa-karena-desakan (accessed 13 August 2020).

Jokowi and Jusuf Kalla (Vice President) had no choice other than fulfilling the demand of the groups. Two actions indicated the government's position of compromise. First, Jusuf Kalla engaged with an ABI representative.[10] Second, the government of Indonesia asked the National Police of Indonesia to launch an investigation in Ahok's case which had been triggered by the MUI fatwa. Once the legal process was finalised, Ahok was jailed for almost two years.

To conclude, MUI played a pivotal role in the 2017 Jakarta gubernatorial elections through its fatwa. Without the MUI fatwa on blasphemy, the final result of the elections would have probably been different since the satisfaction rate of Ahok's first mandate in Jakarta was quite high (around 85 percent).[11] Through its fatwa, MUI effectively deployed identity politics and also the politics of ummah (populism) to attack the image of Ahok and prevent him from being re-elected governor of Jakarta.[12]

The 2014 and 2019 Presidential Elections

MUI has been aware of the importance of general elections in post-reform Indonesia as a political mechanism to compete for political leadership and has approached them as an opportunity to implement the interests of the ummah. For example, having a Muslim president is not only one of the highest such interests, but also an outright demand of some Muslim groups. Therefore, MUI sees itself responsible for creating the optimal circumstances to ensure the election of a Muslim president. The discursive influence granted by their authority to issue fatwas and religious advice enables MUI to provide theological justification for Muslim political leadership at the national level.

In the Suharto era, the role of MUI was to provide an Islamic justification for the re-election of Suharto in each general election. This comes as no surprise, as MUI, together with other Islamic organisations, was sponsored by Suharto's party, Golkar, to legitimise his leadership. Repositioning as the guardian of the ummah after Suharto's resignation, MUI was no longer seen as the pro-government ulama organisation and has gradually gained the trust of the Muslim community. Instead of being dictated by political power, MUI seeks to impose its influence on others, especially on the government of Indonesia. Although MUI is not attached to and has no formal alliance with any political party, it endorses presidential candidates who have an

[10] For an Indonesian-language account, see https://www.jpnn.com/news/perwa kilan-massa-akhirnya-temui-wapres-jk (accessed 7 August 2020).

[11] For an Indonesian-language account, see https://www.merdeka.com/peristiwa/ jokowi-belum-cairkan-dana-bansos-buat-mui-sebesar-rp-3-m.html (accessed 8 August 2020).

[12] See https://www.cnnindonesia.com/nasional/20190116095933-32-361159/saat-isu-sara-benamkan-kepuasan-publik-pada-kerja-ahok (accessed 8 August 2020).

Islamic programme. Its endorsement is not based on political and professional merits, but plays instead on identity politics, as MUI is trapped in the narrow political subjectivity of Islamic identity. The political alignment of MUI to Muslim candidates and politicians threatens Indonesia's pluralism and religious diversity.

Although all candidates were Muslims in the 2014 presidential elections, MUI still thought it of importance to issue a particular fatwa so as to guide Indonesian Muslim to vote Islamic leaders. This is because MUI considers their political advocacy as part of *dakwah* (proselytisation) and its overall duty to implement *amar ma'ruf nahi mungkar* (commanding right and forbidding wrong).[13] The fatwa on electing Muslim political leaders was issued in 2009 following the respective presidential elections (MUI 2011: 878). The fatwa defines a Muslim leader not simply as one who professes Islam as their religion, but one who should be qualified through the purity of their *aqidah* (Islamic faith) and was subsequently utilised in the 2019 presidential elections. Earlier in 2014, Jokowi was assumed to not be Islamic enough by some Islamist groups, although his vice-presidential candidate, Jusuf Kalla, featured well in their books. This was due to the fact that the political party backing Jokowi, the PDI-P (Partai Demokrasi Indonesia Perjuangan, Indonesian Democratic Party of Struggle) is perceived by Islamist groups as an *abangan* party that, according to Clifford Geertz's definition (Geertz 1976), reflects Javanese syncretism rather than the *santri* stream of Islam which is more in line with formal Islamic education.[14] Other Islamist organisations such as the Front Pembela Islam (FPI, Islamic Defenders Front) and the Forum Umat Islam (FUI, The Muslim Community Forum) accuse the PDI-P of ties to the Partai Komunis Indonesia (PKI, Indonesian Communist Party). Despite Jokowi not being considered Islamic enough according to the MUI fatwa on Islamic leadership 2009, he was the winner of the 2014 presidential elections with the support of Nahdlatul Ulama.

In the 2019 presidential elections, MUI's position was more dynamic since Jokowi cleverly employed political anticipation and appointed Ma'ruf Amin (the General Chairman of MUI) as his vice-presidential candidate. As the general chairman of MUI, Ma'ruf Amin was very critical of Jokowi and a close ally to former president Susilo Bambang Yudoyono (2004–9 and

---

[13] For further elaboration on commanding right and forbidding wrong in Islam, see Cook (2004; 2003).

[14] In his book *The Religion of Java*, Clifford Geertz categorises the Javanese people into three streams (*aliran*): *abangan*, *santri* and *priyayi*. The term *abangan* represents the peasant community and Javanese syncretism. The term *santri* represents Islamic groups who are products of an Islamic education system. The term *priyayi* is used to refer to the Javanese bureaucrats and aristocracy. For more information, see https://www.rsis.edu.sg/rsis-publication/rsis/indonesian-presidential-election-2019-abangan-santri-and-priyayi-three-streams-in-indonesias-electoral-politics/ (accessed 3 May 2021).

2009–14) in his capacity as Wantimpres member (Dewan Pertimbangan President, Presidential Advisory Body). Learning from the blasphemy case against Ahok in the 2017 Jakarta gubernatorial election, he asked his party to support Amin as his vice-presidential candidate in the 2019 elections. For the PDI-P itself, the choice of Ma'ruf Amin was in line with their strategy to preserve the national leadership after Jokowi. Given Ma'ruf Amin's seniority – he was seventy-six when he became Jokowi's running mate in the 2019 presidential elections – it is unlikely that he would follow the traditional course of Indonesian politics and run for president in 2024.

However, the appointment of Ma'ruf Amin as the vice-presidential candidate was opposed by some members of MUI, who saw alternatives in Bachtiar Natsir (Vice Secretary General of MUI), Tengke Zulkarnaen (Vice Secretary General of MUI) or Muhyiddin Junaidi (Vice General Chairman of MUI), among others. As a result, they gave their electoral support to Prabowo, the opponent of Jokowi. MUI was therefore divided into two groups, the first supporting Jokowi because of Ma'ruf Amin and the second supporting Prabowo. Within MUI, Ma'ruf Amin's supporters were mostly elites with Nahdlatul Ulama background and Prabowo's elites with Muhammadiyah background. Ma'ruf Amin's followers supported Jokowi because his political partner was an ulama, which was seen as highly beneficial for the ummah. The MUI elites who did not support Ma'ruf Amin stated that they did not want an ulama to be the object of Jokowi's political game. From their perspective, Jokowi was not a serious advocate of Islam and the ulama, and Ma'ruf Amin was the victim in a strategic political game. Notwithstanding this internal MUI split, since the 2017 gubernatorial elections it has become clear that MUI has successfully instrumentalised its authority to issue fatwas in order to set Indonesia on a trajectory of Islamic populism that polarises society along the lines of identity politics.

The Halal Project and Minorities' Response to Islamic Populism

The halal certification was originally raised by President Suharto in the early 1990s to address the aftermath of Dancow's milk products contamination with lard in East Java (Girindra 2008). The incident sparked a decline in Indonesian Muslim consumers buying from Dancow and other food and drink companies. MUI was very eager to promulgate a state policy on halal and hoped that they would be granted the highest authority on the matter. MUI was requested by Suharto to establish an institution to monitor the lawfulness of halal production. Established in 1989, LPPOM (Lembaga Pengkajian Pangan, Obatan-obatan dan Kosmetika, The Assessment Institute for Foods, Drugs and Cosmetics Majelis Ulama Indonesia) has for long been the sole halal certifier in Indonesia.

Although halal certification is not mandatory, producers had felt theologically and morally pressured to pursue their halal certification from LPPOM. The halal certification is not merely a technical issue, but an aspect of Islamic ideology (Fischer 2011). The halal project means that Indonesian Muslims who live in a non-theocratic Muslim state should not only consume lawful goods but endorse the shari'ah doctrine in the legal and public sphere of Indonesia. LPPOM rose to prominence when Ma'ruf Amin was a member of the Presidential Advisory Body of Susilo Bambang Yudoyono (2004–14). Apart from having been the sole halal certifier in Indonesia, LPPOM created a new halal life-style (Farid, Effendi and Nadia 2011; Ali Hidaefi and Jaswir 2019).

Nonetheless, in 2014, Indonesia officially passed State Law No. 33/2014 on Halal Product Assurance.[15] Although this law can become the legal foundation for the shari'atisation of goods in Indonesia, for MUI its issuance was a major setback, as the authority with which it had been vested for the past three decades was transferred to the State Halal Body, called BPJPS (Badan Penyelenggara Jaminan Produk Halal). MUI considers State Law No. 33/2014 a betrayal of their consistent efforts in the halalisation project in Indonesia. Back in the 1990s, the state had no interest in the matter, only to annex it as it grew popular. MUI had practised a monopoly in undertaking halal certification, and the passing of the state law put an end to that. As a consequence, MUI is only authorised to publish halal-related fatwas under the authority of BPJPH (Badan Penyelenggara Jaminan Produk Halal, Halal Product Assurance Organising Agency).

This brings a new dimension to the process of shari'atisation in Indonesia. From the first operation of LPPOM as halal certifiers in 1989 to 2014 or 2018, the shari'atisation of production and consumption has taken place in the cultural domain, but after the legislation of State Law No. 33/2014, the shari'atisation of production and consumption takes place at the state level. This law gives the state the authority to interfere in the halal issue which should be a private matter within Islamic doctrine. It authorises the state to enforce what Indonesian people should drink and eat according to the doctrine of shari'ah. This is the first time that the state can intervene in the private matters of its Indonesian citizens.

The state legislation on halal alarmed minorities in Indonesia. Weary of MUI's authority, minorities channelled their criticism towards the government, pointing at its lack of neutrality and weak law enforcement. When MUI issued the blasphemy fatwa against Ahok, minorities understood that the fatwa not only targeted Ahok, but generally delegitimised minority groups from becoming political leaders in Indonesia. Similarly, when Indonesian law-makers envisioned the creation of an international halal hub that invites foreign investment, economic benefit was prioritised over citizens' rights. The state policy on halal product assurance favours the emergence of a certain religious norm in society. Non-Muslims and human rights activists question the relevance of such a policy in a non-Islamic state. Halal

---

[15] See https://www.iseas.edu.sg/wp-content/uploads/pdfs/ISEAS_Perspective_2019_108.pdf (accessed 18 August 2020).

is a religious private issue; therefore, making it public through a state law affects the neutrality of the public sphere, forcing non-Muslims to recognise the supremacy of shari'ah law.

Minorities denounce that they were not consulted during the halal certification legislative process in 2013–14, which undermines the essence of democracy. When a legal draft is officially registered as state law, all citizens are subject to that law. The law-makers of Indonesia ignored the fact that, although halal certification relates to the rights of Indonesian Muslims, it regulates the life-style of non-Muslims as well. Since the implementation of the halal law in October 2019, minorities worry about the emergence of food-based segregation and exclusivism in their communities. They believe that State Law No. 33/2014 should be implemented for Muslim consumers and producers only, as it follows their particular religious norm. Some efforts were invested to request the Constitutional Supreme Court to undergo a judicial review of the law, but to no avail. Human rights activists also argue that the rationale to protect the rights of Muslims to consume halal food in a Muslim-majority country is a misnomer. Usually, it is minority groups who seek such state protection, as in the case of Singapore, Thailand and many European countries.

Concluding Remarks

MUI has become the main proponent of Islamic populism and identity politics in the post-reform era of Indonesia. Although MUI is not a political party, it exerts influence on Indonesian politics through two effective tools: fatwas and religious advice. Not only do they have broad reception among politicians and the Muslim community; they are also used as sources of Islamic legitimacy.

MUI's recognition of Pancasila does not guarantee their respect for state neutrality, since MUI believes that the shari'ah can protect the rights of minority groups. In light of the cases elaborated above, minorities are most affected by MUI's strong influence on social and political affairs. So far, there has been no significant movement to counter the trajectory that MUI has set regarding Islamic leadership and life-style in Indonesia. Moreover, due to its increasingly strong bargaining position with the government, MUI is likely to remain influential in the future. If MUI's gauging of national leadership does not alarm the government of Indonesia, the country is facing a difficult situation. The promotion of Islamic populism and identity politics not only affects the quality of national leadership, but also the relationship between Indonesia's diverse religious and ethnic groups. Compelling *umat Islam* to elect Muslim leaders closes the space for other citizens of Indonesia who are not part of *umat Islam*. In this regard, the democratic principle of the Pancasila state that treats all citizens as equal regardless of their religion is under threat.

References

Adams, W. (2004), *Pola Penyerapan Fatwa Majelis Ulama Indonesia (MUI) Dalam Peraturan Perundang-Undangan 1975–1997*. Jakarta: Departemen Agama.

Adams, W. (2012), 'Fatwa MUI Dalam Prespektif Hukum Dan Perundangundangan', in Nahar Nahrawi, Nuhrison M. Nuh, Asrorun Ni'am Sholeh and Abidin Zainal (eds), *Fatwa Majelis Ulama Dalam Perspektif Hukum Dan Perundang-Undangan*, 3–17. Jakarta: Puslitbang Kehidupan Keagamaan Badan Litbang dan Diklat Kementerian Agama RI.

Al-Barghouti, T. (2008), *The Umma and the Dawla: The Nation State and the Arab Middle East*. London: Pluto Press.

Ali Hidaefi, F. and Jaswir, I. (2019), 'Halal Governance in Indonesia: Theory, Current Practices and Related Issues', *Journal of Islamic Monetary Economics and Finance* 5(1): 89–116.

Bin Bayyah, A. (2007), *Sina'at al-Fatwa Wa Fiqh al-Aqalliyat*. Lebanon: Dar al-Minhaj.

Cook, M. (2003), *Forbidding Wrong in Islam: An Introduction*. Cambridge: Cambridge University Press.

Cook, M. (2004), *Commanding Right and Forbidding Wrong in Islamic Thought*. Cambridge: Cambridge University Press.

Darmaputera, E. (1988), *Pancasila and the Search for Identity and Modernity in Indonesian Society: A Cultural and Ethical Analysis*. Leiden and Boston: Brill.

van Dijk, C. (1981), *Rebellion Under the Banner of Islam: The Darul Islam in Indonesia*. The Hague: Martinus Nijhoff.

Farid, M., Effendi, U. and Nadia (2011), 'Produk Unik Bersertifikat Halal Apa Tujuannya?' *Jurnal Halal*, 8–9.

Fealy, G. and Barton, G. (eds) (1996), *Nahdlatul Ulama: Traditional Islam and Modernity in Indonesia*. Melbourne: Monash Asia Institute, Monash University.

Federspiel, H. M. (2009), *Persatuan Islam: Islamic Reform in Twentieth-Century Indonesia*. Singapore: Equinox Publishing.

Feith, H. (2006), *The Decline of Constitutional Democracy in Indonesia*. Jakarta: Equinox Publishing.

Fischer, J. (2011), *The Halal Frontier: Muslim Consumers in a Globalized Market*. New York: Palgrave Macmillan.

Formichi, C. (2012), *Islam and the Making of the Nation: Kartosuwiryo and Political Islam in Twentieth-Century Indonesia*. Leiden: KITLV Press.

Girindra, A. (2008), *Dari Sertifikasi Menuju Labelisasi Halal*. Jakarta: Pustaka Jurnal Halal.

Hallaq, W. B. (2005), 'Ifta' and Ijtihad in Sunni Legal Theory: A Development Account', in Muhammad Khalid Masud, Brinkley Messick and David S. Powers (eds), *Islamic Legal Interpretation, Muftis and Their Fatwas*, 33–43. Oxford and New York: Oxford University Press.

Hasyim, S. (2014), 'Council of Indonesian Ulama (Majelis Ulama Indonesia, MUI) and Its Role in the Shariatisation of Indonesia', unpubl. PhD diss., Free University Berlin.

Hasyim, S. (2016), 'The Council of Indonesian Ulama (MUI) and Aqidah-Based Intolerance: A Critical Analysis of Its Fatwa on Ahmadiyah and "Sepilis"', in Tim Lindsey and Helen Pausacker (eds), *Religion, Law and Intolerance in Indonesia*, 211–33. New York: Routledge.

Hosen, N. (2016), 'Race and Religion in the Jakarta Gubernatorial Election 2012', in

Tim Lindsey and Helen Pausacker (eds), *Religion, Law and Intolerance in Indonesia*, 180–94. New York: Routledge.

Ismail, F. (1995), 'Islam, Politics and Ideology in Indonesia: A Study of the Process of Muslim Acceptance on the Pancasila'. Montreal.

Lindsey, T. (2012), 'Monopolising Islam? The Indonesian Ulama Council and State Regulation of the 'Islamic Economy', *Bulletin of Indonesian Economic Studies* 48(2): 253–74.

LTN, Pengurus Besar Nahdlatul Ulama PBNU. Lajnah Ta'lif wan Nasyar (2011), *Ahkam Al-Fuqaha, Solusi Problematika Hukum Islam Keputusan Munas Dan Konbes Nahdlatul Ulama (1926–2010)*. Surabaya: Khalista.

Maarif, Ahmad S. (1996), *Islam Dan Politik: Teori Belah Bambu, Masa Demokrasi Terpimpin, 1959–1965*. Jakarta: Gema Insani Press.

Mada, Universitas Gadjah (1970), *Angkatan Oemat Islam 1945–1950: Beberapa Tjatatan Tentang Pergerakan Sosial*. Seminar Sedjarah Nasional II. Universitas Gadjah Mada.

Majelis Tarjih dan Tajdid Pimpinan Pusat Muhammadiyah (2018), *Himpunan Putusan Tarjih Muhammadiyah*. Yogyakarta: Suara Muhammadiyah.

Mandaville, P. G. (2002), *Transnational Muslim Politics: Reimagining the Umma*. New York: Routledge.

Mardjono, H. (2001), *Umat Islam Menggugat: Pelaksanaan Pasal 29 Ayat 2 UUD 1945, Tentang Jaminan Negara Atas Kemerdekaan Tiap-Tiap Penduduk Untuk Memeluk Agamanya Masing-Masing Dan Untuk Beribadat Menurut Agamanya Dan Kepercayaannya Itu*. Yayasan 'Koridor Kebenaran'.

Masud, M. K., Messick, B. M. and Powers, D. S. (eds) (1996), *Islamic Legal Interpretation*. Cambridge, MA, and London: Harvard University Press.

Mudzhar, M. A. (1993), *Fatwa of the Council of Indonesian Ulama: A Study of Islamic Legal Thought in Indonesia 1975–1988*. Jakarta: INIS.

MUI (1982), *Majelis Ulama, Ummat Dan Pembangunan*. Jakarta: Sekretariat Majelis Ulama Indonesia.

MUI (2005), *Kongres Umat Islam Indonesaia IV: Proses Dan Dinamika Permusyawaratan*. Jakarta: BPKUII IV.

MUI (2011), *Himpunan Fatwa MUI Sejak 1975*. Jakarta: Erlangga.

MUI (n. d.), *Mengawal Aqidah Umat: Fatwa MUI Tentang Aliran-Aliran Sesat Di Indonesia*. Jakarta: Sekretariat Majelis Ulama Indonesia.

Nakamura, M. (2012), *The Crescent Arises Over the Banyan Tree: A Study of the Muhammadiyah Movement in a Central Javanese Town, c. 1910–2010*. Singapore: Institute of Southeast Asian Studies.

Peterson, D. (2020), *Islam, Blasphemy, and Human Rights in Indonesia: The Trial of Ahok*. New York: Routledge.

Porter, Donald J. (2004), *Managing Politics and Islam in Indonesia*. London and New York: Routledge Curzon.

Qibtiyah, A. (2018), 'Pengakuan Ulama Dan Isu Perempuan Di Majlis Tarjih Dan Tajdid Muhammadiyah', in Syafiq Hasyim and Fahmi Syahirul Alam (eds), *Demokratisasi Fatwa, Diskursus, Teori Dan Praktik*, 193–211. Jakarta: ICIP.

Saleh, F. (2001), *Modern Trends in Islamic Theological Discourse in Twentieth Century Indonesia*. Leiden: Brill.

Shalehuddin, Wawan S. (2018), *Fiqh Mu'amalah: Kumpulan Keputusan Dewan Hisbah Persatuan Islam*. Bandung: Persis Press.

MIGRATION AND ISLAMISM IN BANGLADESH: THE RISE OF TRANSNATIONAL IDENTITIES

Nazneen Mohsina

The contemporary Islamist discourse in Bangladesh is impossible to understand without situating it in the context of different global developments. The movement of ideas, symbols and people demonstrates how Islam has been and is still being used to mobilise political support from the masses and legitimise revolt in Muslim countries such as Bangladesh. This chapter examines the instrumental role that migration has played in shaping Islamist movements in Bangladesh. Bangladeshi diasporas have not only returned with ideas to change the system in their homeland, but also travelled to foreign lands to participate in violent conflict (termed jihad) and to serve the Muslim ummah (the global community of Muslims). The chapter opens with a brief discussion of the political implications of globalisation on Islamist movements in Bangladesh. The second part offers a historical overview of the geopolitical context in which Bangladesh became an independent nation-state and how the dependence on Middle Eastern petro-dollars has led to the endorsement of an Islamic element to nationalism in the country. It surveys the conflicts at the heart of the country's search for a national identity. The third part looks at the phenomenon of international migration and the transformations in identity that it brings about, particularly how the Bangladeshi diaspora turns to the global ummah as a renewed source of political identity. Addressing the patterns of Islamism and the migration-Islamism nexus within a historical perspective, this chapter argues that the unevenness of globalisation and international migration has strengthened Islamist movements in Bangladesh and the appeal to transnational identities.

Globalisation, Islamism and New Quests for Identity

Globalisation can be understood as a set of processes that cut across national boundaries, making people and institutions experience the world in more integrated configurations of time and space (McGrew, Hall and Held 1992). It projects social, political and economic activities across frontiers and regions. The phenomenon is marked by the migration of populations, increasing interconnectedness between societies, transmission of ideas, capital, goods and information, and decreasing barriers to effective global communication. Another apparent outcome of globalisation is the diffusion of power from states to non-state actors, caused by the extraordinary information revolution, which, in turn, has caused the rise of transnational social movements (Nye 2011). The transformations and processes that globalisation enabled have important political implications. For example, experiments with supranational political forms have institutionalised forums for thinking beyond the nation-state, while transnational social movements have permitted politics to become mobile (Mandaville 2003). Similarly, globalised cities have become sites of profound shifts in identity, and new dynamics of migration have engendered travelling identities (ibid). These unprecedented global currents have enabled distant events to impact communities as the interdependence on foreign investment and powers increased. Additionally, the hegemony of national and statist forms of political identity have not only been called into question, but also given rise to discrepant ideas and visions of non-Western politics and polities (ibid).

These developments have triggered a vital quest for identity, community and legitimacy within and against the rapidly changing environments that it has created (ibid). This has led to religious revivalism in many parts of the world. One such manifestation of this is Islamism – a 'movement that conceives Islam as a political ideology' (Roy 1994: ix). Almost unanimously, the ultimate goal of Islamist organisations is to establish an Islamic state or 'a moral society of God's *shari'a* (law) for the service of the oneness of God' (Moussalli 2003: 19). Despite this, it must be noted that Islamists are not a homogenous group. Islamism is a heavily contextual phenomenon whose major goal is to express and redress the numerous grievances held by disparate Muslims across societies. For instance, Islamist groups differ on the optimal geographic frontiers of the desired Islamic state – whether within the traditional nation-state, or in the form of a transnational entity – and the means to achieve it. While the precedents of contemporary Islamism can be traced back to the advent of various Islamic reform movements of the nineteenth and early twentieth centuries, Islamism is generally acknowledged as having ascended onto mainstream politics since the 1970s, when it became consolidated as a global political force following the Iranian Revolution, the Soviet invasion of Afghanistan and the consequent jihad of the Afghan Mujahedeen (Gerges 2009).

Even when physical movements do not occur, individuals are ever more conscious of politics, ideas, actions and events in other parts of the world, due to the information revolution caused by developments in communication technologies. The ease in communication has effectively resulted in the compression of space and time. Due to increased interconnectivity and networking, people are increasingly affected and/or influenced by what is happening in other parts of the world. Intensified global social associations have connected distant localities in such a way that local events are shaped by events taking place miles away, and vice versa. Thus, for instance, Asian Muslims often reflect philosophical and ideological trends prevalent in other parts of the world. Also, with the effects of the communication revolution, there has been a diffusion of command and control. This has permitted an extensive range of voices to enter the public sphere. As a result, Muslims from diverse backgrounds have amalgamated within trans-local spaces, leading to the amplification of their thoughts and ideas.

These developments have had important transformative effects in the context of Islamist movements. They have allowed interconnectivity – both within nation-states and also across national boundaries. This has enabled Islamists to share information, recruit and collaborate with each other easily and, in turn, acted as a force multiplier, enhancing the Islamists' power. Also, as the internet permits covert communication and anonymity, it has enabled banned, clandestine Islamists to reach their target audience and operate successfully. In Bangladesh, there has been a proliferation of online Islamist materials in local languages, including Bengali – which the Bangladeshi Islamists are 'localising' to spread their ideology, issue religious injunctions, influence the public and recruit individuals.

Islamists in Bangladesh, like those elsewhere in the world, are heterogeneous. According to Riaz (2008), there are three broad categories of Islamists in Bangladesh: (1) those who participate in the existing political system, (2) those who work within the democratic political system but do not take part in elections, and (3) those who reject constitutional politics and remain clandestine. They function in a fluid environment where different ideologies occasionally cross-fertilise and present a complex picture of evolving structures, transnational and domestic linkages, operational and tactical capabilities, and sources of funding and training (Riaz 2008). The emergence of Islamism in Bangladesh is contingent on the country's nation-building process and internal conflict for a national identity, as well as on the geopolitical context that shaped its political trajectory. While domestic factors have played their part, globalisation can be regarded as one of the key factors in the rise of Islamist movements in Bangladesh. Islamists in Bangladesh have largely been inspired by foreign ideas and/or described as responding to external actions and events. These influences arrived through a number of channels, some of which were inadvertent consequences evolving from, for example, short-term migration, while others have been fostered by external entities (Riaz 2009). As the world became more globalised, national economies became increasingly integrated through global trade. Often, economically strong states use their economic strength as leverage to carve out political opportunities in vulnerable states (Nye 1990). One such illustration is the case of Bangladesh and the Middle East. The discovery of oil in the Middle East and Bangladesh's dependence on the Middle East for financial aid has shaped Bangladesh's history, politics and society to a large extent.

Nationalism and the Emergence of Islamism in Bangladesh

Bangladesh, the world's fourth-largest Muslim-majority country, emerged as a constitutionally secular country in 1971, after a decade-long ethno-linguistic movement to secede from Pakistan. It is home to 'a population of about 140 million where about 88% are Muslims and over 98% of them speak in Bangla' (Bangladesh High Commission, Brunei Darussalam, n. d.). Its religious minorities include Hindus, Buddhists, Christians and animists. The Hindus, its largest minority, have maintained social, cultural and eco-nomic links with their co-religionists in West Bengal, India, and constitute an important 'vote-bank' of the current party in power, the Awami League (AL) (Hossain 2012). Bangladesh has a parliamentary government led by Prime Minister Sheikh Hasina (as of 2017). She is also the daughter of Sheikh Mujibur Rahman, the founder of the nation and the then-leader of AL, which had led the struggle for independence.

Political Islam took shape in Bangladesh in the seventeenth century under the British rule, against the backdrop of a sociological distinction of its Muslim population; it has since played an important role in the nation-building process (Hasan 2012). Given the country's demographics, political history and sporadic use of Islam in political discourse, Bangladesh has tended to be susceptible to identity conflicts involving ethnicity and religion: Muslim versus Bengali (Alam 1993). Various political parties in Bangladesh have exploited this ethno-religious fault-line, the legacy of which still persists.

Bangladesh's nationalism project has hinged on a recurring tension between two constructs – the 'Bengali' and the 'Bangladeshi' identities. While Bangladeshi nationalism is explicitly Islamic in character, Bengali national-ism is rooted in the Bengali ethno-linguistic identity and undermines the role of religion. The development of the 'Bengali' identity can largely be attrib-uted to two factors: on one hand, there is the syncretic secularist traditions present in the early history of Bengal and the rise of the Language Movement in East Pakistan (present-day Bangladesh) in the 1950s. The movement advo-cated for the recognition of the Bengali language as an official language of the then-Dominion of Pakistan. It inspired the development and celebration of the Bengali language, literature and culture and re-affirmed the ethno-national consciousness of the Bengalis, which eventually catalysed the rise of nationalist movements in present-day Bangladesh, leading to its independ-ence. On the other hand, the 'Bangladeshi' identity was forged by taking recourse to Islamic loyalties that were introduced during the Islamist move-ments against British colonialism and crystallised during the movement for Pakistan, and then later by the process of Islamisation set in motion by the military regimes of General Zia and General Ershad.

During Bangladesh's struggle against West Pakistan, calls for Bengali nationalism, democracy, socialism and secularism were made. While people responded to appeals of Bengali nationalism, the other three slogans were largely alien to them, imposed from above. Nevertheless, secularism was enshrined as a principle in the 1972 Constitution, largely as a response to the Islamic parties' opposition to Bangladesh's independence and collaboration with the Pakistani military. As secularism was imposed as a top-down approach, merely as a state directive, it was not internalised by a large segment of Bangladeshis. Also, the rationale and processes that made it a state principle became a disputed matter. Many perceived that it was incorporated into the Constitution to downgrade Islam in the affairs of Bangladesh at the behest of (Hindu) India. Cracks appeared in the language-ethnicity formulation of national identity, and the search for an alternative construction got under way. As Bengali nationalism started losing influence as the chief marker of identity, Muslim identity regained prominence to differentiate from the Hindus of West Bengal, India.

After the independence from Pakistan in 1971, the original vision of socialism and secularism for the country of the first president of Bangladesh, Sheikh Mujibur Rahman, came under threat immediately after the government faced formidable economic challenges. Its separation from Muslim Pakistan had weakened support from most other Muslim countries, including oil-producing Middle Eastern countries, while others such as the United States preserved its distance from Bangladesh because of its socialist rhetoric (Griffiths and Hasan 2015). As Bangladesh's liberation movement was the product of ethno-lingual nationalism, Islamic countries perceived it as a negation of Islamic ideology or disowning of Muslim identity, despite the fact that Bangladesh had a majority-Muslim population. Most of the Muslim countries raised deep suspicion about the legitimacy of Bangladesh's Liberation Movement. They perceived the creation of Bangladesh as a dismemberment of Pakistan and an attempt to divide the Islamic world. In order to reconstruct the war-ravaged economy, the country needed an undisrupted flow of external aid. The oil boom in the early 1970s and the unprecedented oil-price hike in 1973 followed by the worldwide recession pushed Bangladesh to foster relations with Arab countries. Both states were acting pragmatically: while the Arab states wanted to exert influence, through soft power, in one of the largest Muslim nations in the world, Bangladesh desperately needed Middle Eastern petro-dollars to sustain its economy. Thus, Mujib began to endorse an Islamic element to nationalism in Bangladesh (Rahim 2007). He participated in the meeting of the Organisation of the Islamic Conference (OIC) held in Pakistan in 1974, even though his regime was avowedly secular. He also sent a group of Bangladeshi doctors to assist his Arab 'allies' during the Yom Kippur war in 1973 against Israel. Additionally, during the 1970s, oil companies in the Middle East recruited Bangladeshis as labour to work in the oil fields. Hence, the course of promoting religion as a basis for national identity had already commenced with the Awami League prior to the violent military coup of 1975, when Mujib was killed.

After the assassination of Mujib, General Ziaur Rahman established the Bangladesh Nationalist Party (BNP) in 1978 and introduced Bangladeshi nationalism, which is explicitly Islamic in character and contains a blend of culture and religion. It stresses that Muslim distinctiveness was the basis of the movement for the creation of Pakistan in 1947,[1] from which Bangladesh emerged as a sovereign state in 1971. It was during the two subsequent army administrations led by Ziaur Rahman (1975–81) and his successor General Hussein Muhammad Ershad (1982–90) that measures were taken to invoke Islamic nationalism and tarnish the leaders' legitimacy against the backdrop of growing Islamic revivalism.

The military regimes, like their predecessor, were tremendously dependent on foreign support, the bulk of which came from the Middle East (Alam 1993). To win the endorsement of Middle Eastern countries, Zia reinstated the previously banned Jamaat-e-Islami Bangladesh (JIB),[2] whose leaders had strong networks with the Middle East, and several other Islamist parties on the political scene of Bangladesh (Enayetur 2001). General Ershad, who came to power through a military coup in 1982, followed Zia's 'Islamisation' strategy and for some time was able to consolidate his power. By the time he was overthrown in 1990, the restoration of Islam in Bangladeshi society and polity had been formally explained in several amendments to the constitution. First, 'bismillahi rahmanir rahim', which translates to 'in the name of Allah, the most forgiving, the most merciful' was inserted at the beginning of the constitution. Second, 'socialism' and 'secularism' were replaced with 'social justice' and 'absolute trust and faith in almighty Allah'. Third, Islam was declared the state religion.[3] On a social level, Islamic nationalism manifested itself by the hanging of posters in government offices with quotes from the Qur'an, the displaying of Qur'anic verses and the Prophet's advice in public places, the flying of Eid-Mubarak festoons next to national flags during Eids, the issuance of messages by the head of state or government on religious occasions such as Eid-e-Miladunnabi, Shab-e-Barat and Muharram, as well as offerings of *munajat* (prayer) on special occasions. More importantly, a new division of religious affairs was established together with the Islamic foundation (with an extensive network of research facilities), an Islamic university (with an Islamic research centre attached to it), as well as a Zakat fund (headed by the president) and the Bangladesh Madrasah education board.

After 1990, when democracy was established in Bangladesh, both the AL and the BNP courted Islamist parties to form governments at different points of time. Nevertheless, the AL is generally associated with Bengali nation-

---

[1] The Partition of 1947 resulted in the creation of the Union of India and the Dominion of Pakistan, splitting Hindus and Muslims. The Dominion incorporated West (present-day Pakistan) and East (present-day Bangladesh) Pakistan.

[2] In this chapter, I will refer to the contemporary Bangladesh Jamaat-e-Islami party by its historical name, Jamaat-e-Islami Bangladesh, to avoid confusion

[3] Islam was declared the state religion in June 1988; however, Bangladesh's legal and judicial system is based on secular British law.

alism, while the main opposition party, the BNP and numerous Islamist parties such as the Bangladesh Jamaat-e-Islami (BJI) have invigorated a Muslim identity for Bangladesh. As such, Bangladesh has been polarised between the right-of-centre BNP and the left-of-centre AL.

During the Mujib administration, Islamist parties could not play an active role in Bangladeshi politics, because the principle of secularism circumscribed any communal politics in the country (Riaz 2008). However, since the military regime had removed secularism from the constitution, it was no longer a hindrance for Islamists to re-emerge. This also served to create an aura of political legitimacy for the regime's rule (ibid). Popular attachment to Islam in Muslim-majority Bangladesh was exploited by these undemocratic regimes which lacked a widely accepted public mandate to govern the nation. A major ramification of the Middle Eastern influence included the long-term effect of the growth of Saudi-funded charities and institutions (ibid). These organisations offered generous reserves through various Islamist groups to build mosques and run madrasahs and Islamic NGOs – which served to not only neutralise the effect of existing secular organisations, but also preached and promoted a puritanical interpretation of Wahhabi Islam (Hasan 2014). Bangladesh's relationship with the Middle East also facilitated the migration of large numbers of Bangladeshi workers to Middle Eastern countries where they were immersed in Wahhabi orthodoxy (ibid).

It is plausible to argue that Bangladesh's dependence on Saudi Arabia re-opened the doors of political Islam in Bangladesh and facilitated its expansion in multiple ways. While the Bangladeshi Supreme Court reasserted the constitutional secular principle in 2010, the collective impact of the constitutional amendments by the military regimes, coupled with developments beyond national borders, caused a culture war between the secular, liberal civil society and its increasingly Islamic identity. This caused a fundamental shift in the state's ideological orientation (Hashmi 2011) and has arguably contributed to a societal environment conducive to the rise of Islamism. Today, sections of the populace are drawn to Islamism in their quest for a new identity for Bangladesh.

Moreover, in 2013, Bangladesh's identity conflict turned from a political dispute to a social crisis, during the secularist-led Shabagh movement and the Islamist-led counter-movement that followed (Hossain 2015). The Shabagh movement demanded the death penalty for Abdul Quader Mollah, who had been sentenced to life-imprisonment, and others convicted by the International Crimes Tribunal of Bangladesh for war-crimes during the 1971 Liberation War.[4] It also called for a ban on religion-based political parties

---

[4] In 2010, the AL-led government of Bangladesh established a special *ad hoc* court to adjudicate crimes committed during the Liberation War that led to the creation of Bangladesh in 1971. The trials garnered much criticism for allegedly being unfair and biased against members of political opposition parties, especially the Islamists who opposed separation from Pakistan in 1971 (Chopra 2015).

and all the institutions and media outlets associated with them (Sajjad and Härdig 2016). Tens of thousands of Bangladeshis across the country joined the protests. This triggered a counter-movement led by a socio-religious group, Hefazat-e-Islam,[5] demonstrating solidarity in the face of perceived persecution stemming from the war crimes trials, and resisted changes in what they regarded as norms, values and beliefs foundational to Bangladesh (Hossain 2015). Since then, the perceived mutual exclusivity of the religious and secular identities of Bangladeshis have reinforced political and social polarisation (ibid). Correspondingly, migrant Bangladeshis, too, expressed solidarity with the Shabagh protests (and counter-protests) through social media outlets such as Facebook and Twitter, as well as symbolic solidarity demonstrations in countries such as Australia, Malaysia and the United States, among others.

Migration, the Embrace of Islamism and Solidarity with the Ummah

Migration is one of the key drivers of globalisation and an avenue for Bangladeshi youths, particularly from the lower strata of society, to escape the lack of employment opportunities and socio-economic mobility in the country (Rahman 2017). There has been a phenomenal growth in international migration, from labour and economic migrants to political exiles and refugees of humanitarian disasters. Since the 1970s, the country has experienced large-scale migration of mostly low-skilled blue-collar workers to the oil-rich Middle Eastern countries (ibid). Towards the late 1980s, the newly industrialised Southeast Asian nations also became a new migration destination for them (ibid). According to estimates of the Bangladeshi Bureau of Manpower, Employment and Training (BMET) (2018), more than eleven million low-skilled Bangladeshi labourers migrated overseas for work as of 2017. Among these, around 80 percent went to the Middle East, whereas more than 15 percent went to Southeast Asia, and the rest went to other regions (ibid). Today, remittances from migrants are one of the biggest sectors of Bangladesh's foreign exchange earnings. Statistics published from the World Bank show that Bangladesh is the eighth-highest remittance-receiving country in the world – making migration a formidable force in regard to the development of Bangladesh (The World Bank 2016).

---

[5] Hefazat-e-Islam, formed in 2010, gained prominence when it managed to mobilise a counter-protest during the Shabagh Movement. The government cracked down on the Hefazat protesters and more than fifty people were killed according to Human Rights Watch. Following the arrest and execution of key leaders of Jamaat-e-Islami, Hefazat-e-Islam took advantage of the vacuum left in the Islamist space of Bangladesh and is now an umbrella to many madrasahs and Islamic institutions in Bangladesh. It has considerable support in major Bangladeshi cities, especially Chittagong and Dhaka.

International migration is widely assumed to precipitate transformations of identity, including religious identity. Research on Muslim migrants
in non-Muslim nations has underlined religious minority status and the
stigmatisation of Islam in elucidating trends towards literalist, strict and
puritanical Islam (Schmidt 2004). This is because migration leads to the re-
assertion and re-evaluation of religious values. In his research on Muslim
migrants, Roy argues that, when confronted with an environment where
the institutional anchors for the practice of Islam are absent, immigrants
seek a 'pure' Islam which focuses on a strict return to its 'original and true'
tenets (Roy 2006: x). Additionally, as Muslims cross international borders,
they confront a vast diversity of Muslim cultures and practices (Donnan
and Ahmed 1994). In view of these encounters, they re-evaluate their own
approach towards Islam (ibid). A more scriptural slant towards Islam, one
that is not ostensibly endowed with the vagaries of specific native cultures,
becomes particularly compelling to migrants who see the culturally inflected
variety of Muslim practices (ibid). Under these conditions, there is a desire to
abandon superfluous cultural influences and adhere only to the fundamental
tenets of Islam. A faction of this group embraces the belief that Islam should
guide both social and political life.

Bangladeshi migrants are not outside of this scenario. In 2015 and 2016,
two groups of Bangladeshi migrant labourers in Singapore were arrested
under the Internal Security Act and deported back to Bangladesh for Islamist
terrorism-related activities (Hussain 2016). While the majority of the first
group of twenty-seven individuals subscribed to radical Al-Qaeda (AQ)
ideologues like Anwar al-Awlaki, some members also accepted elements of
the Islamic State (IS) ideology (Kok 2016) and had plans to join them in the
Middle East. A number of them also contemplated returning to Bangladesh
itself to wage war against the government; they had sent donations to
domestic extremist groups in the country (ibid). The second group of eight
members professedly belonged to a group called Islamic State of Bangladesh
(ISB), with at least two more members in the group who were in Bangladesh
(Ng 2016). The ISB cell had initially intended to join IS in the Middle East,
but due to the difficulty of travelling there, they concentrated on returning
to Bangladesh, using violence to oust their government and establishing an
Islamic State there under IS's self-declared caliphate (ibid). Bangladesh also
saw its worst terrorist attack in July 2016, when IS-directed Neo-Jamaat-
ul-Mujahedeen Bangladesh (Neo-JMB) members seized the Holey Artisan
Bakery in Dhaka and killed eighteen foreign nationals (Marszal and Graham
2016). Two of the five attackers involved had been radicalised in Malaysia
(Lim 2016).

This migration-Islamism nexus is not a new phenomenon in Bangladesh.
In fact, migration has historically played an instrumental role in shaping
Islamist movements in the country. During the repressive rule of the British
Raj, Islamism had become a focal point largely due to two historic events,
both of which were direct implications of migration: the Faraizi movement

of 1818[6] and the Tariqah-i-Muhammadiya[7] movement during the 1820s and
1830s (Riaz 2009: 79–100). These movements advocated a puritanical doctrine of Islam which condemned components of popular Islam as erroneous
(ibid). They demanded the creation of a Muslim Caliphate, the establishment
of *tawhid* and abolishing 'traces of animistic and Hindu beliefs and practices
from Muslim society' (ibid). Although the movement subsided soon after,
traces of its ideologies lingered for some time. Due to its success in mobilising the masses in various districts to engage in jihad and raise funds for the
cause, it presented the idea that Islam, as a political force, could and should
provide a voice to the oppressed (ibid). Moreover, it provided the foundation
for the conflict in identity whereby Bangladeshis are divided between choosing ethnicity or religion as the prime marker of identity.

As mentioned above, millions of Bangladeshis migrate to foreign countries on short-term employment contracts, with the overwhelming majority
going to the Middle East. With their limited understanding of the social
undercurrents there, the migrants conclude that these states embody ideal
Islamic societies, as the Middle East is conventionally thought to be the home
of authentic Islam (Kibria 2008). The presence of regressive societal values
and stringent understandings of Islam in the birthplace of the faith are commonly misconstrued as true Islam (ibid). Hence, they often return with an
altered idea of Islam, due to the social system of these states (ibid). Upon
their return to Bangladesh, they engage in visible acts of piety and asserted
their newly gained religious principles within their families and the wider
public (ibid). They also attempt to replicate these ideals by making charitable
contributions to and/or establishing madrasahs which teach and propagate
these doctrines (ibid). Although unpremeditated, this has opened doors
to puritanical and often intolerant interpretations of Islam in Bangladesh,
which often encourage the push for the establishment of shari'ah laws and
an Islamic State (ibid).

Bangladeshis have historically not only returned to their homeland with
ideas to change the existing system in Bangladesh, but there have also been
cases in which they travelled outside for jihad, which has had dire implications for Bangladesh. Indeed, the roots of modern-day extremist Islamist
violence in Bangladesh can be traced back to the 1980s, when Bangladeshi

---

[6] According to Banglapedia (2015), the initiator of the Faraizi movement, Shairatullah,
  had migrated to Mecca in 1799 and stayed there for twenty years to study religion.
  The movement had a profound relation with Saudi Arabia's Wahhabi tradition. It
  gained the greatest momentum in places where the Muslim peasantry was under
  the oppressive domination of Hindu *zamindars* (landlords) and European indigo
  planters. After the death of Shariatullah in 1840, the movement lost its momentum.
[7] According to Khan (2006), Sayyid Mir Nisar Ali alias Titu Mir, the leader of this
  movement in Bengal had gone to Mecca where he met Ahmad (the leader of the
  movement in the Indian sub-continent) who inspired Titu Mir to free his fellow
  countrymen from un-Islamic practices and foreign domination.

volunteers joined the Afghan jihad against the Soviet Union (Riaz 2008). During the Cold War, the US actively supported the Taliban mujahidins who branded the Soviet–Afghan war as jihad, justifying the involvement of foreign nationals (ibid). Riaz notes:

> Approximately 3,000 Bangladeshis were motivated to travel in several different branches to fight in Afghanistan and alongside with other volunteer Mujahedeen from all over the globe [. . .] In 1988, a delegation of 10 self-proclaimed Ulama (Islamic scholars) from Bangladesh visited Afghanistan. The returnees from the Afghan war maintained a close contact with the Taliban and became jubilant when the Mujahedeen captured Kabul in 1992. (2008: 82)

The ramifications of Bangladeshis joining the Afghan war were severe for the security of Bangladesh. Some of these Afghan jihad veterans returned to Bangladesh and formed Harkat-ul-Jihad-al-Islami (HuJi-B), which has been instrumental in expediting the formation of other major Islamist militant groups in Bangladesh; many of them have been inspired by and have connections to transnational terrorist groups and participate not only in local, but also global militant Islamist movements (ibid).

Another prominent representative of transnational Islamist ideology that has emerged in the political arena of Bangladesh due to migration is the urban-based Islamist organisation Hizb-ut Tahrir Bangladesh (HTB), which is linked to the London-based international operation of the HT. HT launched its Bangladesh chapter in 2001, at the initiative of a lecturer at Dhaka University who was introduced to HT while studying in England (Riaz 2009). The organisation had gained considerable strength in various public and private universities in Bangladesh before it was banned in 2009. Nonetheless, the group continues to covertly operate in the country (Khan 2017).

Increased globalisation has not only led to a decrease in the importance of the traditional state, but it has also led to the fragmentation of cultures and an increased importance on non-territorial aspects such as faith. Expounding on globalisation's effect on religion, Beyer (2001) has argued that globalisation can effectively mobilise people across social cleavages. That is to say, globalisation makes religion's two major metiers – societal and communal – stronger. By bridging distances, globalisation has led to the reimagining of the ummah as a renewed form of political community (ibid).

Ummah in general denotes the community of Muslims. Some Muslim scholars also refer to the whole of humanity as the ummah. The concept, derived from the Qur'an, was put in practice by the Prophet Muhammad when Medina, the first Muslim state, was established in the seventh century. According to some researchers, ummah refers to a global community based on a shared faith (Islam) and the enactment of its laws (Hassan 2006). However, this community is now absorbed in the nexus of different countries, where, in numerous instances, Islam is not the major religion (ibid).

Therefore, it is argued that national identity has superseded the ummah identity. Even though it has no universal political implementation today, this notion has important political functions (ibid). It represents a utopian ideal in which the racial, ethnic or national differences among the global or transnational community of believers are irrelevant.

Kundnani (2008) explains that 'Islamic political identity is based on the individual actively choosing to join the community of believers rather than accepting inherited tribal, ethnic or national filiations' (2008: 50). Therefore, it is contingent on individuals to choose whether to give utmost loyalty to Islam or to their respective nation-states. Other scholars such as Al-Ahsan (1992) proclaim that all Muslim nation-states develop this identity crisis. In the context of Bangladesh, the contest between the reinforcement of cultural identity and Muslim identity is represented through the battle between Bengali and Bangladeshi identity, respectively.

These crises of identity for Muslims prevail not only in Muslim-majority states but also around the world. In fact, the notion of ummah may resonate in particularly meaningful ways for migrants who confront the complex realities and denotations of national membership. Various studies have revealed that migration plays a vital role in changing and creating strong political ideas – often in the context of a revival of Ummahism (Kibria 2008; Rai 2006).

With migration, Muslims often find themselves in settings where Islam is not normative and/or systemised, often unlike in the societies back home (Donnan and Ahmed 1994). As religion can be a source of comfort and means to cope with the considerable emotional and psychological strains of being overseas, migrants become inclined to turn to religion and seek solidarity with the Muslim ummah in the host countries (ibid). Furthermore, increasing Islamophobia around the world has entailed the development of Muslim 'ethnicisation' (Kibria 2008). Specifically, in the face of intensified hostility and scrutiny, some Muslims cultivate a greater and more self-conscious sense of collective identity *as Muslims* (ibid). This in turn could potentially foster political attachment to a global brotherhood of Muslims and trigger interest in the cultivation and support of Islamist movements and organisations.

One of the key traits of transnational Islamist movements is the emphasis on 'Muslim identity' as opposed to national identities. Reference to the ummah and the duties and responsibilities of the Muslim community remain dominant to their discourse. For instance, transnational terrorist outfits in Bangladesh often manipulate the reference of ummah and exploit Muslim anxieties over perceived threats to their identity, values and ways of life, as well as sentiments towards fellow Muslims suffering in Myanmar, Syria, Yemen, Palestine, Afghanistan and Indian-administered Kashmir. Their propaganda materials recurrently include horrifying images of Muslim civilian deaths and destruction which in turn aids them in their narrative as the defenders of the ummah. Indeed, following the Gulshan attack in Dhaka's diplomatic zone, the IS released a video showing three Bangladeshi men purportedly standing in IS territory, speaking against what they claimed were brutal Western foreign policies towards Muslim countries.[8] They justified the heinous Dhaka attack as an act of revenge for their perceived Western assault on the Muslim ummah (Chowdhury 2016).

Can Bangladesh Turn Away from its Islamist Trajectory?

Throughout the Muslim world, transnational political Islam preaches the return to the golden age of Islam against the backdrop of the colonisation of much of the Islamic world and its aftermath, which is perceived to have stripped Muslims of their glory and power. In other words, transnational political Islam could be described as a reactionary movement to colonisation and globalisation, which is seen as neo-imperialist and exploitative in nature. This is particularly applicable in Bangladesh, where levels of inequality continue to steadily rise and a sizeable proportion of its population lives in poverty or extreme poverty. Thus, sections of Bangladesh which are eco-nomically deprived feel that the presence of the West-dominated capitalist agendas is not only exploiting them, but also eroding the traditional Muslim values of Bangladeshi society.

Bangladesh's poor economy also affects Bangladeshi migrants, the major-ity of whom fall in the low-status foreign workers category. These workers are often discriminated and belittled because of their nationality. For instance, stigmatisation of Bangladeshis in the Middle East is particularly strong, exceeding that of other South Asians (Kibria 2008). They are widely labelled and seen in the Middle East as *miskins* (beggars) or people from a *miskin* nation (ibid). Similarly, in Singapore, they are derogatorily called 'banglas' (Gwynne 2013). These labels imply a potent mixture of prejudice and naturalised inferiority which legitimises the discrimination and mal-treatment of these workers. This, in turn, generates reflexivity and incites greater awareness of the salience of being from Bangladesh as an indicator of their status and identity. Tsuda (2001) argues that international migration is one means by which identities become 'nationalised and globally located' (2001: 413). This essentially means that migration spurs reflexivity about the meaning and significance of national affiliation, in tandem with an intensi-fied awareness of the global order. As they develop consciousness of the (low) significance of Bangladeshi national identity, migrants become aware

---

[8] It is also important to realise that Western foreign policy has been held up as a punching bag not just for Islamists or jihadists, but also for secular individuals who protest the intrusion of Western (especially American) involvement in their domestic affairs. A good example of this consists of the Latin American Countries. American actions have been held responsible for deposing their democratically elected leaders (Chile). Thus, while one group of people hold Anti-American sentiments for whatsoever reasons, jihadists take it a step further by demanding violent action for revenge.

of the negative connotations that mark Bangladesh as a nation in the global arena. Hence, they start to prefer their other identity – that of Muslim – and turn to Islamist movements (which provide a set of ready-made answers to the questions of personal identity, as well as political and societal issues) as an alternative political ideology to change the current scenario and a means to prosperity and order.

In conclusion, I have explored how dependence on other states in the international system – namely, the Middle Eastern region – paved the way for political Islam to recur in Bangladesh. I have argued that Islamist ideologies in Bangladesh gained approval from the public because of other aspects of globalisation, such as developments in communication technologies, migration, an evolving perception of the ummah and uneven globalisation. Increased interconnectivity among the Muslim ummah has predisposed Muslims to not only pose questions about their identity, but it has also allowed them to amalgamate their ideas and consolidate power. Today, Islamist organisations in Bangladesh appropriate and localise universalistic ideologies and messages put forth by transnational Islamist organisations and employ various approaches to establish an Islamic state in Bangladesh. The diffusion of power, whereby non-state actors can challenge the power of states, has also added a new dimension to this.

Transnational communications media and historical antecedents will continue to play a pivotal role in influencing the mentality of Bangladeshi society. The influence and significance of the Islamists, especially those that characterise Islam as a transnational political ideology, will be dependent on both domestic and global political developments. If global politics emboldens the reinforcement of the sense of Muslim victimhood, the Islamists' appeal to Bangladeshis will plausibly increase in strength. This dismal situation will also create fertile ground for the radicalisation of frustrated minds in Bangladesh, for whom the perception of Islamic justice has much appeal. In this way, transnational Islamists can potentially utilise Bangladesh as a new battlefield in their battle against the West, associated with perceived exploitation and inequality.

References

Aḥsan, A. (1992), *Ummah or Nation? Identity Crisis in a Contemporary Muslim Society*. Leicester: The Islamic Foundation.

Alam, S. S. (1993), 'Islam, Ideology and the State of Bangladesh', *Journal of Asian and African Studies* 29(1/2): 88–106.

Bangladesh High Commission, Brunei Darussalam (n. d.), http://www.hcbangladesh.org.bn/about_bangladesh.html (accessed 3 May 2021).

Beyer, P. (2001), *Religion in the Process of Globalization*. Würzburg: Ergon.

Bureau of Manpower, Employment and Training (n. d.), Bureau of Manpower, Employment and Training (BMET), http://www.bmet.gov.bd/BMET/stattistical DataAction# (accessed 3 May 2021).

Carlile, L. (2015), 'Bangladesh's Democratic Backsliding: Time to Act Before It's Too

Late', *The Diplomat*, https://thediplomat.com/2015/11/bangladeshs-democratic-backsliding-time-to-act-before-its-too-late/ (accessed 3 May 2021).

Chowdhury, S. (2016), 'In New Video, ISIS Warns of More Bangladesh Attacks', *The Indian Express*, http://indianexpress.com/article/india/india-news-india/slamic-state-militants-more-attacks-in-bangladesh-is-video-2898404/ (accessed 3 May 2021).

Donnan, H., and Ahmed, A. S. (1994), 'Islam in the Age of Postmodernity', in A. S. Ahmad and H. Donnan, *Islam, Globalization and Postmodernity*, 1–20. London and New York: Routledge.

Enayetur, R. (2001), 'Bengali Muslims and Islamic Fundamentalism: The Jamat-i-Islami Bangladesh', in R. Ahmed, *Understanding the Bengal Muslims*. New Delhi: Oxford University Press.

Ganguly, S. (2006), *The Rise of Islamist Militancy in Bangladesh*. Washington, DC: United States Institute of Peace.

Gerges, F. A. (2009), *The Far Enemy: Why Jihad Went Global*. Cambridge: Cambridge University Press.

Griffiths, M., and Hasan, M. (2015), 'Playing with Fire: Islamism and Politics in Bangladesh', *Asian Journal of Political Science* 23(2): 226–41.

Gwynne, J. (2013). 'Slutwalk, Feminist Activism and the Foreign Body in Singapore', *Journal of Contemporary Asia* 43(1): 173–85.

Hassan, R. (2006), 'Globalisation's Challenge to the Islamic Ummah', *Asian Journal of Social Science* 34(2): 311–23.

Hasan, M. (2012), 'Historical Developments of Political Islam with Reference to Bangladesh', *Journal of Asian and African Studies* 47(2): 155–67.

Hasan, M. (2014), 'Transnational Networks, Political Islam, and the Concept of Ummah in Bangladesh', in R. A. Jeffrey, *Being Muslim in South Asia*, 224–48. New Delhi: Oxford University Press.

Hashmi, T. (2011), 'Islamism beyond the Islamic Heartland: A Case Study of Bangladesh', in I. Ahmed, *The Politics of Religion in South and Southeast Asia*. London: Taylor & Francis.

Hossain, A. A. (2012), 'Islamic Resurgence in Bangladesh's Culture and Politics: Origins, Dynamics and Implications', *Journal of Islamic Studies* 23(2): 165–98.

Hussain, Z. (2016), '8 Bangladeshi men detained under Singapore's ISA for planning terror attacks back home', *Straits Times Singapore*, http://www.straitstimes.com/singapore/8-bangladeshi-men-detained-under-singapores-isa-for-planning-terror-attacks-back-home (accessed 3 May 2021).

Khan, S. E. (2017), 'Bangladesh: The Changing Dynamics of Violent Extremism and the Response of the State', *Small Wars and Insurgencies* 28:1: 191–217.

Kibria, N. (2008), 'Muslim Encounters in the Global Economy: Identity Developments of Labor Migrants from Bangladesh to the Middle East', *Ethnicities* 8(4): 518–35.

Kok, L. M. (2016), '27 Radicalised Bangladeshis Arrested in Singapore under Internal Security Act', *Straits Times Singapore*, http://www.straitstimes.com/singapore/courts-crime/27-radicalised-bangladeshis-arrested-in-singapore-under-internal-security-act (accessed 3 May 2021).

Kundnani, A. (2008), 'Islamism and the Roots of Liberal Rage', *Race and Class* 50(2): 191–214.

Mandaville, P. (2003), *Transnational Muslim Politics: Reimagining the Umma*. New York: Routledge.

Marszal, A. and Graham, C. (2016), 'Gunmen Attack Restaurant in Diplomatic

Quarter of Bangladeshi Capital', *The Telegraph*, http://www.telegraph.co.uk/news/2016/07/01/gunmen-attack-restaurant-in-diplomatic-quarter-of-banglades hi-ca/ (accessed 3 May 2021).

McGrew, T., Hall, S. and Held, D. (1992), *Modernity and its Futures*. Cambridge: Polity Press.

Ministry of Foreign Affairs (2011), http://www.mofa.gov.bd/index.php?option=com_content&view=article&id=46&Itemid=54 (accessed 3 May 2021).

Moussalli, A. S. (2003), *Moderate and Radical Islamic Fundamentalism: The Quest for Modernity*. Gainesville, FL: University Press of Florida.

Ng, K. (2016), '8 Bangladeshis Took Radical Turn after Arriving in Singapore', *Today*, https://www.todayonline.com/singapore/isa-detentions-8-bangladeshis-issued-2-year-orders-detention-says-mha ISA Detentions' (accessed 3 May 2021).

Nye, J. (1990), 'Soft Power', *Foreign Policy* 80: 153–71.

Nye, J. (2011), *The Future of Power*. New York: Public Affairs.

Rahim, A. (2007), 'Communalism and Nationalism in Bangladesh', *Journal of Asian and African Studies* 42(6): 551–72.

Rahman, M. M. (2017), *Bangladeshi Migration to Singapore*. Singapore: Springer Nature Singapore Pte Ltd.

Rai, M. (2006), *The London Bombings: Islam and the Iraq War*. London: Pluto Press.

Riaz, A. (2008), *Islamist Militancy in Bangladesh: A Complex Web*. London: Routledge.

Riaz, A. (2009), 'Interactions of "Transnational" and "Local" Islam in Bangladesh', in P. Mandaville (ed.), *Transnational Islam in South and Southeast Asia: Movements, Networks, and Conflict Dynamics*, 79–100. Seattle: The National Bureau of Asian Research.

Roy, O. (1994), *The Failure of Political Islam*. Cambridge, MA: Harvard University Press.

Roy, O. (2006), *Globalized Islam: The Search for a New Ummah*. New York: Columbia University Press.

Schmidt, G. (2004), 'Islamic Identity Formation among Young Muslims: The Case of Denmark, Sweden', *Journal of Muslim Minority Affairs* 24(1): 31–45.

The World Bank (2016), http://www.worldbank.org/en/topic/migrationremittances diasporaissues (accessed 3 May 2021).

Tsuda, T. G. (2001), 'When Identities Become Modern: Japanese Emigration to Brazil and the Global Contextualization of Identity', *Ethnic and Racial Studies* 24(3): 412–32.

ISLAMISM IN MINDANAO, SOUTHERN PHILIPPINES: MODERATES, RADICALS AND EXTREMISTS

Nathan Gilbert Quimpo

On 29 March 2019, the Bangsamoro Autonomous Region in Muslim Mindanao (BARMM) was formally inaugurated, replacing an autonomy arrangement that the Philippine government had set up in 1989, which had not quite succeeded in bringing peace to Mindanao – the Autonomous Region in Muslim Mindanao (ARMM). The establishment of BARMM brought into fruition, albeit much delayed, the central component of the peace agreement signed in 2014 by the Philippine government and the Moro Islamic Liberation Front (MILF), known as the Comprehensive Agreement on the Bangsamoro (CAB).

Many Filipinos hope that the peace pact and the establishment of BARMM will lead to a more lasting peace in Mindanao, Southern Philippines, which has been wracked by armed conflict between government forces and Moro[1] separatist rebels for several decades. The war has become one of the bloodiest and most protracted ethnic conflicts in Asia. About 150,000 people have been killed, and hundreds of thousands have been forced to leave their homes.

Whether Mindanao will actually have a lasting peace remains a big question mark. For one, the Philippine government has to ensure peace not just with the Islamist MILF, but also the Moro National Liberation Front (MNLF), which had led the Moro separatist struggle basically along a nationalist orientation, in its early decades. The government signed peace agreements with the MNLF in 1976, then again in 1996, but both of these pacts failed to bring about peace in Mindanao. Moreover, a big challenge for the MILF is how to deal – and probably contend – with traditional Muslim politicians who are steeped in the ways of patronage politics and warlordism, in pushing for much-needed political reforms in Muslim Mindanao.

---

[1] The Moros, comprised of thirteen ethno-linguistic groups in Mindanao and adjacent islands, are a mainly Muslim minority in the Philippines, the only predominantly Christian country in the Association of Southeast Asian Nations.

But perhaps a much more immediate and urgent challenge to peace for both the government and the MILF has to do with confronting an extreme form of Islamism: jihadism. In the 1980s, with the establishment of the MILF by a group that had broken away from the MNLF, Islamists emerged as a major force in the Moro struggle. Since then, however, variants of Islamism – moderate, radical and extremist/jihadist – have been competing with one another for the hearts and minds of the Moro fighters themselves and of the Moro masses. In the 1990s and 2000s, the extremist group Abu Sayyaf became very notorious and much dreaded for its ruthless killings, bombings, kidnappings and other acts of terror. More recently, jihadists affiliated with the Islamic State of Iraq and Syria (ISIS)[2] attacked the city of Marawi and controlled a good part of it for several months. The Marawi jihadists were eventually crushed, but new ISIS-affiliated groups have sprouted in different parts of Mindanao.

In a previous essay (Quimpo 2016), I briefly discussed the ideological positions of the major Moro rebel groups in the course of examining why the decades-old Moro insurgency in Mindanao has remained difficult to resolve. In the current paper, I focus on the development of Islamism[3] in the Moro struggle – its emergence, the inroads of jihadism, the deradicalisation of the MILF and the possible resurgence of jihadism – as well as the factors that have brought about the twists and turns in Islamism's development. I also discuss the roles that the Philippine state and other actors have played in how Islamism has evolved in Mindanao.

I argue that international developments, such as the spread of Islamist ideas, especially those of radical Islamist thinkers, and the Soviet–Afghan war and its immediate aftermath, as well as domestic developments – breakdowns in the Mindanao peace process – were the main factors for the rise of Islamism in the Moro struggle and, later, for the major inroads of its violent extremist form, jihadism. Islamism supplanted Moro nationalism as the dominant ideology in the Moro struggle in the 1990s. International factors, as well as the growth in strength of the MILF, contributed to its radicalisation. In the thick of the war on terror, the MILF de-radicalised and took on a more moderate stance due to a combination of state repression and inducements, tremendous international and domestic support for peace and development efforts, and the charismatic leadership of MILF leader Salamat Hashim. The rise of ISIS to global prominence, another breakdown in the Mindanao peace process and President Rodrigo Duterte's lacklustre initial peace efforts led to a revival of sorts of jihadism in Mindanao. Global developments bode well for the ascendance of a moderate form of Islamism within Moro ranks. But intensified counter-terrorist operations will not suffice to defeat jihadism in Mindanao. How the national government and BARMM

---

[2] ISIS is also known as the Islamic State (IS), the Islamic State of Iraq and the Levant (ISIL) and Daesh.

[3] Some scholars use *political Islam* or *Islamic fundamentalism* in place of *Islamism*.

work together for development and reform will play a crucial role in ridding Mindanao of this violent extremist form of Islamism.

Historical Background

Islam came to the Philippines in the early 1300s via the southern islands and spread quickly. The Sultanate of Sulu was established in the mid-1400s and the Sultanates of Maguindanao and Buayan (in central Mindanao) in the 1500s. By the time the Spaniards started to colonise the Philippines in 1565, the thriving sultanates had expanded their reach through most of Mindanao and the Sulu archipelago (Majul 1973).

Throughout the more than three centuries of Spanish colonial rule in the Philippines, the Muslims fiercely fought the Spaniards in a long series of 'Moro Wars' and managed to remain largely unsubjugated. The Spaniards contemptuously referred to the Muslims in Mindanao as *Moros*, after the Muslim Moors (Moros, in Spanish) who had conquered and ruled large parts of Spain starting in 711 and were only finally vanquished by the Christian Spaniards in 1492. Detesting the Mindanao Moros as they did their long-time archfoes back home, the Spanish colonialists mobilised the Christianised *indios* to fight the Moros, thus planting the seeds for present-day 'Christian-Moro' prejudices.

After the United States started to colonise the Philippines in 1898, the Moros once again forcefully resisted, but were finally subjugated by the Americans. The Moro areas in Mindanao were first administered as the 'Moro Province', but this was later subdivided into several provinces. To help spur the development of Mindanao, the Americans encouraged Filipinos from the northern and central parts of the Philippines (Luzon and Visayas) to resettle in Mindanao under a 'homestead programme'. By 1948, just two years after the Philippines gained independence, only 32 percent of the population of Mindanao were Muslims, a very sharp drop from 76 percent in 1903.

In its efforts at nation-building, the newly independent Philippine state undertook a policy of 'national integration' towards all ethnic minorities, Moros included, seeking to make them adapt to the laws, norms and culture of the majority-Christian Filipinos. At the same time, the government further promoted transmigration to Mindanao; thus, the influx of Christian settlers from Luzon and Visayas intensified. According to Gowing (1979: 210), integration and the influx of settlers constituted two ways by which the Moros were being insidiously assimilated into the Philippine nation: 'Integration takes away the Moro religious and cultural identity; migration and resettlement programs take away their land'.

In 1968, the Jabidah massacre – the killing of Moro recruits (possibly as many as sixty-eight) being covertly trained by the Philippine government for an invasion of Sabah, Malaysia – greatly helped ignite Moro separatism. Two months after the massacre, Udtog Matalam, a former governor of

Cotabato province, established the first separatist organisation in Mindanao, the Muslim Independence Movement (MIM), later renamed the Mindanao Independence Movement. Starting in late 1969, groups of rebellious young Moros, coming from different ethno-linguistic groups, underwent military training on Pangkor Island, Malaysia, and then in Sulu. In Malaysia, the trainees formed the Moro National Liberation Front, with Nur Misuari, a former student leader then political science lecturer at the University of the Philippines, as chairman. They adopted the name 'Moro', a pejorative that the Spaniards had used against Mindanao Muslims, as it evoked awe, dread and even fear among the Moros' foes.

In the early 1970s, land disputes between the Moros and Christian settlers took a particularly violent turn. Paramilitary units of powerful 'Christian' landlords and warlords attacked Moro communities, forcing them to flee and abandon their lands. In turn, the private armies of traditional Muslim warlords pounced upon settler communities. But the Muslims, who were now down to just 20 percent of the population of Mindanao, continued to lose ground.

When President Ferdinand Marcos declared martial law in September 1972, the Moros, led by the MNLF, launched their war for liberation. Charging that 'Filipino colonialism' was waging a 'genocidal campaign' against the Moro people, the MNLF called for the secession of Mindanao and the establishment of an independent 'Bangsamoro Republik'. With an armed force of 15,000 men, the MNLF fought pitched battles against government forces in Moro and adjacent provinces, even capturing some towns and holding them for days. The armed conflict between government and Moro rebel forces was at its most intense in the early years of martial law; most of the war's casualties were registered during this period.

Appalled by the mounting deaths of Muslims, especially women and children, in Mindanao, foreign ministers of the Organisation of the Islamic Conference (OIC)[4] called on the Philippine government to find a peaceful solution to the Mindanao conflict through negotiation with the MNLF. Facing the threat of an oil embargo by the Arab countries, Marcos was soon forced to negotiate with the MNLF (Majul 1985).

In December 1976, the Philippine government and the MNLF signed the Tripoli Agreement, a peace pact that was supposed to end over four years of intense fighting between the government and Moro rebel forces and that provided for the establishment of 'autonomy for the Muslims in the Southern Philippines' covering thirteen provinces. The peace pact quickly collapsed, however, as Marcos unilaterally set up two 'autonomous regions' covering only ten provinces.

[4] Now the Organisation of Islamic Cooperation.

MILF and the Emergence of Islamism

Prior to the signing and quick collapse of the Tripoli Agreement, the MNLF had already suffered from a number of setbacks, such as the failed attempt to take over the city of Jolo in 1973; the surrender of many MNLF governments to the government; and the resort to kidnapping and banditry by some MNLF fighters. Since 1975, MNLF chairman Nur Misuari had been mainly based in Tripoli, dependent on funding from Libyan leader Muammar Gaddafi (Tiglao 2000).

The MNLF split into two in December 1977, several months after the collapse of the Tripoli Agreement. Dissidents within the MNLF who were critical of Misuari's leadership, led by Salamat Hashim, established the 'new MNLF'. In their 'Instrument of Takeover', they castigated the 'old' MNLF leadership for moving away from an Islamic standpoint and towards a 'Marxist-Maoist' orientation, and for developing a 'mysterious, exclusive and arrogant' style of leadership (Jubair 2014: 154–5). The ethnic divide played a part in the split. Misuari, who hails from Sulu Island, is a Tausug. With Hashim being a Maguindanao, the great majority of those who joined the 'new MNLF' were Maguindanao, Maranao and Iranun living in Central Mindanao.

In March 1984, the 'new MNLF' renamed itself the Moro Islamic Liberation Front. Jubair (2014: 156) provides the rationale for the name change:

> While there were other important reasons, the most compelling was the need to emphasise the Islamic orientation of the group as contrasted to the secular-nationalist line pursued by the MNLF. Islam thus became the official ideology of the MILF, which would guide all its affairs and activities.

The establishment of the MILF marked the rise of Islamism in the Moro struggle. The MILF adheres to the central tenet of Islamism – the belief that 'Islamic law or Islamic values should play a central role in public life' (Hamid and Dar 2016).

For Islamists, Islam is not just a religion; it is an all-embracing ideology, a total way of life. Through the Qur'an and the shari'ah (Islamic law), Islam sets norms on moral, political and economic conduct for individuals and for society as a whole. In the Islamists' view, for Muslims to be able to live in a truly Islamic way, political power has to reside in Muslims who are true to the faith. Thus, for Islamists (at least back in the 1980s), it would be impossible for a Muslim to lead a truly Islamic way of life under a non-Islamic system of government (Esposito 1992; Roy 1994).

Islamism is in part a reaction to secularisation, Westernisation, modernisation and globalisation, which Islamists believe have led to a decline of Islam and to moral decay in Islamic countries and societies. The MILF, which has been very critical of the MNLF's 'secular-nationalist' perspective, regards secularism as a serious departure from the Islamic way of life as it 'enslaves man in his quest of satisfaction for the insatiable self' and 'leads him to many evil ways like impiety, alcoholism, materialism, and other acts of hedonism' (Jubair 2014: 265).

The rise of Islamism within the Moro struggle can be attributed to several other factors apart from the setbacks in the Moro struggle – mainly developments in the global arena: the spread of Islamist ideas in the Islamic world, the 1979 Islamic Revolution in Iran and the Soviet-Afghan War (1979–89). While still a student in Cairo in the early 1960s, Hashim was profoundly influenced by the writings of the Islamist thinkers Sayyid Qutb and Syed Abul Ala Mawdudi, especially Qutb (Lingga 1995; Quimpo 1999). After the Iranian revolution, Hashim was very much inspired by the ideas of its leader, Sayyid Ruhollah Khomeini, and hoped to follow in his footsteps (Lingga 1995). In solidarity with the anti-Soviet resistance, the 'new MNLF'/ MILF sent hundreds of its cadres to fight in the Islamic International Brigade in Afghanistan in the early 1980s and established links with many Islamist groups from all over the world (Tiglao 2000; Cook and Collier 2006). Another factor for Islamism's rise was the charismatic leadership of Hashim, who was deeply respected by Moros, especially the Maguindanaos, not just as a political leader, but also as an *alim* (scholar of Islamic religion and law).

Like a typical Islamist movement, the MILF advocated for the establishment of 'a true Islamic community' governed by the shari'ah and of an 'Islamic system of government' (Hashim 1985: 8–9). By continuing to adhere to armed struggle, the MILF could then be considered still radical in its behaviour. But there were declarations clearly indicating political and ideological moderation:[5]

- While still calling for independence for the Bangsamoro (Moro nation), the MILF stated that it was open to 'a meaningful autonomous government' under Philippine sovereignty (9).
- As a means to achieve MILF's objectives, jihad was defined mainly as 'struggle in the way of Allah' (9), not as armed struggle.
- The Moro struggle was not a movement against Christians or against datuism – the system of traditional leadership in Moro society (1).
- Under the Islamic government, all sectors would be afforded 'full freedom to pursue their own particular creed, faith or ideology', albeit 'to the extent warranted by Shariah laws and the traditions of Prophet Muhammad' (28).

Abu Sayyaf Jihadism

The entity now known as the 'Abu Sayyaf' or 'Abu Sayyaf Group' originally started out as al Harakatul al Islamiyah (Islamic Movement). Abu Sayyaf

---

[5] Here I use the conventional meaning of the term 'moderate': 'one who seeks gradual change by working within the existing political system'.

was the *nom de guerre* of its chief founder and ideologue, Abdurajak Janjalani, an *ustadz* (religious teacher) in Basilan, who had reportedly briefly taken part in the anti-Soviet resistance in Afghanistan. Somehow, the repeated reference by the military and media to the 'Abu Sayyaf Group', and not the movement's actual name, stuck (Ugarte and Turner 2011).

Apart from the spread of Islamist thinking and the Soviet-Afghan war, the collapse of the peace talks between the Corazon Aquino government and the MNLF in 1988[6] was a major factor in the emergence of the Abu Sayyaf. Angered by what they perceived to be the government's treachery, on the one hand, and Misuari's feckless leadership, on the other, some Muslim youth and disgruntled MNLF fighters gravitated towards Janjalani, a forceful speaker. The Abu Sayyaf (also known as al Harakatul al Islamiyah) came to the fore in the early 1990s. Its forces operated mainly among the Yakans and Tausugs in Basilan, Sulu and the southern part of the Zamboanga peninsula.

From the very start, the Abu Sayyaf was extremist in both ideology and behaviour. While the MNLF and the MILF had opened up to the possibility of regional autonomy, the Abu Sayyaf advocated for complete secession and the establishment of an Islamic state adhering strictly to the shari'ah. Jihad – meant as war – was the means for achieving this objective. The Abu Sayyaf instilled in its members and followers that this jihad was a personal obligation of Muslims. In this war, the Abu Sayyaf regarded as its enemies all Christians – combatants and non-combatants – as well as Muslims who did not agree with their interpretation of jihad. It engaged in out-and-out terrorism: indiscriminate killings (including beheadings), bombings, raids, ambushes and kidnappings. It rejected any peace negotiations with the government (Wadi 2003). Contrary to the military's early depictions, the Abu Sayyaf has never been a tight, formal organisation, but more a network of amorphous groups, each bound by a chain of personal ties to its leader.

Anthropologist Charles O. Frake (1998) drew up an identity matrix of the Moro rebels, contrasting the Abu Sayyaf, in its early years, with the MNLF and the MILF. He described the MNLF as being dominated by Tausugs, led by a non-traditional university-educated elite and identified with secular Islam; and the MILF as being Maguindanao-dominated, led by Muslims from the established political elite, secular but sometimes employing 'Islamicist' rhetoric.[7] On the other hand, the Abu Sayyaf was 'militantly Islamicist', and its leadership did not come from the established or university-educated elite. It was not typically viewed in terms of ethno-linguistic identification, but in

---

[6] The Aquino government subsequently proceeded with the unilateral establishment of the Autonomous Region in Muslim Mindanao (ARMM).

[7] disagree in great part here with Frake's characterisation of the MILF. Although Hashim did come from an elite clan, he was seen much more in terms of his religious identity, apart from his rebel background/identity. Moreover, the MILF was deeply, not superficially, Islamist.

the context of the long 'outlaw' history of Basilan and neighbouring islands, as being '"like outlaws", but outlaws with an agenda and an ideology' (48).

International terrorist organisations, principally Al Qaeda, provided substantial funding to the Abu Sayyaf in its early years. But its main conduits to the Al Qaeda were soon apprehended – Mohammed Jamal Khalifa, Osama bin Laden's brother-in-law, in the US in late 1994, and Ramzi Yousef, the mastermind of the 1993 World Trade Center attack, in Pakistan in early 1995. As foreign funding dwindled, the Abu Sayyaf intensified its kidnappings for ransom (Taylor 2017a).

After Abdurajak Janjalani was killed in a shoot-out with Philippine police in Lamitan, Basilan, in December 1998, his younger brother Khadaffy took over as Abu Sayyaf leader. Although Khadaffy lacked his brother's charisma and authority, the Abu Sayyaf persisted. Disputing the popular view that the Abu Sayyaf was factionalised and reduced to banditry after Abdurajak's death, Taylor (2017) writes that its forces in Basilan 'continued to adhere to his teachings and maintained a degree of coordination among themselves'. In Sulu, however, the Abu Sayyaf was reduced to 'a host of bands competing for kidnapping victims, exercising their initiatives with a seemingly entrepreneurial spirit, employing networking skills to extend their reach, outsourcing certain aspects of their venture [. . .], all hoping to "score the big one"'.

In the 1990s, with the MILF in overwhelming control of Moro rebel forces in Maguindanao and Lanao del Sur and with the Abu Sayyaf competing with the MNLF in the island-provinces of Basilan, Sulu and Tawi-Tawi, Islamism replaced Moro nationalism as the dominant ideological influence within the Moro rebel ranks.

The Abu Sayyaf, which the US had already declared a 'foreign terrorist organisation' (FTO) in 1997, became the main target of the war on terror in Southeast Asia soon after the US launched the global war on terror. Although the Abu Sayyaf still managed to conduct major terrorist attacks, including a ferry bombing near Manila,[8] the war on terror exacted a heavy toll on the extremist group. In September 2006, Philippine Marines killed Khadaffy in a gunbattle in Patikul, Sulu, but it was only a few months later that they were able to confirm this. By early 2007, Philippine security forces had nearly wiped out the top leadership of the Abu Sayyaf in both Basilan and Sulu (Taylor 2017a). For a decade, the threat posed by the Abu Sayyaf was widely seen as being on the decline. Moreover, some of the actions being attributed to the Abu Sayyaf were believed to be actually the handiwork of armed groups appropriating its name.

---

[8] In February 2004, the Abu Sayyaf, working with the Rajah Solaiman Movement (RSM), bombed a passenger ferry in Manila Bay, killing 116 people – the deadliest terrorist attack in Philippine history. The RSM is a small extremist group composed of Christian converts to Islam.

The Radicalisation of the MILF

The Philippine government (under President Fidel Ramos) and the MILF began exploratory talks in August 1996, and in July 1997 the two sides signed an agreement on general cessation of hostilities. These developments would have seemed to be indications of moderation on the part of the MILF. Not quite so.

The MILF, in fact, was then undergoing a certain degree of radicalisation. Ashour (2009) defines radicalisation as 'a process of relative change in which a group undergoes ideological and/or behavioural transformations that lead to the rejection of democratic principles [. . .] and possibly to the utilisation of violence, or to an increase in the levels of violence, to achieve political goals'.[9] During this period, the MILF developed close ties with radical Islamist and even terrorist organisations, was much more influenced by radical Islamist thinking and conducted military training in its camps, in cooperation with international terrorist groups. It also reverted to its original goal of secession from the Philippine state.

The international factors behind the emergence of Islamism in Mindanao cited earlier contributed to the MILF's radicalisation. In the late 1980s and early 1990s, the Soviet–Afghan War and its chaotic aftermath played a most crucial role. The involvement of MILF fighters in actual combat in Afghanistan was minimal, but they benefited greatly from military training in Pakistan and Afghanistan during and immediately after this war. As mentioned earlier, the MILF forged links with many Islamist groups from all over the world. Among these were radical and even extremist groups such as Al Qaeda and Jemaah Islamiyah (JI). Out of gratitude to the JI for helping train MILF fighters in Afghanistan, the MILF acceded to the JI proposal for training camps to be set up in MILF areas in Mindanao. When the training began in 1994, MILF fighters were the initial trainees. By 1998, the JI and the MILF were running a full-fledged military academy in the MILF's Camp Hubaidiyah, at the far edge of Camp Abubakar, the MILF headquarters, with trainees – Islamist radicals and extremists – from other parts of Southeast Asia (International Crisis Group 2004; Collier and Cook 2006; Taylor 2017b). Cook and Collier (2006) referred to these training camps as 'terror camps'.

The continued spread of Islamist ideas, particularly those of radical Islamist theorists, helped deepen radical thinking within the MILF. As mentioned earlier, MILF leader Hashim had already been influenced by the radical Islamist ideas of Qutb and Mawdudi in his student days. In the 1980s and 1990s, many radical and extremist Islamists, including Al Qaeda, adopted Qutb and Mawdudi as their intellectual beacons and came up with interpretations of these theorists' ideas that suited their own objectives. The

---

[9] Unlike Ashour, however, I distinguish between *radicalism* and *extremism*. I associate the latter with advocacy of extreme measures or views. In the 1990s and early 2000s, the MILF was radicalised, but did not become an extremist group.

constant referencing to these thinkers by other Islamist groups impacted the MILF.

The growth in strength of the MILF was another major factor for its radicalisation. By the mid-1990s, the MILF had become the country's biggest rebel force. In June 1999, Philippine defence officials estimated that the MILF had over 15,000 fighters. The MILF itself claimed to have 120,000 mujahideen forces, armed with automatic rifles, light and heavy machine guns, artillery, anti-tank and anti-aircraft weapons as well as grenades and grenade launchers (Quimpo 1999). In the areas it controlled, the MILF maintained thirteen major camps, a few of which were the size of a small Philippine province, plus thirty-three satellite camps (Quimpo 2000).

In the 1990s, it was not yet too clear to the outside world that the MILF was radicalising. Although there were media reports of MILF links with, and even funding from, international terrorist organisations, the MILF denied them and dismissed them as Western propaganda. Reports about the presence of foreign mujahideen fighting alongside the MILF were likewise denied (Crescent International 1999b). Prior to 9/11, the MILF had largely succeeded in keeping secret the participation of foreign trainers and trainees in military training in its camps. While disavowing ties to international terrorist organisations, it maintained links and a tactical alliance with the Abu Sayyaf, a blatantly terrorist organisation (Quimpo 1999).

Outside of the espousing of the radical ideas of Qutb and Mawdudi and the links with the Abu Sayyaf, there were hardly any obvious signs of radicalisation. The MILF did articulate certain changes in its objectives and means. As late as 1993, the MILF still advocated the full implementation of the 1976 Tripoli Agreement which provided for regional autonomy. But by the latter part of the 1990s, it had reverted to the original MNLF objective of secession, as in the early 1970s. Moreover, it explicitly called for the establishment of an Islamic state in an independent Bangsamoro. While it hoped to achieve independence through peace negotiations, it remained prepared for the resumption of war in the event that it failed to gain independence (Quimpo 1999).[10] These signs of apparent radicalisation, however, did not ring alarm bells as they were widely interpreted as mere tactical manoeuvring in the peace negotiations.

The MILF's radicalisation was by no means through-and-through. In the mid-1990s, the MILF had rejected efforts by an Al Qaeda representative to unify the MILF and the Abu Sayyaf, citing ideological and tactical differences

[10] In its pursuit of independence, the MILF even sought to achieve belligerency status by trying to gain government recognition of its camps. 'The perimeter and outer defenses of our 46 camps', explained Hashim, 'cover about half of Mindanao. It is not possible to keep these areas secret. If these territories governed by the MILF are recognized by the Philippine government, we are closer to our objective. For these are territories we can legally claim even if we go by the laws of the enemy' (Crescent International 1999a; Quimpo 2000).

and criticising the Abu Sayyaf for engaging in anti-Islamic activities (Taylor 2017a).[11] Moreover, the MILF's decision to embark on peace negotiations and agree to a general ceasefire was most untypical of radical Islamists and extremists elsewhere, who generally called for unrelenting war.

The De-radicalisation of the MILF

As the war on terror unfolded in Mindanao, US and Philippine intelligence gathered more and more information about the MILF's training camps and its links with international terrorist organisations. It seemed that it was just a matter of time before the MILF would be included in the FTO list and become the primary target of the war on terror in the Philippines, supplanting the Abu Sayyaf.

In January 2003, MILF chairman Hashim wrote to US President George W. Bush through the US Embassy, asking for Washington's assistance in the Mindanao peace process. In May, the White House responded, expressing its willingness to help, 'provided that the MILF renounced terror'. Hashim quickly replied, stating emphatically that the MILF had 'repeatedly renounced terrorism publicly as a means of attaining its political ends'. Hashim's communications with Bush were the first clear signal that the MILF was de-radicalising and undergoing a process of moderation. Soon after, the MILF pursued a negotiated political settlement more vigorously.

De-radicalisation, says Ashour (2009), 'is another process of relative change within Islamist movements, one in which a radical group reverses its ideology and de-legitimises the use of violent methods to achieve political goals, while also moving towards an acceptance of gradual social, political and economic changes within a pluralist context'. Common causative factors of de-radicalisation are charismatic leadership, state repression, interactions with the 'other' as well as within the organisation and selective inducements from the state and other actors. Moderation, writes Schwedler (2011: 359), is 'movement from a relatively closed and rigid worldview to one more open and tolerant of alternative perspectives'.

A combination of state repression and inducements, tremendous domestic and international support for peace and development efforts, as well as Hashim's charismatic leadership were the main factors behind the de-radicalisation of the MILF.

The state's carrot-and-stick approach evolved in an unusual fashion. Before the war on terror, the government was largely unaware of the JI-MILF training camps. The Ramos government had provided the initial inducements (the carrot) through its peace and ceasefire overtures to the MILF. When the administration of President Joseph Estrada declared 'all-out war' (the stick) against the MILF in March 2000, this was not actually triggered

---

[11] The Abu Sayyaf also rejected the proposed merger, claiming that the MILF was more concerned about making money than waging jihad.

by the training camps. The MILF had earlier succeeded during the peace negotiations in getting the government to recognize seven MILF camps, an important step towards gaining belligerency status. The government sought to reverse its error. At the culmination of the 'all-out war', military forces overran and destroyed Camp Abubakar. The fall of the MILF headquarters showed up weaknesses in the MILF's combat capabilities and shattered the illusion of its main camps' invulnerability. After Estrada was forced to resign amid a corruption scandal, President Gloria Macapagal Arroyo re-opened peace talks with the MILF (the carrot again).

As the war on terror unfolded in Mindanao, US and Philippine intelligence uncovered the MILF's extensive links and collaboration with international terrorist groups. Exercising some restraint, the Arroyo government did not endorse the idea of including the MILF in Washington's FTO list. In February 2003, however, the Arroyo government launched military operations against the MILF (the stick again), accusing the latter of harbouring a notorious kidnap-for-ransom gang. The military captured and dismantled the Buliok Complex at the Maguindanao-Cotabato boundary, the MILF's new head-quarters. The two big military setbacks – Camp Abubakar and the Buliok Complex – proved crucial in convincing the MILF leadership that it could not possibly defeat the government militarily.

Through the ups and downs of the government-MILF peace process, many international and domestic organisations – donor agencies, peace and human rights groups, and so on – assisted or undertook various peace and development initiatives in Moro areas. Members of the diplomatic community and other representatives of foreign governments and intergovernmental organisations frequently met with MILF representatives and extended their own support, too (see Jubair 2007). Such great outpouring of support helped deepen the MILF's commitment to the peace pact.

Although some MILF commanders wanted to continue the armed struggle and the links with terrorist groups, Chairman Hashim managed to lead the MILF towards de-radicalisation. He repeatedly said: 'The most civilised and practical way to solve the Bangsamoro Problem in Mindanao is through a negotiated political settlement of this conflict' (Jubair 2007: 17). After Hashim's sudden death (of natural causes) in July 2003, it took another two years before the new MILF leadership laid down a policy of cutting off all links with JI, Abu Sayyaf and other terrorist groups (Quimpo 2016).

Due to grave blunders of the Arroyo and Benigno Aquino III governments, the de-radicalisation of the MILF has not translated into concrete peace dividends. In 2008, Arroyo's peace panel worked out with the MILF panel an extraordinary document, the Memorandum of Agreement on Ancestral Domain (MoA-AD). Negotiating all too secretly, however, the government side did not undertake proper vetting. Eventually, MoA-AD failed to withstand the constitutional challenge. The signing of the MoA-AD fell through. Arroyo, then under threat of impeachment on fraud and corruption charges, abandoned the pact. In 2014, the government under President Benigno

Aquino III signed a Comprehensive Agreement on the Bangsamoro (CAB) with the MILF. A botched counter-terrorist operation in Mamasapano, Maguindanao, in January 2015, however, threw a monkey wrench into the peace process. The operation resulted in the killing of forty-four specially trained police commandos, among others. Amid the anti-Muslim/anti-Moro hysteria that ensued, Congress failed to pass an enabling legislation for CAB, the Basic Bangsamoro Law (BBL).

ISIS in Mindanao and the Battle of Marawi

After the killing of most of Abu Sayyaf's top leaders and after the MILF's cutting-off of links with terrorist groups, jihadism declined in Mindanao. In 2014, however, reports and videos on various Moro groups pledging allegiance to ISIS and its leader Abu Bakr al-Baghdadi started to appear. In April 2016, the official newsletter of ISIS, *Al-Naba*, announced that an Abu Sayyaf leader, Isnilon Hapilon, had been designated emir of all ISIS forces in Southeast Asia. Until late 2016, however, Philippine military spokesmen repeatedly denied, at least officially, the existence of ISIS in Mindanao.

In May 2017, government security forces attempting to capture Hapilon clashed with ISIS-affiliated groups in Marawi City, Lanao del Sur. Among the jihadist groups were the Islamic State of Lanao, headed by the Maute cousins (Abdullah and Omar), and Hapilon's Abu Sayyaf faction. The government forces expected to wipe out the ISIS jihadists in a quick operation, but the latter turned out to be a much bigger group than previously thought, and the fighting dragged on. President Duterte imposed martial law over the whole of Mindanao. Ill-prepared for urban warfare, the military resorted to artillery bombardment and air strikes to flush out the militants. The siege of Marawi extended over five months, becoming the longest urban battle and longest siege in Philippine post-war history. Over 1,000 were killed, including forty-two foreign jihadists; 1,780 hostages were rescued. Much of the center of Marawi was turned to rubble.

The main factors for the revival of jihadism in Mindanao were the rise of ISIS on the global scene and the breakdown of the Mindanao peace process following the Mamasapano tragedy. These were aggravated by the lacklustre initial peace initiatives undertaken by President Aquino's successor, Rodrigo Duterte, and his underestimation of the ISIS threat.

ISIS gained global prominence in 2014–15, following its capture of large swathes of territory in Iraq, Syria and Libya, and its terrorist attacks in Europe and North America. After proclaiming itself a worldwide caliphate in June 2014, ISIS established *wilayahs* (provinces) of its 'caliphate' in various countries. Many jihadist groups, including erstwhile Al Qaeda affiliates, swore allegiance to ISIS. Southeast Asian jihadists soon aspired to having their own *wilayah*.

The post-Mamasapano peace impasse created a vacuum which the ISIS-affiliated groups, particularly the Maute group, exploited. The Maute cousins were former MILF fighters who had become disgruntled with the movement's leadership. Mohagher Iqbal, the head of the MILF's peace panel, says: 'One of the reasons why these groups are cropping up is because of the frustration of the people [with the peace process]'. He acknowledges that the failings in the peace process have somewhat eroded the MILF's legitimacy, especially among the Moro youth (Fonbuena 2017).

Many Filipinos believed that Duterte, as the country's first president from Mindanao, would finally lead the way to bringing about a just and durable peace in Mindanao. His peace efforts, however, proved wanting. He failed to give priority, or even much attention, to the enactment of an enabling law for CAB, during the early part of his presidency. He campaigned vigorously for a shift to a federal system of government, which requires a constitutional revision process that could take several years, without considering how this could stymie the ongoing peace process. He vainly tried to get the MILF and both the Misuari and Sema factions of the MNLF to form a unified panel in negotiating with the government. (Misuari refused.)

Duterte was kept abreast of the organising activities of ISIS-affiliated groups in Mindanao, but he grossly underestimated the threat that they posed. He even resorted to a bit of braggadocio in impugning the group's capabilities. In December 2016, six months before the Battle of Marawi, he revealed during a dinner at Malacañang Palace that the Maute group was in the forest in Lanao and that they were willing to stop fighting if the government stopped their offensive against the group. The Maute group threatened to attack Marawi and burn it down if the government persisted with its operations. Duterte dared the Maute group: 'Go ahead, do it' (Duterte 2016).

The Aftermath of the Battle of Marawi

After the Battle of Marawi, Duterte finally buckled down to re-animate the stalled peace process with the MILF. Despite grumblings from Misuari, Duterte went ahead with the passage of an enabling law for CAB, the Bangsamoro Organic Law (BOL), a revised version of the BBL. In July 2018, Duterte signed the BOL into law. In January 2019, voters in the Moro areas ratified the new law. Two months later, BARMM was formally inaugurated, with MILF chairman Al-Hajj Murad Ebrahim as interim Chief Minister.

The Bangsamoro Transition Authority (BTA), which serves as BARMM's interim regional government, has executive and legislative powers over the region. It is presently composed of eighty members, of which forty-one have been nominated by the MILF and the rest selected by the government. Some of the government appointees are nominees of the MNLF. As a regional legislative body, the BTA is now giving priority to legislating an administrative code and other basic laws on internal revenue, civil service, local government, elections, education and indigenous people's affairs.

Now that it is in the driver's seat in BARMM, the MILF can take the lead in pursuing the development programmes and political and other reforms that it has long advocated for Muslim Mindanao. But it has only three years within which to work on development and reform before elections for the regular regional government take place in 2022. Will the MILF, which has hardly had any experience in fielding candidates in elections and much more in winning elections, be able to stand up to Muslim Mindanao's traditional politicians, who have long engaged in patronage politics and warlordism?

The MNLF's electoral experience is instructive. After the 1996 peace agreement, the MNLF handily won the ARMM elections in 1996 and 2001 – but only with the full backing of the national government. When such support was withdrawn in the 2005 elections, the ARMM fell under the control of an infamous warlord clan, the Ampatuans, top members of whom perpetrated the Maguindanao massacre in 2009.

A much more pressing and urgent problem for BARMM is the threat posed by Islamist extremists. Although Hapilon, the Maute cousins, other jihadist leaders and hundreds of their militants were all killed in the Battle of Marawi, the threat from ISIS is far from over. In April 2019, the *New York Times* reported that, while ISIS's territory in Iraq and Syria was dwindling, the terrorist group was drawing a range of militant jihadists in the Southern Philippines.

Banlaoi (2019) notes that ISIS, far from being a spent force in the Philippines, has been actively regrouping and recruiting and, since the Battle of Marawi, resumed terrorist activity. According to him, ISIS has local branches or affiliated jihadist groups in five provinces – Sulu, Basilan, Maguindanao, Lanao del Sur[12] and Sarangani – and operates in Metro Manila as well. Hatib Hajan Sawadjaan, the leader of the Abu Sayyaf in Sulu, has reportedly replaced Hapilon as the emir of ISIS in Southeast Asia.

Since the Marawi siege and decline of the ISIS in Iraq and Syria, Mindanao has become more of a magnet for foreign jihadists. According to Banlaoi (2019), close to a hundred foreign terrorist fighters, especially from Indonesia, Malaysia, Sri Lanka and Arab countries, are now in the Philippines. They see the Philippines as an ISIS-declared 'new land of jihad'; as a safe haven due to the strong support of several pro-ISIS groups; and as an alternative base, particularly for jihadists experiencing much more severe counter-terrorist measures in their home countries.

In 2018–19, apart from engaging in armed attacks and clashes with military forces, ISIS groups have perpetrated bombings in various cities and towns – Lamitan, Isulan, General Santos, Cotabato and Jolo – sometimes with the assistance of foreign terrorist fighters. The July 2018 Lamitan bombing, which took eleven lives, was the very first suicide bombing by militants in the Philippines. The suicide bomber was a Moroccan national. Abu Sayyaf

---

[12] ISIS in Lanao suffered another setback with the death of Abu Dar, the last surviving leader of the Maute Group, after clashes with the military near Marawi in March 2019.

plotted and carried out the bombing with the help of Malaysian jihadists and the Moroccan. The January 2019 Jolo Cathedral bombing, which killed at least twenty-three and injured more than a hundred people, was again carried out by foreign suicide bombers, this time an Indonesian couple. No less than Sawadjaan has been tagged by the military as being the mastermind of the cathedral blast.

Conclusion

In November 2001, just two months after 9/11, Francis Fukuyama (2001) disputed Samuel Huntington's controversial 'clash of civilisations' thesis, arguing that the so-called civilisation struggle between Islam and the West was not actually what it appeared to be and that the real clash was between Islam and modernisation. In the sixteenth and seventeenth centuries, Fukuyama says, Christian societies in Europe had to grapple with the question of the relation between religion and politics, and with the notion of modern secular liberalism. Islam, he argues further, now confronts a similar dilemma. It now has to contend with the question of secularism and the need for religious tolerance.

Islamism is a manifestation of 'Islam's clash with modernisation' – and, for that matter, with globalisation, too. It has been an arena of contestation among moderates, radicals and extremists; contrary to widespread thinking, it appears that moderates are gaining. In a study on the evolution of political Islam since the late 1970s, Brichs et al. (2017) state:

> In most Islamist groups, the objective of creating an Islamic state governed by sharia throughout the Muslim community has given way to an acceptance of state borders, the co-option of regimes, and the championing of representative democracies. In addition, violent methods have given way to negotiation and non-violent mobilisation.

If one goes by the 'wave theory' on modern terrorism, the extremist form of Islamism, jihadism, may not last beyond a decade or so. In a study of terrorist movements over the past 150 years, covering the anarchist, anti-colonial and new left movements as well as the contemporary 'religious' movement, David C. Rapoport (2001; 2004) contends that terrorist movements have a wave-like life cycle. A new ideology becomes popular. Terrorist groups espousing it arise and engage in terrorist activity. States persecute them. The groups persist and even grow as the ideology remains popular. The wave crests. And then it starts to decline. Terrorist waves last for about the generation. It was estimated that the 'religious wave' which started in the late 1970s would continue for several decades.

The global developments pointed out above bode well for the ascendance of a moderate form of Islamism within Moro ranks in the coming years. It could even have a powerful influence on the BARMM, if the MILF succeeds in making its Islamist imprint. But the threat from ISIS appears to be growing. Without the concerted efforts of the government and BARMM in development and reform, counter-terrorist operations will not be able to stamp out jihadism as a major scourge in Mindanao.

References

Ashour, O. (2009), *The De-Radicalization of Jihadists: Transforming Armed Islamist Movements*. Oxon and New York: Routledge.

Banlaoi, R. (2019), 'Updates on Threats of Violent Extremism in the Philippines', lecture at a public forum on violent extremism, Miriam College, Quezon City, Philippines, 11 March 2019.

Brichs, F. I., Etherington J. and Feliu, L. (eds) (2017), *Political Islam in a Time of Revolt*. Cham, Switzerland: Palgrave Macmillan.

Collier K. and Cook, M. (2006), 'The Philippines' Sanctuaries of Terror', *Project Syndicate*, 2 May 2006, https://www.project-syndicate.org/commentary/the-philippines--sanctuaries-of-terror (accessed 5 May 2021).

Cook, M. and Collier, K. (2006), *Mindanao: A Gamble Worth Taking*. Sydney: Lowy Institute for International Policy.

Crescent International (1999a), 'Bangsamoro Muslims' Determination to Establish an Islamic State', 16–31 March 1999, https://crescent.icit-digital.org/articles/bangsamoro-muslims-determination-to-establish-an-islamic-state (accessed 5 May 2021).

Crescent International (1999b), 'Mindanao Muslims and the Global Ummah', 1–15 April 1999, https://crescent.icit-digital.org/articles/mindanao-muslims-and-the-global-ummah (accessed 5 May 2021).

Duterte, R. (2016), 'Speech of President Rodrigo Duterte during the Wallace Business Forum Dinner', Malacañang Palace, 12 December 2016, https://pcoo.gov.ph/dec-12-2016-speech-president-rodrigo-duterte-wallace-business-forum-dinner/ (accessed 5 May 2021).

Esposito, J. L. (1992), *The Islamic Threat: Myth or Reality?* New York: Oxford University Press.

Fonbuena, C. (2017), 'MILF, Maute Group Battle for Legitimacy', *Rappler*, 3 July 2017, https://www.rappler.com/newsbreak/in-depth/174531-milf-maute-group-peace-process-marawi-crisis (accessed 5 May 2021).

Frake, C. O. (1998), 'Abu Sayyaf: Displays of Violence and the Proliferation of Contested Identities among Philippine Muslims', *American Anthropologist* 100(1): 41–54.

Gowing, P. G. (1979), *Muslim Filipinos – Heritage and Horizon*. Quezon City: New Day Publishers.

Hamid, S. and Rashid, D. (2016), 'Islamism, Salafism, and Jihadism: A Primer', *Brookings*, 15 July 2016, https://www.brookings.edu/blog/markaz/2016/07/15/islamism-salafism-and-jihadism-a-primer/ (accessed 5 May 2021).

Hashim, S. (1985), *The Bangsamoro Mujahid: His Objectives and Responsibilities*. Mindanao: Bangsamoro Publications.

International Crisis Group (2004), 'Southern Philippines Backgrounder: Terrorism and the Peace Process', *Asia Report* No. 80, 13 July 2004, https://www.crisisgroup.org/asia/south-east-asia/philippines/southern-philippines-backgrounder-terrorism-and-peace-process (accessed 5 May 2021).

Jubair, S. (2007), *The Long Road to Peace: Inside the GRP-MILF Peace Process*. Cotabato: Institute of Bangsamoro Studies.

Jubair, S. (2014), *Bangsamoro: A Nation under Endless Tyranny* (4th edition). Kuala Lumpur: IQ Marin SDN BHD.

Lingga, A. S. M. (1995), *The Political Thought of Salamat Hashim*, unpubl. MA thesis, University of the Philippines.

Majul, C. A. (1973), *Muslims in the Philippines*. Quezon City: University of the Philippines Press.

Majul, C. A. (1985), *The Contemporary Muslim Movement in the Philippines*. Berkeley: Mizan Press.

Quimpo, N. G. (1999), 'Dealing with the MILF and Abu Sayyaf: Who's Afraid of an Islamic State?' *Public Policy* 3(4): 38–62.

Quimpo, N. G. (2000), 'The Thorny Issue of the MILF Camps'. *Philippine Daily Inquirer*, 31 May–2 June 2000.

Quimpo, N. G. (2016), 'Mindanao: Nationalism, Jihadism and Frustrated Peace', *Journal of Asian Security and International Affairs* 3(1): 1–26.

Rapoport, D. C. (2001), 'Modern Terror: The Four Waves', *Current History* 100(650): 419–25.

Rapoport, D. C. (2004), 'The Four Waves of Modern Terrorism', in Audrey Cronin and Lames Ludes (eds), *Attacking Terrorism: Elements of a Grand Strategy*, 46–73. Washington, DC: Georgetown University Press.

Roy, O. (1994), *The Failure of Political Islam*. Cambridge, MA: Harvard University Press.

Schwedler, J. (2011), 'Can Islamists Become Moderates? Rethinking the Inclusion-Moderation Hypothesis'. *World Politics* 63(2): 347–76.

Taylor, V. (2017a), 'Evolution of the Abu Sayyaf Group: Part 1', *Mackenzie Institute*, 21 April 2017, http://mackenzieinstitute.com/evolution-abu-sayyaf-part-1/ (accessed 5 May 2021).

Taylor, V. (2017b), 'Evolution of the Abu Sayyaf Group: Part 2', *Mackenzie Institute*, 24 April 2017, http://mackenzieinstitute.com/evolution-abu-sayyaf-group-part-2/ (accessed 5 May 2021).

Ugarte, E. and Turner, M. (2011), 'What is the "Abu Sayyaf"? How Labels Shape Reality', *Pacific Review* 24(4): 397–420.

Wadi, J. (2003), 'They've Come This Far', *Newsbreak*, 1 January 2003, http://archives.newsbreak-knowledge.ph/2003/01/01/they%E2%80%99ve-come-this-far/ (accessed 5 May 2021).

HINDU ORIENTALISM: THE SACHAR COMMITTEE AND OVER-REPRESENTATION OF MINORITIES IN JAIL

Irfan Ahmad

With the release in 2006 of the Sachar Committee Report (SCR), instituted by the Government of India, the social-economic backwardness of Muslims became a public issue. Discussing responses to the SCR, this chapter sheds light on the interrelationships among democracy, minorities and 'inclusive development'. My principal contention is that behind the reluctant, perhaps even insincere, implementation of the SCR under the Congress administration and its near dumping under the Modi administration was the successful mobilisation of Re-Orientalism. This Re-Orientalism – or what Mita Banerjee, Lisa Lau and Ana Mendes allude to as 'Hindu Orientalism' – stigmatised the relative deprivation of Muslims vis-à-vis other communities by deploying tropes of 'Islamic terrorism', 'fanaticism', 'Muslim appeasement', 'separatism', 'disloyalty to the nation' and so on – tropes supplied by British colonialism. That this Re-Orientalism won was not inevitable. An anti-Orientalist alternative notion of democracy – democracy as an ethos resonant with suffering and mutual care – did exist, but it was sacrificed to prolong the ceremonial, mediatised, arithmetic, corporate national democracy. I conclude with theoretical observations about the limits and possibilities of the term 'Re-Orientalism'.

According to the 2011 census, of India's population of 1.21 billion, Muslims constituted 14.2 percent, Hindus 79.8 percent, Christians 2.3 percent and Sikhs 1.7 percent. Followers of Buddhism and Jainism, religions that evolved in India, accounted for 0.7 and 0.4 percent, respectively. While the share of people of other religions and persuasions was 0.7 percent, the total of those who did not mention their religion was 0.2 (Rukmini and Singh 2015).

Of the states and territories that comprise the Indian Union, the state with the largest number of Muslims is Uttar Pradesh (UP) where in 2001 Muslims formed 18.5 percent of the population. UP is also the most populous state. The share of Muslims in Lakshadweep was the highest at 95.5 percent (its total population was 65,000). In Jammu and Kashmir, Muslims formed

66.9 percent of the state's population, in Assam 30.9 percent, in West Bengal 25.3 percent and in Kerala 24.7 percent. Other states with significant Muslim populations are Bihar (16.5 percent), Jharkhand (13.9 percent), Karnataka (12.2 percent) and Uttaranchal (11.9 percent). The national capital of Delhi had 11.7 percent (Shaban 2018: 2).

As a community, Muslims are diverse along multiple lines. In terms of schools of thoughts (*madhab* rather than sects, cf. Shaban 2018: 5), while most Muslims in North India belong to the Hanafi school, the majority of Muslims in Kerala in the south follow the Shafi'i *madhab*. Within the Hanafi school, there are further differences, for example, between the followers of Imam Reza and those who pledge their allegiance to the Deobandi interpretation of Islam. Those who describe themselves as Ahl-e-hadith do not follow any of the four schools as they claim to rely directly on the *salaf*, the Prophet and his companions. India also has a significant population of Muslims who are Shi'as, of which the main branches are Twelve-Imam Shi'ism, Ismailis and Zaidis. There are also forms of social stratification along the lines of *biradri*, erroneously called castes. Historically, Urdu as a language of trade, bazaars, literature and much else was the lingua franca used by people across religious differences and through the length and breadth of undivided India. Politicised along religious lines since the nineteenth century and manifest, above all, in the ethnic anti-Urdu and anti-Muslim slogan 'Hindi, Hindu, Hindustan' (Ahmad 2008; Pandey 1990) after 1947, officially and unofficially the language was almost killed. The Indian journal *Seminar* (1987) aptly described the case of Urdu as 'linguistic genocide'. Currently, Urdu is mostly the language of the poor, largely in North and Western India. Muslims in Kerala and Tamil Nadu speak languages that belong to a family entirely different from languages in North India. However, it should be noted that until the early twentieth century Muslims in Kerala and Tamil Nadu wrote Malayalam and Tamil in Arabic script (Sadiq 2018). In socio-economic terms, Muslims are one of the poorest segments of India's population. Jeremy Seabrook and Imran Siddiqui offer a glimpse of their condition. While doing research for their book about the Muslim slums of Kolkata, a local activist told them: 'There is no visible prison [here], but that does not mean these people are free. Mobility is not prevented by checkpoints, military posts, and armed guards; but the exit from misery, ignorance, and want is policed by discrimination and prejudice' (Seabrook and Siddiqui 2011: 248–9). Constituting merely 5 percent, currently, there are only twenty-seven Muslim members in the lower house of India's Parliament for which elections were held in the summer of 2019.

At the reviewers' advice and for readers unfamiliar with India, the 'contextual' notes above aim to orient them. Verily, 'context' seems self-evident. It is not. Philosophically, it may lead, *inter alia*, to debates on relativism versus universalism. Contrary to its rendition by Dilley (2001: 440) as 'a form of social action', contextualisation is indeed deeply political. For instance, whereas certain things need to be specified or situated in their contexts, other things may appear 'normal', requiring no contextualisation. Subject to what they are tailored to, contexts can simultaneously be acts of enabling and disabling, of violent destruction and mutual accommodation.

Beyond the divides of right-wing, Hindu nationalist, on one hand, and liberal secular, on the other, most political and intellectual discussions – by Western and 'indigenous' actors alike – begin with the assumption of Muslims as a 'foreign' and 'undesirable' entity. The concomitant assumption is that India – itself assumed as purely Hindu with Muslims emptied out – has 'always' and 'originally' been Hindu. A context that assumes so is already violent. And it is less about the past and more about the present and the future, which crafters of context assume, often implicitly and akin to doxa. In important ways, this essay precisely demonstrates and undoes this violent assumption, which informs not simply discussions on the history of Islam in India (prior to as well as after the creation of Pakistan in 1947 and of Bangladesh in 1971), but also nearly everything, including the socio-economic, linguistic, cultural, political and demographic conditions of Muslims (Ahmad 2019c).

Notably, the regnant premise about Hindus as indigenous is of recent origin and diametrically opposite to the one prevalent in the nineteenth century. No less interesting is the fact that, as a term, 'Hindu' itself is not indigenous. Stemming from the river Indus, the Greek and Persian used Hindu to refer to people beyond the Indus. Hindu was not strictly a religious label, as people of other faiths across the Indus were also called Hindu (Sen 2005). Building on earlier works, especially on German Romanticism and a Bible-inspired history of monogenesis, as well as his own works on Sanskrit and the Vedas, the philologist and Orientalist Max Müller (1823–1900) held that the Indo-German or Indo-European ancestral language originated in Central Asia, the original Aryan homeland. While one clan of the white-complexioned Aryans migrated to Europe, another moved southeast towards India and conquered the dark-skinned indigenous *dasa* population. With no mention of Islam in his definition of India, Müller used Aryan as both racial and linguistic category. According to historian Romila Thapar (1996, see also van der Veer 1999), the upper-caste Hindu elites readily embraced Müller's Aryan theory. It offered, *inter alia*, prestige to the colonised as they saw themselves belonging to the same stock as the coloniser. Thus, authors like Nirad Chaudhuri who extolled the British Empire and largely despised Islam, upheld the racist Aryan theory according to which the 'true home' of Hindus was in Southern Russia. Chaudhuri viewed himself 'racially as a displaced European' (in Almond 2015: 92, 3). Thapar mentions how educated Indians such as Keshab Chander Sen and B. G. Tilak also upheld this Aryan theory. Theosophist Col. Olcott, sympathetic to Hindu nationalism and in search for a 'spiritual East' (contra a 'materialist West'), altered Müller's theory to say that Aryans (by which he meant Hindus) were not only indigenous to India, but that they 'were also the progenitors of European civilization' (in Thapar 1996: 9). Olcott's view currently works as a consensus and the long-held theory of India's invasion by the Aryans is nearly a stigma (except among some academics). Practising 'ethnic democracy' (Khalid 2019), the current government led by Mr Narendra Modi is set to turn the bill it had introduced earlier into a law. This law makes Hindus, Sikhs, Buddhists, Jains and Christians from Afghanistan, Bangladesh and Pakistan elegible to become Indian citizens, while rendering stateless millions, mostly Muslims in Assam, who have lived in India for generations (Apoorvanand 2019; Salam 2019). The law is premised on the bogus tenet of 'them-Muslims' as foreign and 'us-Hindus' as indigenous.

Introduction: India as Super Powerless and *The White Tiger*

Nationalism is thus not the answer to orientalism as implied in [Edward] Said's book. Rather, *nationalism is the avatar of orientalism in the later colonial and postcolonial periods.*

Breckenridge and van der Veer (1993: 12, italics mine)

Although separated by only two years, there has been little conversation between the Sachar Committee Report (2006) and Aravind Adiga's (2008) novel *The White Tiger.*

Set up in 2005 by the Prime Minister's office as a High-Level Committee headed by Justice Rajinder Sachar and widely known as the Sachar Committee Report (SCR),[1] its aim was to present evidence-based analysis of the economic, social and educational status of Muslims, who, according to the 2001 Census, constituted 13.4 percent of the total population, and to 'identify areas of interventions by the Government to address' (SCR 2006: 2, iii). Titled *Social, Economic and Educational Status of the Muslim Community of India: A Report,* it was submitted by the committee in November 2006. Drawing on academic literature and a wide variety of government and non-government data and reports, including the 2001 census and the National Sample Survey, the SCR (2006: 237) concluded that 'while there is considerable variation in the conditions of Muslims across states [. . .] the Community exhibits deficits and deprivation in practically all dimensions of development. In fact, by and large, Muslims rank somewhat above SCs/STs but below Hindu-OBCs, Other Minorities and Hindu-General (mostly upper castes) in almost all indicators considered'.

In the economy, the ratio of the working population among Muslims was lower than in comparison to all other Socio-Religious Communities (SRCs). This ratio was even higher in the countryside. Most Muslims worked in the informal economy and were self-employed in street-vending, transport equipment business, traditional artisanship and related petty trade and busi-

---

[1] In addition to Sachar as its Chairman, the committee consisted of six members: Saiyid Hamid, T. K. Oommen, M. A. Basith, Rakesh Basant, Akhtar Majeed and Abusaleh Shariff, the last being its Member-Secretary.

nesses. Their access to bank credit was fairly low. Compared to Scheduled Castes (SCs) and Scheduled Tribes (STs), Other Backward Classes (OBCs) and Hindu Upper Castes who constitute 40, 36 and 49 percent, respectively, of the regular, salaried employment, Muslims' percentage was only 27. In the Indian Administrative Services (IAS), Muslims' ratio was only 3 percent, and even lower in the Indian Foreign Service. Their percentage in the Indian Police Service was slightly better: 4 percent. In the Railways, Muslims formed 4.5 percent of the workforce, mostly at the lower levels. In the private sector their condition was not much better, either. The literacy rate among Muslims was far lower than the national average. In comparison to all other SRCs, Muslims' dropout rate was the highest and the average years of school attendance the lowest. As for tertiary education, in the leading colleges of the country, of fifty graduates only one was Muslim – a figure far lower than among Dalits (former untouchables). In relation to all other SRCs, the level of unemployment among Muslim graduates was the highest. In villages and urban areas where Muslims constituted more than the national average in the total population – Muslim-concentrated areas – public facilities such as metaled (*pakka*) road, transportation, hospital, postal and telegraph facilities were abysmal. Educational and financial infrastructures in such areas were likewise poorer (SCR 2016; Hansen 2007; Kundu 2016; Robinson 2008; Raina 2007).

At the time when the Sachar Report was published, of the 539 Members of Parliament (MP, of the lower house), only thirty-six were Muslims. After the 2014 elections, the number of Muslim MPs was reduced to an all-time low, at a mere twenty-two (Shaikh 2014). One of the few positive things that the SCR brought to public debate was that the rate of infant mortality was far lower among Muslims than in other communities. And unlike Hindus, Muslims were more receptive to the birth of female children (Basant and Shariff 2010: 8).[2]

In documenting the status of Muslims, the SCR noted that, of the four Indian states where their condition was 'particularly grave', Bihar was one. And Adiga's novel about rising India begins in Bihar: in Laxmangarh, a village in the district of Gaya. Early on in the novel, Balram, the protagonist born in a low, *halvai*, non-twice born caste, describes how his father, a rickshaw-puller, died due to lack of medical care at the government hospital. When his father, suffering from tuberculosis, was taken to the hospital, there was no doctor available. At the hospital, Balram meets two people whom he calls 'Muslim men'. One of them had an open wound on his leg and was sitting on newspapers he had spread over the grassy ground. He invited Balram and his brother to sit beside him. The Muslim fellow empathised with Balram and his father's condition. To Balram, he also unveiled how corruption worked in practice, the absence of the doctor being one of its many manifestations. This episode demonstrates the poor condition of the lower

---

[2] For a summary account of the SCR, see Basant and Shariff (2010); Raina (2007).

castes and Muslims, both denied medical treatment. However, as the novel progresses, so does Balram's ambition to fervently join the rising India and thereby participate in what Mita Banerjee (2011) as well as Lisa Lau and Ana Mendes (2011) allude to as 'Hindu Orientalism'. This exactly is the point at which the shared marginality of Muslims and Dalits in the novel starts to unfold parallel to each other, with almost no convergence.

Having joined as driver-servant the family of an upper-caste industrialist businessman – the Stork and his son Ashok, with whom he would later go to New Delhi and murder him to run away with his money in order to launch his own taxi company in Bangalore – Balram knew well that his success depended on removing the existing driver-servant: 'a grim-looking fellow named Ram Persad'. In Balram's own account, Persad was a better driver. He was honest. The family trusted him to the point that, wearing dark glasses, Pinky Madam, the American-Christian wife of Ashok, played Badminton with him. That she preferred Persad to Balram as her sporting partner generated in Balram 'hatred' against Persad. For Balram to rise, Persad must disappear. And disappear he does.

Balram hatches a scheme to dislodge Persad. To confirm his new knowledge which he received from the cook, that in the past week Persad stopped eating during the day and left the house always exactly at the same time, Balram stealthily follows him one evening to discover that he goes to pray in the mosque and to break his fast. It is the month of Ramadan. Persad is depicted as follows: 'Now, this Mohammad Mohammad was a poor, honest, hardworking Muslim, but he wanted a job at the home of an evil, prejudiced landlord who didn't like Muslims – so, just to get a job and feed his starving family, he claimed to be a Hindu! And took the name of Ram Persad'. Balram calls the 'secret' he has discovered a 'scam', because the Nepali guard whom the Stork employs was tasked to 'check' Persad's background. As if he himself were the Stork, Balram slaps the guard for not having verified the details of Mohammad's life. In the wee hours of the following morning, 'without a word to me, he [Persad] began packing. All his things fitted into one small bag'. Balram thinks:

> [W]hat a miserable life he's had, having to hide his religion, his name, just to get a job as a driver – and he is a good driver, no question of it, a far better one than I will ever be. Part of me wanted to get up and apologise to him right there and say [. . .] You never did anything to hurt me. Forgive me, brother. (93)

Balram not only never apologises to Mohammad, for robbing him of his job and making him disappear from the Stork's house, he also makes him disappear from his own life – *ergo*, the narrative. Balram and Mohammad shared a life and space, as both lived in the same dilapidated, segregated servant room in the otherwise sprawling bungalow of the Stork. Mohammad's disappearance in the midst of India's rise as a future economic giant and superpower is thus triple. First, like his parents and Balram himself initially,

Persad remains poor, while India achieves tremendous economic growth (in statistical terms). Second, as India begins to be visible on the international stage, Mohammad's own name becomes invisible.[3] Third, Balram expels Mohammad from the rest of his narrative to fully secure the invisibility of the latter.

This chapter is divided into three parts. The first part enunciates the argument about Hindu Orientalism and identifies the strategies of its operation. In the second part, I demonstrate the argument by discussing the responses to the SCR. Here I focus on the responses from the Hindutva formations, especially the Bharatiya Janata Party (BJP) and the Rashtriya Swayamsevak Sangh (RSS). The RSS is the ideological fountainhead of anti-Muslims ethnic Hindu nationalism, which praises the Nazi ideology (Ahmad 2019a). I dwell on the responses from L. K. Advani, key leader of the BJP. I then discuss the response from RSS's English mouthpiece, *Organiser*, as well as one of its key contemporary ideologues – Rakesh Sinha, a teacher at the University of Delhi. I close this section with a discussion of the opposition by Narendra Modi's Gujarat Government to the implementation of the Scholarship Scheme recommended by the SCR. Having demonstrated the Re-Orientalist opposition to the SCR and its eventual dumping by the current Union Government, in the second section I show that the victory of Re-Orientalism was not inevitable. Returning to Balram and Mohammad, I suggest there existed a possible path other than the triumph of Re-Orientalism. But the rampant notion of democracy – mediatised, ceremonial, statistical and corporate-driven – blocked this path. In the final and concluding part, I return to the key argument of the chapter to conduct a critique of the idea of Re-Orientalism to situate its theoretical relevance differently.

The Argument: Strategies of Hindu Orientalism

Although Mohammad as an individual stands erased from the rest of the narrative, his religion does not. It appears many a time. At the far end of the novel, after killing his boss Ashok by thrice ramming a bottle into his skull, Balram observes: 'The blood was draining from the neck [of Ashok] quite fast – I believe this is the way the Muslims kill their chicken' (246).[4] And shortly afterwards in Bangalore, where Balram had established himself as a successful entrepreneur in the taxi business, when his driver, a Muslim called Asif, kills a boy in an accident, Balram observes:

---

[3] Adiga's depiction of Mohammad changing his name due to discrimination and fear resonates with non-fictional reality. In Gujarat, the model of 'development' that Modi promised to replicate nationally as Prime Minister, many Muslims changed their names out of fear. See the report in *The Indian Express* (Saiyed 2009) and Ahmad (2013b).

[4] All page numbers within round brackets *sans* author are from Adiga (2008).

> I have come to respect Muslims, sir. They are not the brightest lot, except for
> those four poet fellows, but they make good drivers, and they are honest people,
> by and large, although a few of them seem to get *this urge to blow trains up every*
> *year*. I was not going to fire Asif over this. (267, italics mine)

The passage above is striking on many counts. The blowing up of trains is
a direct reference to so-called Islamic terrorism, integral to Indian and international politics (Ahmad 2017a). To begin with, Balram takes it as a 'fact'
that it is Muslims who blow up trains. It is well known that activists of the
RSS and its Hindutva affiliates perpetrated many terrorists attacks, such
as the one in Ajmer Dargah (Singh 2017). Yet, Adiga attributes terrorism
to Muslims who have 'this urge'. And this urge appears not only once in a
while. It is almost perpetual: 'every year'. Furthermore, Balram's reference to
'respecting Muslims' is equally striking. In the novel Adiga nowhere speaks
of respecting Hindus. Indeed, characters are never explicitly identified as
Hindus. In contrast, Muslims are. In the village hospital where his father
dies, Balram describes people, one with an open wound on his leg, as 'a
couple of Muslims'. Likewise, when walking through the second-hand book
bazaar in Delhi, he calls one bookseller 'the Muslim uncle'. It is this Muslim
uncle who tells Balram about the poets in which he is interested: Rumi, Iqbal,
Mirza Ghalib. There is also a fourth poet whose name the protagonist does
not remember. Again, they are not simply poets; instead Balram calls them
'Muslim poets'. Sanjay Subrahmanyam (2008) writes:

> The falsity in *The White Tiger* goes much further. It means having a character
> who cannot read Urdu, and certainly has no notion of Persian, tell us that his
> favourite poets include Jalaluddin Rumi and Mirza Ghalib. It means having
> someone who can't read English being able to recall a conversation in which his
> interlocutor speaks of books by James Hadley Chase, Khalil Gibran, Adolf Hitler
> and Desmond Bagley.

There is more to *The White Tiger* than Subrahmanyam's reading of it along
the lines of falsity. I suggest that Adiga enacts what Lisa Lau and Ana Mendes
(2011), following Mita Banerjee (2011), allude to as 'Hindu Orientalism'.
Hindu Orientalism is a set of practices and discursive strategies rooted in
what Lau (2009: 572) calls 'Re-Orientalism'. The role of old Orientalism,
'the relationship of the dominance and representation of the Oriental by the
non-Oriental or Occidental' now is 'taken over [. . .] by other Orientals [. . .]
This process of Orientalism by Orientals is [. . .] 'Re-Orientalism'. In the case
of India and Bollywood, Banerjee (2011: 127, 130) enunciates the working of
Hindu Orientalism as follows: 'it re-Orientalises India for the western audience, and it re-Orientalises Hindu India for the benefit of Hindu mainstream
audiences in India, marginalising Muslims in the process'. 'An Orientalist
gaze on the Orient and a Hindu gaze on India's Muslim communities', thus,
she continues, 'may converge'.

Shifting from the realm of aesthetics, a key concern of Banerjee, to the electoral politics that Adiga writes about, the contours of Re-Orientalism take on new dimensions. What Subrahmanyam detects as falsity in Adiga is nourished by the sheer power that India as an emerging superpower – a democracy unlike the rival emerging superpower China, to which Adiga addressed his letters (itself an Orientalist trope gaining increasing currency among young Indians) – bestows on its Hindu majority to orientalise Muslims for the enjoyment of its assumed Hindu core, as well as for Western desire. And unlike old-style Orientalists who mastered the languages and knowledge of religions of the Orientals in order to Orientalise them, Re-Orientalism through Hindu Orientalism requires no such mastery or knowledge.[5] The number 786 – some Muslims begin a piece of writing with that number, which is the total numerical value of all letters used in the phrase *bismillāh hirrahman-ir-rahīm* ('in the name of God, the most Gracious, the most Merciful'; see Ahmad 2017b) – thus becomes what 'Muslims think [. . .] is a magic number that represents their god'. Balram thus can write about Rumi, Ghalib and Iqbal without knowing the script of the language in which those poets wrote. It is not simply that Balram is not familiar with the language, he instead transfers his non-familiarity onto an 'unfamiliar other' who resides not in the human kingdom, but in the kingdom *animalia*. To Balram: 'Some books were in Urdu, the language of the Muslims – which is all just scratches and dots, as if some crow dipped its feet in black ink and pressed them to the page'.[6]

In the old Orientalism of the eighteenth or nineteenth century, Muslims were surely an important Other, but not many Muslims lived in the society whence European Orientalists came. The Other lived elsewhere. In Hindu Orientalism, Muslims become the Other in spite of cohabiting in and sharing the same space. Unlike European Orientalists who Orientalised Muslims elsewhere as symbolic Other, Hindu Orientalism renders Muslims the Other symbolically as much as empirically. The co-evalness (Fabian 1991) between Hindus and Muslims is denied and erased in a single stroke, and Muslims are swiftly transported to a space and time outside of India as a nation-state of Hindus as the so-called indigenous dwellers. Historically, this act of Re-Orientalism is a loyal borrowing from the British-style Orientalism, for instance, of W. W. Hunter and J. D. Anderson (1913), notably the former's *The Indian Musalmans: Are They Bound in Conscience to Rebel against the*

---

[5] Not all Orientalists in the colonial era mastered the language of people about whom they wrote. Colin Mackenzie, for instance, wrote about India without knowing the local language. He relied on Brahman interpreters (see Dirks 1993).

[6] Compare this to the remark by Modi when he compared the state-directed killings of Muslims in Gujarat in 2002 to puppies being run over by a moving car – literally, 'the child of a dog', as the Hindi words he used were 'kuttē ka bachcha', a slur (in Ahmad 2019a).

Queen? (1871).[7] To classify their colonial rule as legitimate, even desirable, the British fashioned the myth that they were not the first outsiders to rule India: Muslims were outsiders, too (Nasr 1999: 581). Adiga reproduces this Orientalist trope: 'For this land, India, has never been free. First the Muslims, then the British bossed us around'. And, again, in his interaction with the bookseller, Balram calls 'the Muslim uncle' in which his beard becomes the marker of his Muslimness and foreignness at once:

> He shook his head, but I kept flattering him, telling him how fine his beard was, how fair his skin was (ha!), how it was obvious from his nose and forehead that he wasn't some pigherd who had converted but true-blue Muslim who had flown here on a magic carpet *all the way from Mecca*, and he *grunted with satisfaction*. He read me another poem, and another poem. (217, italics mine)

Notice that the novelist not only turns the Muslim character into someone 'foreign', but he also makes him proud of his foreignness. And in Hindu Orientalism Muslims cannot be 'natural', 'normal', 'banal':

> A great poet, this fellow Iqbal – **even if** he *was* a Muslim. (By the way, Mr. Premier: Have you noticed that all four of the greatest poets in the world are Muslim? And yet all the Muslims you meet are illiterate or **covered head to toe in black burkas** or **looking for buildings to blow up**? It's a puzzle, isn't it? If you ever figure these people out, send me an e-mail). (35, italics in original, my italics in bold)

A re-Orientalised prejudice against Muslims as violent, fanatic, terrorists and oppressing their own women is packaged as a curious puzzle to be unpacked by none other than the Chinese Premier!

I hope to have made a plausible case for the relevance of Re-Orientalism via Hindu Orientalism in Adiga's novel. Now is the time to make my argument clearer. It is my contention that the effective and substantial amelioration of the backwardness and poverty of Muslims that both *The White Tiger* and the Sachar Committee Report describe – the latter by suggesting many policy measures, some of which the United Progressive Alliance (UPA) led by the Congress adopted – failed to materialise because the Re-Orientalism I described above triumphed over the empirically (SCR) and literarily (*The White Tiger*) demonstrated deprivation and marginality of Muslims. In order to substantiate this argument, I turn to the responses to the SCR from within (Congress and other constituents of the UPA) as well as from without (the BJP-led National Democratic Alliance, NDA). I focus on the latter.

---

[7] Barely a few months after 9/11, the New Delhi-based Rupa & Co. published Hunter's (2002) book, eliminating its subtitle.

Responses to the Sachar Committee Report

The SCR should be analysed along with the report of the National Commission on Religious and Linguistic Minorities (also known as Ranganath Misra Commission Report, hereafter RMCR), submitted a year after the SCR, in 2007. Tasked with identifying socially and economically backward segments among minorities (religious and linguistic) and suggesting measures to address them, the RMCR put forward the proposal of reservation for Muslims in government jobs along the pattern available to the OBCs (Alam 2014). No less significant was the 2011 Prevention of Communal and Targeted Violence (PCTV) Bill drafted by the National Advisory Council. The backdrop to the bill was not only the 2002 anti-Muslim Gujarat pogrom, but also a series of 'riots' before and after, in which Muslims suffered the most, in terms of lives, assets and sources of livelihood. In her brilliant ethnography of Hindutva in Rajasthan, Mathur (2008: 12, 28, 184) shows how on many occasions police and Hindutva activists jointly participated in violence against Muslims and how the culprits responsible for violence went unpunished. In some cases, police even shared sweets with rioters and joined them in chanting anti-Muslim slogans.[8] In early 2014, however, the government withdrew the bill, and no further progress has been made (Ahmed 2019) as of April 2018. The aim of the bill was:

> To respect, protect and fulfill the right to equality before law and equal protection of law by imposing duties on the Central Government and the State Governments, to exercise their powers in an impartial and non-discriminatory manner to prevent and control targeted violence, including mass violence, against Scheduled Castes, Scheduled Tribes and religious minorities in any State in the Union of India, and linguistic minorities in any State in the Union of India . . . (cited in Ahmed 2019: 167–8)

As if it had anticipated the trope of Re-Orientalism as a response to it, the SCR, like the objective of the bill cited above, painstakingly argued how taking policy steps to overcome the backwardness of Muslims was an affirmation of the universal constitutional obligation rather than the promotion of sectional interests. The measures it suggested to address the backwardness of Muslims and their near absence in India's development comprised *general* and *community-specific* ones (SCR 2006: 237–8). In particular, the SCR stressed that for Muslims to gain equality the focus should be placed on

---

[8] In a 2004 interview, Paul Brass, an American political scientist who has studied India for decades, observed that politicians of all parties, including the Congress, produced riots as political acts. 'But make no mistake about it [. . .] in the last ten or fifteen years, the main perpetrators of Hindu-Muslim violence are the members of the BJP, the RSS, and other organisations in the Hindutva family' (in Shah 2004: 4–5).

the *general* measures. To this end, the SCR proposed forming of 'an Equal Opportunity Commission (EOC) to assure all the underprivileged (including Muslims) that discrimination [. . .] would be dealt with expeditiously'; to develop an agreed Diversity Index to ensure diversity along SRC and gender lines in a variety of spaces; and to create a National Data Bank to gather data and to establish an autonomous Assessment and Monitoring Authority to see equity delivered to all marginalised SRCs, including Muslims (Basant 2016: 21; Hasan 2009). As if this was still inadequate, Sachar himself cited a ruling of the Supreme Court: 'We conceive the duty of this Court to uphold the fundamental rights and thereby honor the sacred obligation to the *minority communities who are our own*' (in Sachar 2010: xv, italics mine).[9]

Praised by many as a 'myth-buster' (Hansen 2007: 51), a harbinger of a new discourse on India's minorities (Basant 2016: 18) and a 'valuable' document 'unparalleled in terms of data collation and putting together all these in one single volume' (Jodhka 2007: 2996), the SCR boasted many laudable features; however, Re-Orientalism eventually triumphed, leading to its near banishment under the new and current regime of Narendra Modi voted to power in May 2014 (Shariff 2017).

L. K. Advani, key leader of the BJP and projected to become the next Prime Minister at that time, was hostile to the very idea of forming a committee such as the SCR. In his eyes, its formation was an 'appeasement of minorities' and, therefore, no less than a 'political crime' (OneIndia.com 2006). When its findings were made public, he outright dismissed them, describing it as the 'worst kind of vote bank politics [. . .] by the Congress party' (*Rediff.com*). Although M. N. Sriniva (in the 1950s) had coined the term 'vote bank' in relation to Karnataka where he did his fieldwork (Bjorkman 2015; Guha 2008) and although initially it had no 'natural' association with Muslims, from the 1980s onwards, 'vote bank' was invested with a new valence implying 'Muslim vote bank', which was not well received by the BJP. To the other leaders and organisational wings of Hindutva, the recommendations of the SCR were 'anti-national', leading them to denounce the chair of the committee, Rajinder Sachar, as 'caring for terrorists' (Hansen 2007: 51). If Sachar himself were not a Hindu, the phrase 'caring for' would have been likely dropped.

Rakesh Sinha, a Professor of political science at the University of Delhi as well as the Director of India Policy Foundation, is regarded as 'the most authentic and well read RSS ideologue' (Sinha 2017). He described the SCR as an exemplification of minorityism and 'a fraud on the nation' (in Basant 2016: 19, 36, 40). In contradistinction to the brief remarks that Advani made in 2007, in 2013 Sinha elaborated his sharp opposition to the SCR. In some

[9] Without defining the term, the Indian Constitution mentions 'minorities' four times. It figures in relation to Articles 29 and 30 (Mustafa 2017). See the demand below by an ideologue of the RSS to revoke Article 30 to bring Muslims into 'national mainstream'.

ways, his opposition compressed the entirety of modern Indian history vis-à-vis Muslims and the attendant Orientalism. If one could assemble a set of keywords (as used by Raymond Williams 1983) central to his opposition, they would read: 'Muslim separatism', 'Jinnah', 'Sir Syed Ahmad Khan' (called 'actual father of the two-nation theory'), threat to the 'unity and integrity of the nation' against which 'nationalist forces' must fight. Claiming to have read the report from cover to cover, Sinha doubted the accuracy of facts and figures in the SCR. However, he offered no evidence to validate his doubt. Nor did he discuss the facts and figures to show how they were inaccurate. He directed his attack elsewhere, alleging that the SCR's 'intentions are highly objectionable. It is not only unconstitutional; it will eventually lead to creation of a *nation within a nation*. The recommendations of the committee are on communal lines and will divide the country. This is a result of the vote bank politics' (italics mine). Sinha issued a call to . . .

. . . *deconstruct the psychology* that Muslims are separate from others in this country. To enable this, *Article 30 of our constitution needs to be revoked*. This will enable the integration of the Muslims into the national mainstream [. . .] It is the mindset of false identity politics that needs to be demolished [. . .] This has to be countered and the mindset should be deconstructed. (Sinha 2013, italics mine)

As is obvious from this quote, Sinha views Muslims as the object of a problem to be resolved through the 'science' of psychology which manifests itself in a mindset which he aims to deconstruct, among others, by expelling Article 30 of India's Constitution. To recall, Article 30 grants rights to 'all minorities, whether based on religion or language [. . .] to establish and administer educational institutions of their choice'. Re-Orientalist premises and thoughts such as Sinha's show their full force in the response to the SCR published in the *Organiser*, the English mouthpiece of the RSS. Claiming to be the custodian of 'unadulterated patriotism', its readers include power-elites of all hues, including members of parliament and business elites. And its readers are spread over fifty-seven countries, notably in the UK, USA and Canada (*Organiser* 2017).

A search for 'Sachar Committee' on *Organiser's* website (on 3 April 2017) yielded thirteen stories published between 6 August 2006 and 28 February 2015. The first story predates the publication of the SCR by a few months, while the last one is well over six months after the installation of the Modi government in 2014. It is possible to conduct a content analysis of all thirteen stories. For my purpose, this is not necessary, however. I aim to capture the key statements of the *Organiser's* opposition by focusing on select articles. An assemblage of keywords from the titles of the thirteen stories (see Figure 7.1) would leave readers believe that the SCR had nothing positive and that it was the result of a 'perverse mindset' connected to Muslim fanaticism, terrorism, separatism and appeasement of disloyal minorities, thereby leading to the 'subjugation of Hindus'; therefore, the Sachar committee must be banned. As

Organiser

Title	Date
Preamble Ad Controversy : It is no 'Treason', Mr Sachar	28 Feb 2015
The self-damage imposed by Muslim on themselves	06 Nov 2013
Sachar to Ranganath Cannibalizing Hindu society	31 Jan 2010
From Sachar to Ranganath Misra A period of minority assertion, Hindu subjugation	31 Jan 2010
Sachar does not like nconvenient questions	06 Jul 2008
Sachar stats only prove an old theorem Committee wants to take the trough to the horse	28 Jan 2007
Sonia, Singh and Sachar?escalating separatism	28 Jan 2007
Controversy	
Sachar report defies logic, Muslims are better off Tales of backwardness and creation of political myths	31 Dec 2006
The Moving Finger Writes	
The Sachar report and appeasement	31 Dec 2006
Sachar report and terror crescent UPA engineering a festering division like Minto-Morley in 1909	24 Dec 2006
Opinion	
Sachar report and after Compulsory education, not reservation *Free Muslims from fanatic clergy*	03 Dec 2006
Column	
Sachar panel: Product of a perverse mindset	13 Aug 2006
Disband Sachar Committee	
It's only dividing the people	06 Aug 2006

Figure 7.1 Screenshot of Stories about the Sachar Committee Report from the website of the *Organiser*, the RSS Mouthpiece, 2006–15.

for the backwardness and disempowerment of Muslims, so keywords from the *Organiser* tell us, Muslims themselves are responsible.

The first story (dated 6 August 2006) demanded the termination of the committee itself, because by finding out through what it described as 'communal headcount' the lower representation of Muslims in government services, especially in the police and armed forces, Justice Sachar attempted to divide the country. Referring to the warning by M. K. Narayanan, National Security Adviser, that 'terrorists *may have infiltrated* the armed forces', the *Organiser* story mentioned the 'recent arrests' of three soldiers and two policemen by Srinagar police, 'with *likely* links with the Lashkar-e-Toiba' (sources of both not given). Disregarding 'may have' and 'likely', the *Organiser* took these statements already as 'facts' to argue that infiltration was not done from 'outside' but from 'inside'. Naming the two Kashmiri policemen, it went on to say that their 'arrests once again bring to the limelight the religious identity of the culprits (Islamic) and the religious dimension of the challenge

India is facing both internally and externally'. The *Organiser* appealed to the government to 'discourage collection of employment statistics in any sector on communal lines' and to immediately 'disband the Sachar Committee' (*Organiser* 2006a).

A few weeks after the publication of the SCR, the *Organiser* published an article titled 'Sachar Report and Terror Crescent'. It charged Sachar with supporting violence. In its reading, the Sachar committee 'had as its mandate the same task last given to Lord Minto and Mr Morley in 1909 (of engineering a festering division within Indian society between Muslims and the rest) [round brackets in original]'. Notice that the article draws on Carl Schmittian's (1996) dualistic line between foe and friend by pitting Muslims against the rest. In the process it enacts a series of deletions. To introduce representative politics in India, the British had proposed the Morely-Minto reforms, which provided for separate electorates, not only for Muslims, but also for Depressed Classes (former untouchables, now Dalits), Sikhs, Christians and Anglo-Indians. Importantly, representing the Depressed Classes and supporting a separate electorate for them, B. R. Ambedkar fought a bitter battle against M. K. Gandhi who opposed it (Bose and Jalal 2004: 84ff., Keer 1990: 207–8). This erasure by the *Organiser* fits perfectly well with a similar erasure by Sinha, which I cited earlier. In describing Sir Sayyid Ahmad Khan as 'actual father of the two-nation theory' and separatism, and linking both to the SCR, Sinha erased (assuming that he knew) the fact that the foundation of the two-nation theory was laid as far back as 1760, by the British soldier-writer William Watts. The operation of erasure that Sinha performed included deleting the statement that Khan made about Hindus and Muslims as the two eyes of a beautiful bride called India – a statement which Sachar (2016) himself quoted in his preface to a book on SCR. Watts was a member of the Calcutta Council and he had participated in the 1757 Battle of Plassey, which led to the establishment of British rule in India. Given the profound salience of his view, let me quote at length Watts, who in his *Memoires of the Revolution in Bengal* (1760s) wrote:

The two great nations, inhabiting this part of the Indies, differ widely from each other in their complexion, languages, manners, disposition, and religion. The Moguls who are commonly called Moors and Moormen, are a robust, stately, and, in respect to the original natives, a fair people [. . .] they are naturally vain, affect shew and pomp in everything, are much addicted to luxury, fierce, oppressive, and, for the most part, very rapacious. [. . .] The Gentoows [*sic*], or native Indians, are of a swarthy aspect [. . .] less war-like, but more active and industrious than the Moors [. . .] a mild, subtle, frugal race of men, exceedingly superstitious, submissive in appearance, but naturally jealous, suspicious, and perfidious; which is principally owing to that abject slavery they are kept in by the Moors. (cited in Sen 2002: 100; square brackets Sen's)

Returning to the Morely-Minto reforms, the article in the *Organiser* erased, as did Sinha, much of the history to single out Muslims and warned about a single division: the SCR 'will have the effect of creating a new and virulent division between Muslims and the rest of the country'. Finally, the article linked the SCR to terrorism, in which Muslims as a community and across India had begun to participate.

> No longer can it be said that Indian citizens [. . .] are free of the Al Qaeda virus. *Modules and cells of this entity now exist across the country, including in several campuses and even among certain policymakers and business-houses.* Unlike in the 1990s, terrorists are now assured of a local support structure in *most parts of the country*, including in UP, Bihar, Rajasthan, Maharashtra, Andhra Pradesh, West Bengal and Kerala. (*Organiser* 2006b, italics mine)

Another article in the *Organiser* in 2006 did not dispute the findings of the SCR, acknowledging as it did that 'the problem of Muslim backwardness and under representation in public services is a fact'. However, it diagnosed the root cause of the problem in Islam. Without any citation, it referred to a petition, allegedly signed by 8,000 Moulvis (Muslim scholars) of Calcutta in 1835, which opposed the study of Western literature and science by Muslims. In contrast, it stated that no Hindu ever opposed Western education. Since the article identified the very faith of Muslims as the cause of their backwardness, it issued a clarion call to 'free Muslims from fanatic clergy' (*Organiser* 2006c). After the RMCR was published, the *Organiser* in 2010 alarmingly noted how, with the formation of a separate Ministry of Minority Affairs, the rights and privileges of the minorities were being consolidated. It termed the six years of the UPA rule in which such initiatives were undertaken as the period of 'Hindu subjugation' (*Organiser* 2010). The discussion and framing of the issue in the *Organiser* clearly demonstrate how through Hindu Orientalism the issue of Muslims' marginalisation was turned upside down and eventually transformed into an issue of subjugation of Hindus. Such responses as I have discussed so far were not simply verbal and confined to printed words; they were equally manifest in policy practices.

In response to the SCR, the central government launched a prematriculation (grade 10) scholarship scheme for Muslim students based on academic and economic criteria. Those who had scored 50-percent marks in the annual examination and whose parents' annual income was below Rs 1 lakh qualified. Based on these criteria, in Gujarat 55,000 students qualified for it. To this end, the centre would have given 3.75 crore Rs and the state government 1.25 crore. However, as Chief Minister of the state, Modi refused to grant the scholarships on the ground that the scheme discriminated against poor students of other communities. It became a legal issue. While one bench of the Gujarat High Court ruled in favour of the scheme, another ruled against it. In 2013, five years after the scheme had been launched, another bench of five judges upheld it. Dissatisfied, the Modi government filed an affidavit contending that the Sachar Committee (upon whose recommendation the scholarship had been started) itself was 'neither constitutional nor statutory' (Jaffrelot 2016: 239; Nag 2014: 144–5). After becoming Prime Minister and in reference to the recommendation by the RNMC for reservation to Muslims, Modi dismissed any such move on the grounds that India's Constitution did not favour religion-based reservation. Modi's contention, so journalist Khan pointed out, was flawed because the Constitution (Scheduled Castes) Order relating to Article 341 states: 'No person who professes a religion different from the Hindu, the Sikh or the Buddhist religion shall be deemed to be a member of a Scheduled Caste' (in Khan 2015).

Let me close this section by returning to the 2011 Prevention of Communal and Targeted Violence (PCTV) Bill. The Hindutva conglomerate headed by the RSS called it 'anti-Hindu'. To give only one example, in November 2011, the Andhra Pradesh (AP) branch of the RSS sent a memorandum to the Governor of AP, asking for the withdrawal of the PCTV. Signed by seven individuals (two retired Director Generals of Police, two former Army officers, one former judge of the AP High Court, one professor and one communications businessman), the memorandum began with the platitude that 'from times immemorial, the civilization and culture of this country [and followers of . . .] Sanatan Dharma [have] cherish[ed] Ahimsa, tolerance, harmony and peace amidst variety' and that 'Hindus do not, by their very dharma, preach, start or sustain communal violence, riot and killing of "others"'. 'In the guise of protecting minorities', it noted, 'it [the Bill] assumes that the majority community, i.e., Hindus is always the initiator and perpetrator of riots and violence . . .' The memorandum chided the bill because 'it has totally forgotten that religion is a globalised issue now and that there are global strategies to devour smaller religions. The fund flow from outside India seems to have been totally lost sight of by the framers of this bill. *Samuel Huntington's studies have to be kept in mind on this issue*'. Calling the constitution of the National Advisory Council which drafted the bill 'extra-constitutional', it observed that 'a large number of Muslims and Christians and known habitual Hindu-baiting, [and] leftist nominal Hindus' helped formulate the bill (*Samvada* 2011, italics mine).

Using the primary sources of the Hindutva formation, notably its fountainhead, the RSS, this section has shown how the RSS employed Re-Orientalism to subvert the issues of socio-economic backwardness and marginalisation of Muslims by forcibly and non-evidentially linking them to terrorism, separatism, appeasement, anti-Indianness/nationalism and the 'fanaticism' of Islam as a religion. This subversion secured its full completion as the backwardness of Muslims and their deficit in development was erased by foregrounding instead the subjugation of Hindus through a series of Re-Orientalist mechanisms. To close this section, let me state that I focused here on the Hindutva formation, not simply because it was the most vociferous opponent of the SCR, RNMC and PCTV, but also because it acquired power in the 2014 elections. I do not mean to suggest that the Congress party, which instituted these committees and to some extent took policy steps to implement some recommendations of the SCR, was entirely sincere.[10] A committee established by the Congress to inquire into the causes of its debacle in the 2014 elections maintained that its 'minority-appeasement policy' was one important factor (Naqshbandi 2014). And long before the 2014 elections, the Congress itself withdrew the PCTV. Although it created the Ministry of Minority Affairs, its performance in terms of delivery and budgetary allocation was far from satisfactory. In its 2014 report, the committee headed by Amitabh Kundu and appointed to evaluate the post-Sachar performance made this observation (Ghosh 2014; Fazal 2010). Although Singh and Kim (2016) do not use the term 'Hindu Orientalism', they point out the institutional, legal-constitutional and bureaucratic detriments in implementing the SCR.

The (Un)Happiness of Democracy: Over-representation in Jail

The SCR that documented the marginalisation of Muslims by way of their under-representation in key areas of public life, so the media reported, excluded data in the only area where Muslims were over-represented: jails (Ahmad, 2009: 234; Chishti 2006). As the government's own data from 1998 to 2014 show, along with other minorities the ratio of Muslims in prison did indeed exceed their percentage in the total population. The marginalisation of Muslims in the political economy and their over-representation in jail thus raises a question about democracy: why do minorities in democracies stand under-represented in the political economy and over-represented in jail? If one takes prison as a place of unhappiness – not only for the prisoners, but also for the members of their families and communities at large – then the following question arises: does democracy make crimes by the many (the powerful, the corrupt and those belonging to the majority) unnoticeable and unpunished, thereby making them happy? Put differently, does democracy ensure immunity for some from being jailed, even if their crimes are visible? In contrast, does democracy imprison many others, even when there exists no evidence of their crime or when the nature of their crime is far less severe than that of the powerful? Is it that democracy makes some joyful, whereas others are rendered unhappy and invisible?

When the Stork, the Hindu rich upper-caste businessman, bends down to greet and welcome Vijay, son of a pigherd from Balram's village, later to become a politician and finally a businessman, *The White Tiger* christens the gesture as 'marvels of democracy' (86). After the declaration of the result of the elections in which the party of the Great Socialist has won, thereby making the tax-evading business difficult for the Stork and his son Ashok, Vijay and one of his fellows strike a deal with Ashok at the Imperial Hotel

---

[10] Hansen (2001: 9) notes that 'the ostensibly clear distinction drawn today between "secular forces" and "communal forces" is more spurious than many of us would like to believe'.

in Delhi. Unable to do anything but to agree to the deal, Ashok pays an enormous amount of money to Vijay who says: 'I just love to see a rich man roughed up. It is better than an erection' (233). At the very end of the novel, Balram expresses his joy at having become a successful, rich businessman. Although the possibility that the police might catch and imprison him for having murdered Ashok haunts him, he is confident of his escape and in utmost happiness: 'I am now one of those who can't be caught in India. At such moments, I look up at this chandelier, and I just want to throw my hands up and holler, so loudly that my voice would carry over [. . .] all the way to [. . .] America. *I have made it*' (italics in original, 275). The shrillness of Balram's voice and the joy emanating from it is matched only by the silence and grim face of Ram Persad, who, to recall, is actually Mohammad. As India rises and while Balram escapes prison, Mohammads in India perish in jails at rates exceeding their percentage in the total population. Based on government data, a recent study by Ahmad and Siddiqui (2017) argues how democracy has been unfriendly, if not hostile, to minorities as they are over-represented in prisons. At the national level, the percentage of Hindus in jail is far below their ratio in the total population. In some states where Hindus are in a minority – in Jammu and Kashmir, Lakshadweep, Meghalaya, Mizoram and Nagaland – their percentage in jail is higher than their percentage in the population of those states. The condition is similar in the 'democratic' nation-states of the West – Australia, Canada, France, the Netherlands, the UK and the USA (Ahmad and Siddiqui 2017).

Scholars writing about the over-representation of minorities in jail in Western democracies use 'penal democracy' and 'punishing democracy' to describe the structural symbiosis between the Prison Industrial Complex and the over-representation of minorities in democracies such as the USA. They argue that the warehousing of 'criminals' is not about crime *per se*, it is about the entire matrix of political, economic, industrial and media corporations which sustain prisons to secure the immunity of the political order that produces prisoners (Davis 2011; Meiner 2011). Put differently, punitiveness is constitutive of capitalist democracy – hence, the description of it as 'punishing democracy' by Hartnett (2011: 5–6, 11n8), 'police state' by Harcourt (2014: 11) and 'penal democracy' by James (2007: xiv–xv). Scholars also link prisons to nation-building and war-making in international relations (Loyd et al. 2012). Inspired by Foucault's *The Punitive Society*, Harcourt avers that punitiveness in prison characterises society at large.

Cognizant of the merits of this line of thought, however, there is another way to think about democracy and over-representation of minorities in prison. Drawing on memoirs of imprisoned Indian 'terrorists', Ahmad and Siddiqui (2017) argue how their imprisonment also generates a notion of democracy that is an alternative to 'penal democracy' and 'punishing democracy'. At the heart of this alternative is the identification that imprisonment unleashes among fellow humans through a shared vocabulary of injustice, pain, human finitude and vulnerability, thereby generating what Talal Asad

(2012: 56) calls 'democratic sensibility as an ethos'. This ethos emanates from as well as nurtures 'the desire for mutual care, distress at the infliction of pain and indignity, concern for truth more than for immutable subjective rights, the ability to listen and not merely to tell . . .' Judith Butler (2011) has made a similar argument. Writing about the revolt against dictatorship in the Tahrir Square in Egypt, she contends how the bodily vulnerability of protesters, the materiality and possibility of a crackdown by the police and secret agents, as well as their mutual care about eating, sleeping and so on fashioned democratic solidarity among a range of protestors. This notion of democracy, 'democratic sensibility as an ethos', has the potential to re-signify the prevalent election-centric, ceremonial, mediatised democracy characteristic of a 'penal democracy' in such a way that democracy may possibly become itself.

The current regime's dumping of the Sachar Committee is a perfect illustration of the victory of a militarised, mediatised, statistical, ceremonial democracy over 'democratic sensibility as an ethos'. It is the victory of Balram joyously roaring under the glittering chandelier over grim-faced Persad who continues to be impoverished in the midst of India rising. And worse, in order for himself to become visible Balram renders Persad voiceless and jobless first and completes his invisibility by permanently expelling him from the rest of his own life. Had Balram – nay, Adiga – been aware of his Re-Orientalism and instead identified, if only partially, himself with the suffering, humiliation and invisibility of Persad – let me call him by his real name, Mohammad – a new path to confront the tyranny of the Stork and the money-mired ceremonial democracy would have opened up. Blinded by power and money and infatuated with the urge to speak, or rather shout, Balram did not care to simply listen to Mohammad.

Conclusion: Re-situating Re-Orientalism

The publication of the Sachar Committee Report (SCR) in 2006 was a landmark event in the history of modern India, as it brought the backwardness and marginalisation of Muslims in political economy and democratic life to the forefront of the political debate. The Congress government adopted some policy initiatives to address the issues of Muslims' backwardness and their deficit in development. At the same time, the government itself backed away from other initiatives, such as the need for protective discriminations as recommended by the Ranganath Misra Committee, and it withdrew the Prevention of Communal and Targeted Violence (PCTV) Bill. With the victory of the BJP in the 2014 elections and the installation of the Modi administration since then, the SCR and its recommendations have been virtually dumped.

Focusing on the RSS's response to the SCR, I have demonstrated how Re-Orientalism in the vocabulary of Hindu Orientalism was one key factor that led to the stigmatisation of inequality among Muslims. Central to the deployment of Hindu Orientalism vis-à-vis the SCR – especially by

Hindutva formations such as the RSS – were the tropes of Muslim fanaticism, terrorism, separatism and minority appeasement. These tropes, I suggested, are a loyal borrowing from the knowledge system of British-style colonialism: Orientalism. Rather than soberly analyse the SCR, the BJP ethnically-politically read it through a Schmittian-Orientalist divide (central to the 2014 electoral mobilisation; see Ahmad 2019b; Sethi 2019) to make Muslims into the Other of the nation and thereby acquired power.

While the SCR documented the marginalisation of Muslims manifest in their under-representation in key areas of public life, the only domain where the ratio of Muslims exceeded their percentage in the total population was in prison. The marginalisation of Muslims in the political economy and their over-representation in jail thus raises a question about democracy: why are minorities in democracies such as India as well as Western nation-states under-represented in the political economy and over-represented in jail? While largely sympathetic to arguments that construe the over-representation of minorities in the prisons of Western democracies, especially in the US, by characterising them as 'punishing democracy', 'penal democracy' or 'police state', I have instead argued how imprisonment also generates an alternative notion of democracy among inmates, prison officials, as well as the community outside. At the heart of this alternative is the sense of empathy that imprisonment generates among fellow humans, through a shared vocabulary of injustice, pain, human finitude and vulnerability, thereby inaugurating what Talal Asad calls 'democratic sensibility as an ethos'.

I have deployed the character of Balram from *The White Tiger* as exemplifying a militarised, mediatised, ceremonial, Orientalised democracy, on the one hand, and that of Ram Persad (Mohammad) as illustrative of 'democratic sensibility as an ethos', on the other. With the near-dumping of the SCR by the current regime, the victory of Balram seems almost total. However, this victory (if it can be called one) was not inevitable. Had Balram interrogated his Re-Orientalism and instead identified himself with the suffering and invisibility of Persad, probably a new path to confront the tyranny of the Stork and the money-mired, criminal, corrupt, ceremonial democracy would have opened. Intoxicated by the desire for power and wealth beyond all ethical limits and emboldened by the escape that democracy offers him from his crimes, Balram's failure to listen to Mohammad's sufferings and to connect his invisibility to that of countless others, including his own, means the failure of the alternative idea of 'democracy as an ethos' to come into being.

Based on my argument so far, in the rest of this concluding section I present theoretical reflections on the idea of Re-Orientalism, around which this chapter is organised. As is evident, I initially found Lisa Lau's (2009: 571) idea of 'Re-Orientalism' useful for its concern with the 'perpetration of orientalism in the contemporary South Asian English literature'. I agree with her argument that this perpetration is continued, not by the so-called

Occidentals, but by Orientals themselves. The rest of her argument about Re-Orientalism and many of her central premises informing it, however, are poorly conceived and hence in need of radical reformulation. Lau (2009: 590) concludes as follows: 'It is somehow mildly ironic that when the opportunity arose to move away from Orientalism, the direction some diasporic authors have chosen to move in is Re-Orientalism'. In my view, she can find it ironic only because she did not think adequately about the mutual imbrication of Orientalism and nationalism. As a matter of fact, Lau's 2009 article has almost nothing to say about nationalism and its violent notion of nation as home and its polarising logic of 'us-national' versus 'they-anti-national' (Ahmad 2013a). By the phrase 'when the opportunity arose' (Lau 2009: 590), it is safe to infer, she means the formal withdrawal of colonial rule and the take-over of power by the so-called native elites. Since she is concerned with power-holders and the change of hand – from colonial to 'post-colonial' – rather than the constitution and the substance or mechanics of power and the mutual bind among local, regional and international elites over the *longue durée* (Harris 2004), she is driven to such an ironical conclusion. As this chapter's epigraph makes clear, post-colonial nationalism, as much as earlier nationalism, is an avatar of Orientalism, which is limited not only to the diasporic writers in English, as Lau contends, but equally permeates 'home' writers, and not only those writing in English.

If we closely analyse the trajectory of Nirad C. Chaudhuri, as Ian Almond (2015) skillfully does, the distinction between 'home' and 'diaspora' becomes fairly facile. Chaudhuri's Orientalism, especially in relation to Islam, began in India and continued to flourish in Oxford where he later moved and died. Lau takes 'home' and 'diaspora' as two disjointed spaces and then proceeds to examine if and how Orientalism works in those spaces. My argument is that Orientalism itself is a home in its own right – beyond the geography of 'East' and 'West' – and that it possesses the mandate to recruit (and also disown) writers, journalists, academics and others from all over the world. Relevant to this discussion are the names of Fareed Zakaria and Fouad Ajami that Almond writes about. And this Orientalism is sustained by a variety of writers and intellectuals, such as Francis Fukuyama (2007), with no solid training in the languages and cultures of the 'Orient', unlike nineteenth-century Orientalists. Importantly, the contemporary Orientalism is linked to the New World Order and its stability (see Ahmad 2017a). Thus viewed, Orientalism informs and is reproduced by the 'post-colonial intelligentsia', whether based in the 'East' or the 'West'. It pervades nearly every domain of human life, for Orientalism is not simply a literary trope, but a modern form of power (see below) impacting and impacted by tourism as much terrorism, democracy as much as monarchy, (neo)liberalism as much as (neo)populism, proponents of globalisation as much as advocates of nationalism.

In many ways, it will be easy to fault Lau and many other practitioners in the Humanities for confining their discussion of Orientalism to the solitary field of literature – a point that Breckenridge and van der Veer (1993) made over two decades ago. In some ways the historical formation of disciplines itself is limiting (Wallerstein 2003), as they rob readers of the understandings synthetically reached by the social sciences or social studies at large.[11] My point is that this confinement deprives Lau of much analytical richness in her own identification of the otherwise useful concept of Re-Orientalism. We ought to connect the literary to anthropology, philosophy, politics, sociology and international relations (to name only a few), and *vice versa*. Establishing this connection entails overcoming the conceptual blind spots that the term Re-Orientalism has in theorisations such as Lau's.

Lau's argument rests on a distinction between 'diasporic' and 'home' writers. In her tidy schema, those who perpetuate Orientalism belong to the diaspora, mostly residing in the West, especially in the US. That is, 'home' writers do not practice Orientalism. To prove this point she cites *Ladies Coupe* by the home author Anita Nair and *The Mango Season* by the disaporic author Amulya Malladi. How does Malladi perpetuate Orientalism? She does, Lau says, by essentialising and stereotyping Hindu Indian parents' opposition to their daughters 'marrying outside race and caste'. Put differently, Malladi practices Orientalism when she describes it 'barbaric to expect a girl of maybe twenty-one years to marry a man she knew even less than the milkman'. Lau is right thus far. And such a description largely fits with William Watts' description of Hindus in the 1760s, particularly his description of the 'natives [Hindus]' as 'superstitious'. However, it does not occur to Lau that an entire community of Muslims continues to be catalogued as 'homeless' and 'alien' by colonial and post-colonial discourses, beyond the putative divide of 'disaporic' and 'home' authors. Put differently, Lau's Re-Orientalism is silent about, if not averse to, the role of religion in the very constitution and practice of Re-Orientalism.

I have argued earlier in this chapter how British colonialism-Orientalism fashioned the myth of Muslims as 'outsiders' and Hindus as 'native' and 'original' – Watts being only one among many examples. And this dualistic distinction between 'foreign' and 'native' religions was in full play in opposition to the SCR by the RSS-BJP combine. Describing the proposal by the RMCR for the reservation of backward Muslims divisive, the above-mentioned *Organiser* article from 31 January 2010 – 'From Sachar to Ranganath Misra: Period of Minority Assertion, Hindu Subjugation' – reprimanded the RMCR for not distinguishing between Indian and foreign religions. To this end, it focused on the dissenting note by a member of the RMCR, Mrs Asha Das. The *Organiser* (2010) interpreted Das' note as follows: 'There is a difference between religions of Indian origin, and religions

---

[11] Charles Wright Mills (1959: 18–19n2) preferred 'social studies' or 'human disciplines' to the widely used term 'social sciences'. He was dead opposed to 'behavioural sciences', calling it a propaganda term used by social scientists to receive research money from academic foundations and politicians who confused social sciences with socialism.

like Islam and Christianity that have originated outside. And, therefore, the privileges offered to Hindu, Sikh, Jain and Buddhist Scheduled Caste persons can not be extended to Muslims and Christians'. With much satisfaction, the *Organiser* went on to say that the distinction between Indian and foreign religions had, however, become part of the official government document. Arguably, 'diasporic' (e.g., Rajiv Malhotra; see Butalia 2015; Kurien 2006) and 'home' intellectuals alike adhere to this Orientalist distinction. And unlike Orientalism in Malladi's novel, the Orientalism along the axis of religion permeates the textbooks written by 'post-colonial' authors and authorised by the 'post-colonial' government. A supplementary textbook distributed to 42,000 schools in Gujarat states that 'it is better to die for one's religion [which is native/indigenous]' and that 'an alien religion is source of sorrow' (quoted in Butalia 2015: 19). To state the obvious, while the Orientalist dualism between 'foreign' and 'native' religions is at the heart of a massive political mobilisation causing change of the government, the Orientalist trope of Indian women denied choice in choosing their marital partners does not even figure in the manifesto of any political party, let alone in their on-the-ground mobilisations.

The analysis of responses from the RSS-BJP to the SCR also demonstrates the thematic continuity from the colonial-Orientalist discourse of William Watts in the eighteenth century to that of the *Organiser* in the present. There is a thread of continuity about Muslims as violent and Islam as intolerant from Watts ('oppressive', 'rapacious') over W. W. Hunter to the *Organiser* (for the latter two 'fanatic'), and yes, to *The White Tiger* (Muslims' 'urge to blow up trains every year'). Depictions of Islam and Muslims as fanatic, intolerant and violent, on the one hand, and the portrayal of Hindus as a symbol of peace, tranquility, even timidity, on the other, were thus not scattered views of a few administrative-soldier-writers such as William Watts. They were equally central to the Enlightenment and liberalism. Kant described the character of Hindus as *'pusillanimity'*; for him 'Mohammedinism [sic] is distinguished by its *pride*, because it finds confirmation of its faith in victories and in subjugation of many peoples rather than in miracles, and because its devotional practices are all of a fierce kind' (Kant 1998: 6–125, 130, 177–8, 184–5, italics Kant's).[12] Along the same lines, Alexander Dow (d. 1779), an Orientalist-army officer in India, viewed Islam as 'peculiarly calculated for despotism'; as a faith, it 'enslaved the mind as well as the body', whereas 'Tranquility is the chief object' of Hindus (in Sen 2002: 100–1).

The context of Lau's article, as also of the debate on the SCR, is obviously the Global War on Terror (GWOT) and the alleged move by the West to spread democracy (the positive obverse of 'despotism', with which Dow identified Muslims). Both of these themes bear continuity with colonial-

---

[12] For more on the Enlightenment's views on Islam in the German as well as the French Enlightenment, see Ahmad (2013a; 2017c: Chapter 2).

Orientalism. India's not so tacit approval of the bombing of Afghanistan and Iraq and her fervent participation in the GWOT (Ahmad 2009) make it clear that the Re-Orientalism that Lau describes works at the confluence of Indian and Euro-American powers. *Pace* Lau, it has been my contention in this chapter that there is nothing ironic about this confluence. I have also argued that Re-Orientalism is a far more comprehensive practice than can be limited to text and novels. If Said in a narrow way saw Orientalism mostly textually, Lau views Re-Orientalism similarly. Hallaq's (2018) instructive proposal to see and think about Orientalism as a much wider systemic structure constitutive of modern power at large, I suggest, can usefully be extended to Re-Orientalism, including its manifestations through the vocabulary of democracy and the attempts by many 'democrats' to disguise it.

Acknowledgements

My foremost thanks go to S. Rajaratnam School of International Studies, Nanyang Technological University, Singapore, at whose invitation and where I gave the first draft of this chapter as a talk. I presented its subsequent versions at Aliah University, Kolkata where it was delivered as Justice Rajinder Sachar Memorial public talk; at Hyderabad Central University where I presented it to an audience comprising university teachers enrolled for Refresher Course and organised by the Academic Staff College, and at the Centre for Culture, Media and Governance, Jamia Millia Islamia, New Delhi. I thank Mohammad Reyaz, Sudhakar Babu and Biswajit Das respectively for the invitations. I am equally thankful to the audience at the four universities for their questions and feedback.

References

Adiga, A. (2008), *The White Tiger*. New York: Free Press.

Ahmad, I. (2019a), 'Populism: A Political Anthropology Approach', *Public Anthropologist* 1(2): 224–45.

Ahmad, I. (2019b), 'Introduction: Democracy and the Algebra of Warfare-Welfare', in I. Ahmad and P. Kanungo (eds), *The Algebra of Warfare-Welfare: A Long View of India's 2014 Election*, 1–54. New Delhi: Oxford University Press.

Ahmad, I. (2019c), 'Foreword: On Writing History', in Tauseef Ahmad Parray, *Mediating Islam and Modernity: Sir Sayyid, Iqbal and Azad*, vi–xiii. Delhi: Viva Books.

Ahmad, I. (2017a), 'Injustice and the New World Order: An Anthropological Perspective on 'Terrorism' in India', *Critical Studies on Terrorism* 10(1): 115–37.

Ahmad, I. (2017b), 'In Conversation with an Ordinary Indian: *Kaliyuga*, War, End of the World and Hindutva', *Journal of Religious and Political Practice* 3(1/2): 57–74.

Ahmad, I. (2017c), *Religion as Critique: Islamic Critical Thinking from Mecca to the Marketplace*. Chapel Hill: The University of North Carolina Press.

Ahmad, I. (2013a), 'In Defense of Ho(s)tel: Islamophobia, Domophilia and the West', *Politics, Religion and Ideology* 14(2): 234–52.

Ahmad, I. (2013b), 'Modi as Future Indian PM? Development, Camps, the 'Muslim Vote', *Open Democracy*, 30 November 2013, https://www.opendemocracy.net/openin dia/irfan-ahmad/modi-as-future-indian-pm-development-camps-'muslim-vote' (accessed 6 December 2013).

Ahmad, I. (2009), *Islamism and Democracy in India: The Transformation of Jamaat-e Islami.* Princeton: Princeton University Press.

Ahmad, I. and Siddiqui, M. Z. (2017), 'Democracy in Jail: Over-Representation of Minorities in Indian Prisons', *Economic and Political Weekly* 52(44): 98–106.

Ahmed, H. (2019), 'Communal Violence, Electoral Polarization and Muslim Representation: Muzaffarnagar 2013–2014', in I. Ahmad and P. Kanungo (eds), *The Algebra of Warfare-Welfare: A Long View of India's 2014 Election*, 163–96. New Delhi: Oxford University Press.

Ahmad, R. (2008) 'Scripting a New Identity: The Battle for Devanagari in Nineteenth Century India', *Journal of Pragmatics* 40: 1163–83.

Alam, S. M. (2014), 'Affirmative Action for Muslims? Arguments, Contentions and Alternatives', *Studies in Indian Politics* 2(2): 215–29.

Almond, I. (2015), *The Thought of Nirad C. Chaudhuri: Islam, Empire and Loss.* Cambridge: Cambridge University Press.

Anderson, J. D. (1913), *The Peoples of India.* Cambridge: Cambridge University Press.

Apoorvanand (2019), 'The New Citizenship Bill and the Hinduisation of India', *Al-Jazeera*, 12 January 2019.

Asad, T. (2012), 'Thinking About Religion, Belief and Politics', in R. Orsi (ed.) *The Cambridge Companion to Religious Studies*, 36–57. Cambridge: Cambridge University Press.

Banerjee, M. (2011), 'More Than Meets the Eye: Two Kinds of Re-Orientalism in Naseeruddin Shah's *What If?*', in L. Lau and A. Mendes (eds), *Re-Orientalism and South Asian Identity: The Oriental Other Within*, 126–45. New York: Routledge.

Basant, R. (2016), 'Discourses and Perspectives on Muslims in India: Has the Sachar Committee Report Made a Difference', in R. Hasan (ed.), *Indian Muslims: Struggle for Equality of Citizenship*, 17–40. Melbourne: Melbourne University Press.

Basant, R. and Sharif, A. (2010), 'Introduction', in R. Basant and A. Shariff (eds), *Oxford Handbook of Muslims in India: Empirical and Policy Perspectives.* New Delhi: Oxford University Press.

Bjorkman, L. (2013), 'You Can't Buy a Vote': Cash and Community in a Mumbai Election', *MMG Working Paper* 13-01, 1-26. Max Planck Institute for the Study of Religious and Ethnic Diversity, Göttingen, Germany.

Bose, S. and Jalal, A. (2004 [1997]), *Modern South Asia: History, Culture, Political Economy* (2nd edition). London and New York: Routledge.

Brass, P (2006), 'Collective Violence, Human Rights, and the Politics of Curfew', *Journal of Human Rights* 5(3): 323–40.

Breckenridge, C. and van der Veer, P. (1993), 'Introduction', in C. Breckenridge and P. van der Veer (eds), *Orientalism and the Postcolonial Predicament: Perspectives on South Asia*, 1–19. Philadelphia: University of Pennsylvania Press.

Butalia, U. (2015), 'Captive to Their Own Myths', *New Internationalist*, 483 (June): 18–20.

Butler, J. (2011), 'Bodies in Alliance and the Politics of the Street', http://eipcp.net/ transversal/1011/butler/en/print (accessed 3 April 2017).

Chishti, S. (2006), 'Too Many Muslims in Prison, Sachar Edits This out', *The Indian Express*, 25 November 2006, http://archive.indianexpress.com/news/too-many-muslims-in-prison-sachar-edits-this-out/17275/ (accessed 10 January 2007).

Davis, A. (2011), *Are Prisons Obsolete?* Delhi: Navayana.

Dilley, R. M. (2002), 'The Problem of Context in Social and Cultural Anthropology', *Language and Communication* 22: 437–56.

Dirks, N. (1993), 'Colonial Histories and Native Informants: Biography of an Archive', in C. Breckenridge and P. van der Veer (eds), *Orientalism and the Postcolonial Predicament: Perspectives on South Asia*, 279–313. Philadelphia: University of Pennsylvania Press.

Fabian, J. (1983), *Time and the Other: How Anthropology Makes its Object*. New York: Columbia University Press.

Fazal, T. (2010), 'Between 'Minorityism' and Minority Rights: Interrogating Post-Sachar Strategies of Interventions', *History and Sociology of South Asia* 4(2): 145–51.

Fukuyama, F. (2007), 'Democracy and "The End of History" Revisited', in H. Munoz (ed.), *Democracy Rising: Assessing the Global Challenges (A Project of the Community of Democracies)*, 115–20. New Delhi: Vikas.

Ghosh, A. (2014), 'Eight Years after Sachar, Muslims Still Out of Government Jobs and Schools: Panel', *Indian Express*, 22 November 2012, http://indianexpress.com/article/india/india-others/8-yrs-after-sachar-muslims-still-out-of-govt-jobs-and-schools-panel/ (accessed 26 March 2017).

Ghosh, P. and Siddiqui, K. (2016), 'Progress of School Education among Socioreligious Communities in India Post-Sachar', in R. Hasan (ed.), *Indian Muslims: Struggle for Equality of Citizenship*, 194–234. Melbourne: Melbourne University Press.

Guha, R. (2008), 'The Career of a Concept', *The Hindu*, Sunday Magazine, 20 January 2008, http://www.thehindu.com/todays-paper/tp-features/tp-sundaymagazine/The-career-of-a-concept/article15401331.ece (accessed 5 May 2021).

Hallaq, W. (2018), *Restating Orientalism: Modern Knowledge and Sovereign Domination*. New York: Columbia University Press.

Hansen, T. B. (2007), 'The India That Does Not Shine', *ISIM Review*, 17: 50–1.

Hansen, T. B. (2001), *The Wages of Violence: Naming and Identity in the Postcolonial Bombay*. Princeton: Princeton University Press.

Harcourt, B. (2014), 'The Invisibility of the Prison in Democratic Theory', *The Good Society*, 23, (1): 6–16.

Hasan, Z. (2009), 'Muslim Deprivation and the Debate on Equality', *Seminar*, 602, http://www.india-seminar.com/2009/602/602_zoya_hasan.htm (accessed 5 May 2021).

Harris, O. (2004), 'Braudel: Historical Times and the Horror of Discontinuity', *History Workshop Journal* 57: 161–74.

Hartnett, S. (2011), 'Introduction: Empowerment or Incarceration – Reclaiming Hope and Justice from a Punishing Democracy', in S. Hartnett (ed.) *Challenging the Prison-Industrial Complex*, 1–12. Urbana: University of Illinois Press.

Hunter, W. W. (2002), *The Indian Musalmans*. New Delhi: Rupa & Co.

Hunter, W. W. (1871), *The Indian Musalmans: Are They Bound in Conscience to Rebel against the Queen?* London: Trubner.

Jaffrelot, C. (2016), 'The Muslims of Gujarat during Narendra Modi's Chief Ministership', in R. Hasan (ed.), *Indian Muslims: Struggle for Equality of Citizenship*, 235–58. Melbourne: Melbourne University Press.

James, J. (2007), *Warfare in the American Homeland: Policing and Prison in a Penal Democracy*. Durham, NC: Duke University Press.

Jodhka, S. (2007), 'Perceptions and Receptions: Sachar Committee and the Secular Left', *Economic and Political Weekly*, 21 July: 2996–99.

Kant, I. (1998), *Religion within the Boundaries of Mere Reason and Other Writings*. Cambridge: Cambridge University Press.

Keer, D. (1990 [1954]), *Dr. Ambedkar: Life and Mission*. Bombay: Popular Prakashan.

Khalid, S. (2019), 'Q&A: India Is Heading towards a Full Ethnic Democracy', *Al-Jazeera*, 3 May 2019.

Khan, S. A. (2015), 'Scrap Religion-Based Scheduled Caste Reservations, Mr Modi', *Dailyo.in*. 28 October 2015, http://www.dailyo.in/politics/bihar-polls-narendra-modi-reservation-muslims-christians-parsis-jains-scheduled-castes/story/1/7032.html (accessed 1 November 2015).

Kundu, A. (2016), 'Education and Health Facilities and Indian Minorities: Issues of Access and Utilization', in R. Hasan (ed.), *Indian Muslims: Struggle for Equality of Citizenship*, 41–93. Melbourne: Melbourne University Press.

Kurien, P. (2006), 'Multiculturalism and "American" Religion: The Case of Hindu Indian Americans', *Social Forces* 85(2): 723–41.

Lau, L. (2009), 'Re-Orientalism: The Perpetration and Development of Orientalism by Orientals', *Modern Asian Studies* (43): 571–90.

Lau, L. and Mendes, A. (2011), 'Introducing Re-Orientalism: A New Manifestation of Orientalism', in L. Lau and A. Mendes (eds), *Re-Orientalism and South Asian Identity: The Oriental Other Within*, 1–16. New York: Routledge.

Loyd, J., M. Mitchelson and A. Burridge (2012), 'Introduction: Borders, Prisons and Abolitionist Visions', in J. Loyd et al (eds) *Beyond Walls and Cages: Prisons,Borders, and Global Crisis*, 1–15. Athens, GA: University of Georgia Press.

Mathur, S. (2008), *The Everyday Life of Hindu Nationalism: An Ethnographic Account*. Gurgaon, India: Three Essays Collective.

Meiner, E. (2011), 'Building an Abolition Democracy or the Fight against Public Fears, Private Benefits, and Prison Expansion', in S. Hartnett (ed.) *Challenging the Prison-Industrial Complex*, 15–40. Urbana: University of Illinois Press.

Mills, C. W. (1959 [1968]), *The Sociological Imagination*. New York: Oxford University Press.

Mustafa, F. (2017), 'Minority Report', *The Indian Express*. 5 April 2017, http://indianexpress.com/article/opinion/columns/minority-report-4599777/ (accessed 5 April 2017).

Nag, K. (2014), *The NaMo Story: A Political Life* (revised edition). New Delhi: Lotus Collections, Roli Books.

Nasr, V. (1999), 'European Colonialism and the Emergence of Modern Muslim States', in J. Esposito (ed.), *The Oxford History of Islam*, 549–600. Oxford: Oxford University Press.

Naqshbandi, A. (2014), 'Antony Panel Report Lists Out Reasons for LS Poll Rout', *The Hindustan Times*, 17 August 2014, http://www.hindustantimes.com/india/antony-panel-report-lists-out-reasons-for-ls-poll-rout/story-Qlg82GBxRBua7k3TwgSa3M.html (accessed 5 May 2021).

OneIndia.com (2006), 'Advani Blames UPA of Minority Appeasement', http://www.oneindia.com/2006/03/19/advani-blames-upa-of-minority-appeasement-1142844937.html (accessed 12 November 2007).

Organiser (2017), 'About us', http://www.organiser.org/static/about.aspx (accessed 4 April 2017).

Organiser (2010), 'From Sachar to Ranganath Misra: Period of Minority Assertion, Hindu Subjugation', 31 January 2010, http://organiser.org/search.aspx?q=from+sachar+to+ranganath&lang=4 (accessed 5 May 2021).

Organiser (2006a), 'Disband Sachar Committee: It's Only Dividing the People', 6 August 2006, http://organiser.org//Encyc/2006/8/6/Disband-Sachar-Committee-br--br-It-s-only-dividing-the-people.aspx?NB=&lang=3&m1=&m2=&p1=&p2=&p3=&p4= (accessed 5 May 2021).

Organiser (2006b), 'Sachar Report and Terror Crescent: UPA Engendering a Festering Division Like Minto-Morely in 1909', 24 December 2006, http://organiser.org//Encyc/2006/12/24/Sachar-report-and-terror-crescent-br-UPA-engineering-a-festering-division-like-Minto-Morley-in-1909.aspx?NB=&lang=3&m1=&m2=&p1=&p2=&p3=&p4= (accessed 5 May 2021).

Organiser (2006c), 'Sachar Report and After: Compulsory Education, Not Reservation: Free Muslims from Fanatic Clergy', 3 December 2006, http://organiser.org//Encyc/2006/12/3/Opinion-br--br--em-Sachar-report-and-after--em--br-Compulsory-education,-not-reservation-br--em-Free-Muslims-from-fanatic-clergy--em-.aspx?NB=&lang=3&m1=&m2=&p1=&p2=&p3=&p4= (accessed 5 May 2021).

Pandey, G. (1990), *The Construction of Communalism in Colonial North India*. New Delhi: Oxford University Press.

Rediff.com (2006), 'I Don't Expect Vajpayee to Propose My Name for PM: Advani', 10 December 2006, http://in.rediff.com/news/2006/dec/10advani.htm (accessed 5 May 2021).

Raina, B. (2007), 'Sachar Committee Report on Indian Muslims: Right Wing Lies Exposed', *Mainstream*, 24 April 2007, https://www.mainstreamweekly.net/article 96.html (accessed 5 May 2021).

Rukmini, S. and Singh, V. (2015), 'Muslim Population Growth Slows', *The Hindu*, 25 August.

Robinson, R. (2008), 'Religion, Socio-Economic Backwardness and Discrimination: The Case of Indian Muslims', *The Indian Journal of Industrial Relations* 44(2): 194–200.

Sachar Committee Report (2006), *Social, Economic and Educational Status of the Muslim Community of India: A Report*. New Delhi: Cabinet Secretariat, Prime Minister's High-Level Committee, Government of India.

Sachar, R. (2016), 'Preface', in R. Hasan (ed.), *Indian Muslims: Struggle for Equality of Citizenship*, xix–xxx. Melbourne: Melbourne University Press.

Sachar, R. (2010), 'Foreword', in R. Basant and A. Shariff (eds), *Oxford Handbook of Muslims in India: Empirical and Policy Perspectives*, xv–xvii. New Delhi: Oxford University Press.

Sadiq, P. K. (2018), 'Citizenship and Belonging: A Socio-Historical Analysis of Muslim Engagement with Kerala Public Sphere', unpubl. PhD diss., The English and Foreign Languages University, Hyderabad.

Saiyed, K. (2009), 'To Get Job in Surat, Muslim Took Hindu Name, Revealed When He Was Killed', *The Indian Express*, 29 December 2009, http://archive.indianexpress.com/news/to-get-job-in-surat-muslim-took-hindu-name--revealed-when-he-was-killed/560929/0 (accessed 15 November 2013).

Salam, Z. (2019), 'A Kafkaesque Mixture', *Frontline*, 15 February.

Samvada (2011), 'RSS Submits Memorandum to Governor on Communal Violence Bill-2011', http://samvada.org/2011/news-digest/rss-submits-memorandum-to-governor-on-communal-violence-bill-2011/ (accessed 1 April 2017).

Schmitt, C. (1996), *The Concept of the Political*. Chicago: University of Chicago Press.

Seabrook, J. and Siddiqi, I. A. (2011), *People Without History: India's Muslim Ghettos*. Delhi: Navayana.

Seminar (1987), 'Urdu: A Linguistic Genocide', No. 332.

Sen, A. (2005), *The Argumentative Indian: Writings on Indian History, Culture and Identity*. London: Allen Lane.

Sen, S. (2002), *A Distant Sovereignty: National Imperialism and the Origins of British India*. London: Routledge.

Sethi, M. (2019), 'Modi and the Spectre of Terrorism: Crafting the Hindutva Icon', in I. Ahmad and P. Kanungo (eds), *The Algebra of Warfare-Welfare: A Long View of India's 2014 Election*, 91–118. New Delhi: Oxford University Press.

Shaban, A. (2018), 'Introduction', in A. Shaban (ed.), *Lives of Muslims in India: Politics, Exclusion and Violence* (2nd edition), 1–24. New York: Routledge.

Shah, T. (2004), 'Muslims in Hindu Nationalist India: A Conversation with Asghar Ali Engineer and Paul R. Brass', *Centre Conversation* 28: 1–9.

Shaikh, Z. (2014), 'Only 22 Muslims in 16th Lok Sabha', *The Indian Express*, 17 May 2014, http://indianexpress.com/article/india/politics/only-22-muslims-in-16th-lok-sabha/ (accessed 5 May 2021).

Shariff, A. (2017), 'Sachar Report: Shelved and Forgotten', *Frontline*, 29 September.

Singh, M. P. (2017), 'Swami Aseemanand among 7 Acquitted, Three Convicted in 2007 Ajmer Shrine Blast', *The Indian Express*, 9 March.

Sinha, R. (2017), 'Rakesh Sinha: A Brief Introduction', http://profrakeshsinha.blogspot.com.au (accessed 3 April 2017).

Sinha, R. (2013), 'Separate Muslim Universities: Mindsets and Threats': Prof. Rakesh Sinha's Speech Summary', *Samvada.org*, http://samvada.org/2013/news-digest/separate-muslim-universities-mindsets-and-threats-prof-rakesh-sinhas-speech-summary/ (accessed 5 May 2021).

Singh, G. and Kim, H. (2016), 'Between Hegemonic Domination and the Quest for Equality: The Challenges of Managing Religious Diversity in India Today', in A. Dawson (ed.), *The Politics and Practice of Religious Diversity: National Contexts, Global Issues*, 49–66. New York: Routledge.

Subrahmanyam, S. (2008), 'Diary', *London Review of Books* 30(21): 42–43, https://webcache.googleusercontent.com/search?q=cache:5ksSq3T7ovgJ:https://www.lrb.co.uk/v30/n21/sanjay-subrahmanyam/diary+&cd=1&hl=en&ct=clnk&gl=us (accessed 29 March 2017).

Thapar, R. (1996), 'The Theory of Aryan Race and India', *Social Scientist* 24(1): 3–29.

Times of India (2007a), 'Times View: Preferential Treatment Helps No One', 24 January 2007, http://timesofindia.indiatimes.com/edit-page/TIMES-VIEW-Preferential-treatment-helps-no-one/articleshow/1410740.cms? (accessed 15 April 2017).

Times of India (2007b), 'Times View: Talk about Economic Criteria, Not Religion', 22 December 2007, http://timesofindia.indiatimes.com/edit-page/VIEW-Talk-about-economic-criteria-not-religion/articleshow/2641958.cms? (accessed 22 December 2007).

van der Veer, P. (1999), 'Hindus: A Superior Race', *Nations and Nationalism* 5(3): 419–30.

Wallerstein, I. (2003), 'Anthropology, Sociology, and Other Dubious Disciplines', *Current Anthropology* 44(4): 453–65.

Williams, R. (1983), *Keywords: A Vocabulary of Culture and Society* (revised edition). New York: Oxford University Press.

8

THE MAKING AND UNMAKING OF
THE ROHINGYA

Imrul Islam

Around the world, the mosaic of Muslim identity is under attack from institutions that benefit from portraying Muslims as a homogenous community
uniquely susceptible to violence. In China, the Chinese Communist Party
has labelled Islam a 'contagion', necessitating the internment of one million
Uyghur Muslims in 're-education camps' (Levitz 2018); in the United States,
former President Trump's Muslim ban was set into place 'to protect the nation
from foreign terrorist entry' (Bridge Initiative 2018). To this day, Myanmar
continues to whitewash the Rohingya genocide as a counter-terrorism operation against alien insurgents (International Court of Justice 2019).

Using the case of Myanmar, this chapter shows how the transmutation
of Muslim identity led to – and retroactively allowed the state to justify –
genocide in the state of Rakhine. The chapter consists of three parts: first, it
situates the history of the Rohingya within the history of Burma, showing
how the continuity of colonial traits culminated in a violent contestation
of Muslim identity in the country. Second, it traces how political dissent in
Rakhine was weaponised to redefine Rohingya identity in antithesis to the
identity of the Buddhist majority state. And third, it reflects on the crisis of
2017, framing genocide as a project of anachronistic remembering mediated
by structural and epistemic Islamophobia.

The Making of the Rohingya

The Rohingya are not the only ethnic group residing in Arakan (present-day
Rakhine), nor are they the only Muslim minority in the region. Yet, inex-
plicably, they have been singled out by the Myanmar government. Today,
there are more Rohingya in refugee camps in Bangladesh than in Rakhine,
and those who do remain in Myanmar have been sequestered in camps and
registered as Internally Displaced Persons (IDP). Since the exodus, the local
Rakhine government has taken over razed villages, constructing security

bases and government buildings on ancestral Rohingya land (Human Rights Watch 2018). Mosques have been reduced to rubble, and Muslim burial sites bulldozed by the state (ibid). Interestingly, the contemporary move to 'Burmanise' Rakhine has deep roots in the contested colonial history of Myanmar.

Until 1784, the history of Arakan and Burma were largely separate. In central Burma, Buddhism arrived in stages, but became firmly established by 800 AD (Aung-Thwin 1982). In Arakan, by comparison, initial indigenous populations had largely adopted Islam by 1000 AD (ibid). When Arakan split from Burma in 1300 AD, it became a multi-ethnic state comprising Hindus, Muslims and Buddhists. Most of the region's rulers were Muslims, and Arakan's kingdoms had enduring – often rivalrous – histories with the kingdoms in neighbouring Bengal (Buchanan and Charney 2003). In 1885, the British invaded Burma, and ruled until 1948. In these six decades, there were at least four identifiable waves of migrations from British India to Burma, precipitated by both economic and environmental factors.[1]

It was under British rule that one saw the first indications of ethnic schisms develop in Burma. By and large, the British favoured non-Buddhists in Burma, leading to the import of labour from British-ruled India. As a result, non-Buddhist workers were elevated to economic primacy in a largely agrarian society.[2] In 1939, World War II saw Muslims in Arakan ally with the British, while the Buddhist-majority population across Burma sided with the Japanese. This, in turn, provoked deep inter-communal friction, leading ultimately to the fragmentation of the previously mixed Rohingya and Rakhine ethnic communities. As Christie (1998) notes, the British had promised the Rohingya partial independence, but reneged on the promise once the war was over, causing some Rohingya to campaign unsuccessfully for inclusion of the Arakan state into what was then East Pakistan (present-day Bangladesh). When Burma gained independence in 1948, the Rohingya, unlike most of Burma's ethnic groups, were not given full citizenship, although Prime Minister U Nu indicated that 'the Rohingya had equal status of nationality with Kachin, Kayah, Karen, Mon, Rakhine, and Shan' (San Lwin 2012). Indeed, the term Rohingya appears in the official census of 1961, indicating an ongoing process of recognising them as an ethnic group within the country (Bischoff 1995).

This relative tolerance, however, changed when the military assumed control of Myanmar in 1962, abolishing the Constitution and, with it, legal frameworks for the protection of minority rights (Egreteau 2013). Two decades later, in 1982, legislation was passed that made it impossible for the Rohingya to become citizens (Grundy-Warr and Wong 1997). Between 1993

---

[1] For an overview of the famines and cyclones that precipitated the mass migration of communities from Bengal, see Ludden 2011.

[2] See James Baxter's *Report on Indian Immigration* (1941); and Azeem Ibrahim's *The Rohingyas: Inside Myanmar's Genocide* (2018).

and 2008, a series of government orders titled 'Requirements for Bengalis who apply for Permission to Marry' laid out ten requirements for authorities to approve a marriage between the Rohingya, further isolating Rakhine's Muslims (Burmese Rohingya Organization UK 2014). In 2005, a strict two-child policy was enforced in northern Rakhine (Fortify Rights 2014); the same legislation also restricted movement of the Rohingya in Myanmar, blatantly violating Article 12 of the UN Freedom of Movement Act (United Nations 1948). In 2014, as Myanmar refused to count the Rohingya in the official census, the UN accused the government of reneging on its promise:

> [The government] explicitly agreed with the condition that each person would be able to declare what ethnicity they belong to. Those not identifying with one of the listed ethnic categories would be able to declare their ethnicity and have their response recorded by enumerators. (Associated Press 2014)

While the rise of antipathy toward the Rohingya can be traced along the trajectory of the Myanmar state, the broader socio-political determinants of the crisis remain harder to apprehend. Between 1948 and 1980, Myanmar attempted to chart a non-linear course to democracy, becoming by the 1980s one of the most insular countries in Asia (Ware and Laoutides 2018). When it surfaced from four decades of political stagnation, Bamar-Buddhist national-ism emerged as a driving force behind Myanmar's politics, leading, over time, to the codifying of anti-Rohingya animus within the Myanmar Constitution.

During World War II, Buddhist monks had actively participated in the colonial struggle, aligning with Japan to drive the British out of Burma (see Lewy 1972). Following independence, religion continued to play a part in nationhood, with U Nu's victory in 1960 being driven largely by his promise to make Buddhism the state religion, leading to the forceful campaigning of monks on his behalf. For the Burmese, the cultural disinheritance of colo-nial acculturation seems to have inevitably led to a renewed revaluing of Burmese Buddhist identity at a national scale. In this space of post-colonial nation-building, being Burman became synonymous with being Buddhist. Under the military regimes that ruled Myanmar from 1962 until the recent democratisation process, religious freedoms for non-Buddhist minorities remained severely limited: Christians, Hindus and Muslims faced restric-tions on their movement, their ability to construct places of worship and their ability to pray in public (Walton and Hayward 2014). At the same time, the Myanmar military's (Tatmadaw) attempts to preserve national unity were overshadowed by the political, economic and cultural domination of the Burman majority, inevitably leading to the subjugation of minority com-munities in the country. Where the British had elevated non-Buddhists in Burma, a new Myanmar state sought to right the wrongs of the past by con-centrating state power in Bamar-Buddhist circles.

Democratic elections were held in 1990, but the Rohingya, already denied citizenship, were barred from voting. As Myanmar inched towards democratic reforms, Buddhism strengthened as a political tool to power, with monks taking active part in anti-regime protests (ibid). A sub-group of these monks, led by Ashin Wirathu, framed reform along religious lines: Myanmar was to be a nation for the protection of Buddhism, leaving little room for heterox identities in the country. In 2001, the elevating of orthodox religiosity turned into anti-Muslim animus when – spurred on by the rise of Islamophobia in a post 9/11 world – Buddhist monks publicly spoke out about the Taliban's destruction of the Bamiyan Buddhas in Afghanistan. By adopting a distinctly Western 'war on terror' discourse, these monks proclaimed a new identity-based framing of the anti-Muslim riot that was not related to specific economic or political grievances, but rather the belief that Buddhism, and by extension Myanmar, was under attack from Islam (Khalid 2011).

This mephitic brew of illiberalism, nationalism and 'anti-terrorism' discourse led to the codifying of anti-Rohingya animus within the state structure, even as Bamar-Buddhists were elevated to positions of power. In time, as Callahan (2005) has argued, *taing-yin-tha* or indigeneity, became the fulcrum for national unity in Myanmar. Because the Rohingya were considered Bengali immigrants, they were not listed as one of Myanmar's 135 ethnic communities, and because they were not indigenous, the government barred the community from obtaining citizenship (Ware and Laoutides 2018: 181). This process of Burmanisation was mirrored in other state institutions as well, specifically in the sectors of education, land reform and the promotion of Buddhism as the official religion. Over time, *taing-yin-tha* became the *de facto* test for full citizenship (Cheesman 2017), and for the Rohingya, the dual identity of being a Muslim and non-*taing-yin-tha* emerged as an insurmountable barrier to belonging. Ultimately, although the political rhetoric centred on a narrative of 'unity through diversity', the political practice of Burmanisation created a preferential system of governance that promoted ethnic Burmans while disenfranchising minority groups such as the Muslim Rohingya.

In a speech in 1993, former head of the ruling junta, Than Shwe, summarised the state's official position succinctly: 'In the Union of Myanmar, where national races are residing, the culture, traditions and customs, language and social systems may appear to be different, but in essence they are all based on the common blood of Union Kinship and Union Spirit' (Smith 1994: 18). The essential problem with the 'unity narrative', of course, is that it opened legal doors to political exclusion. By redefining political community away from the notion of citizenship, the narrative implied that national membership necessitated a common imagined ancestry. Seen from inside the *taing-yin-tha* truth regime, any claim to be Rohingya came to be viewed not just as falsehood, but also as a dangerous and illegal identity, both politically and juridically unacceptable (Cheesman 2017).

Once the Rohingya had been marked as a non-indigenous entity, the sum total of their existence became dependent on the whims of an illiberal state, reducing any hope of representation to a reclamation of identity. In effect, the Rohingya faced the insurmountable barrier of history: a history that sought to erase their identity as a people by weaponising colonial memory. To Myanmar, the Rohingya became a reminder of colonial trauma and the ravages of empire; to the Rohingya, Myanmar turned into a home that had historically turned a blind eye to the needs and demands of a disenfranchised community. Today, 'Rohingya' remains a contentious term in the country, and Myanmar an intractable conflict characterised by a stalemate of historical narratives through which historical grievances have been weaponised and people mobilised. The psychological conditions created by the prolonged conflict has inevitably led to a cognitive freezing of memories, translating and crystallising ethnocentric narratives to identify an enemy that needs vanquishing (Bar-Tal and Antebi 1992). In this memoryscape, the Rohingya remain a people forgotten, uniquely susceptible to the aggressions of an illiberal state.

The Unmaking of the Rohingya

The study of radicalisation, largely, remains a study of why Muslims commit terror. Of particular concern to the field is the psychological and theological journey of Muslims, often cited as the root causes of the radicalisation process (Kundnani 2014). Rarely mentioned are the social and political circumstances in which Muslims live, how they are subjugated, and how political dissent becomes fodder for Islamophobic hate. Violence perpetrated by Muslims is seen as having no political roots; perpetrators are labelled, too often, as rebels without a cause. In contrast, violence committed against Muslims is often situated in the realm of logic and rationale – an act of last resort to protect the majority against marauding extremists. That anti-Muslim understanding of the world materialised strongly in Rakhine in the years leading up to the genocide.

By the early 2000s, the Rohingya had been effectively rendered apolitical in Myanmar. The community, representing a mere 4 percent of Myanmar's population, had no voting rights, no citizenship and no means to political representation. As violence in Rakhine became inevitable, the Myanmar government sought out allies. On 10 October 2002, the US embassy in Rangoon sent a rare cable home to Washington, DC – rare because it contained intelligence directly from the Burmese military. It asserted that members of the Arakan Rohingya National Organisation (ARNO) had met with Osama bin Laden and had sought weapons training in Afghanistan and Libya (Allchin 2012). On the same day that the cable was sent, the US Senate approved President George W. Bush's war against Iraq. In time, both stories were exposed as myths birthed by Islamophobia.

As Ibrahim (2018) has noted,

A regular motif in the extremist Buddhist narrative is the alleged close links between the Rohingyas and states such as Saudi Arabia, or armed jihadist groups such as Al-Qaeda or ISIS. So far, there is no evidence that such links, if they exist, have led to jihadist violence within Myanmar. (Ibrahim 2018: 146–7)

Long before violence visited Rakhine in 2012, the policies of the illiberal regimes had turned Myanmar into a tinderbox. Burmese society had been polarised along religious lines, the Rohingya had been effectively dehumanised, and religious factions, in particular Bamar Buddhists, organised. In June 2012, the gang rape and murder of a Buddhist Rakhine woman made Myanmar erupt. Ensuing riots killed at least ninety-eight Rohingya and displaced over 75,000 (Human Rights Watch 2012). According to a Physicians for Human Rights report (2013) about the atrocity, Wirathu and other MaBaTha monks had delivered anti-Muslim speeches in affected towns in the days before the violence. Immediately thereafter, Wirathu called the massacre a show of strength. Following the attacks in Meiktila, DVDs were sold in Mandalay, which contained video footage, reportedly shot during the riots, of Muslims being burned and beaten to death (ibid).

Violence returned to the region in late 2012, this time with evidence of direct army involvement. In Kyauk Pyu, the Tatmadaw reportedly shot dead three young Muslims; in Sittwe, where the Rohingya sought refuge, naval ships reportedly pushed them back out to sea (ibid). Wirathu, the leader of the Buddhist far-right organisation MaBaTha, framed the flight of the Rohingya as Muslims deliberately razing their own houses to gain a place in refugee camps run by aid agencies.

As violence raged across Rakhine, in 2012 the director of President Thein Sein's office posted the following message on his Facebook page:

> It is heard that the Rohingya Terrorists of the so-called Rohingya Solidarity Organization are crossing the border and getting into the country with weapons. That is Rohingyas from other countries are coming into the country. Since our Military has gotten the news in advance, we will eradicate them until the end! I believe we are already doing it [. . .] We don't want to hear any humanitarian issues or human rights others. Besides, we neither want to hear any talk of justice nor want anyone to teach us like a saint. (as quoted in Ibrahim 2018: 81–5)

Despite the overwhelming evidence of military and police involvement in the riots, both the US and the EU lauded the regime for its even-handed approach to curbing violence. The EU Foreign Affairs Commissioner went on record stating that:

> We believe that the security forces are handling this difficult intercommunal violence in an appropriate way. We welcome the priority which the Myanmar government is giving to dealing with all ethnic conflicts. (quoted in Reuters 2012)

The events of 2012 can only be described as a precursor to genocide, a coordinated state-backed attempt to drive the Rohingya either from the country, or into refugee camps. Military action sought to strike fear into the hearts of communities, and long after the carnage had subsided, evidence of geno-cidal intent was transparent in the actions of the Tatmadaw. In 2012, after violence had died down, for example, the Tatmadaw exhibited the corpses of Rohingya in Rakhine. According to a Human Rights Watch Report,

> None of the bodies were identified. Local residents took photographs showing some victims who had been 'hogtied' with string or plastic strips before being executed. By leaving the bodies near a camp for displaced Rohingya, the soldiers were sending a message – consistent with a policy of ethnic cleansing – that the Rohingya should leave permanently. (Human Rights Watch 2013: 15)

All this occurred as the world watched in silence. Human Rights Watch warned of genocidal tendencies in Myanmar, and Genocide Watch instituted a genocide alert for the country, but to no avail. Leniency was offered not just to the state, but to non-state actors as well. Wirathu, the *de facto* leader of the Buddhist far right evaded accountability after accusing Muslims of hyperfertility and instructing Buddhists to take up arms if needed to protect the religion of Buddhism from Islamic invasion (Beech 2019). MaBaTha con-tinued to be in operation, despite pushing for laws that made it harder for Buddhist women to marry outside their faith. Sitagu Sayadaw, Myanmar's most respected Buddhist monk, remained a beloved figure despite promis-ing monks under him to the Tatmadaw: 'There are over 40,000 monks in Myanmar [. . .] If you need them, I will tell them to begin. It's easy' (as quoted in Beech 2019).

And so, when the Tatmadaw began a systematic offensive to exterminate the Rohingya in 2016, it surprised no one. After decades of state-sponsored terror, genocide had become inevitable. In 2019, Thant Myint-U, the famed Myanmar historian, wrote on the world's silence concerning the suffering of Muslims in Rakhine:

> When discordant news got in the way – a communal riot here, a clash between the army and insurgents there – it was easily swept aside as peripheral to the main story. The story was too good, a much needed tonic at a time when the Arab Spring was giving way to extreme violence. Burma, at least, was a morality tale that seemed to be nearing its rightful conclusion. (Myint-U 2019: 20)

On 10 December 2019, Aung San Suu Kyi defended her government against accusations of genocide. In her thirty-minute speech, the word 'Rohingya' never appeared, but an old Islamophobic trope did:

> Mr President, on October 9, 2016, approximately 400 fighters of the Arakan Rohingya Salvation Army, known as ARSA, launched simultaneous attacks on three police posts in Maungdaw and Rathedaung townships in northern Rakhine, near the border with Bangladesh. ARSA claimed responsibility for

these attacks, which led to the death of nine police officers, more than 100 dead or missing civilians, and the theft of 68 guns and more than 10,000 rounds of ammunition. Mr President, allow me to clarify the use of the term 'clearance operation' – the military has used this expression in counter-insurgency and counter-terrorism operations after attacks by insurgents or terrorists. In the Myanmar language, *nae myay shin lin yeh* – literally 'clearing of locality' – simply means to clear an area of insurgents or terrorists. (International Court of Justice 2019)

In Myanmar today, ARSA has emerged as justification for genocide, the pall bearers of a violent group of Muslims who have taken up arms against the majority Buddhist population. This precipitates a decade-long project of Islamophobia: a rewriting and categorisation of the Burmese past through perceptions of tyrannical and oppressive Muslims versus traumatised and oppressed Buddhist subjects. The use of the terminology of terrorism is important because it uses isolated incidences of violence by Muslims to justify coordinated attacks against entire communities of Muslims. Myanmar's framing of ARSA's violence as 'Islamic terrorism' bears eerie resemblance to the post-9/11 rush in the US to frame violent actions by Muslims as violence integral to the lived traditions of Islam. Sageman (2014) explains: 'The key assumption behind the "Blame it on Islam" explanation of terrorism is that there is some mysterious process of indoctrination or brainwashing that transforms "vulnerable" or "at risk" naive young people into fanatic killers or true believers' (Sageman 2014: 567).

Myanmar contends, with very little evidence, that ARSA is an Islamist militant group which aggregates the interest of Myanmar's Muslim mosaic to undermine the Buddhist nature of the state (Fair 2018). The international press has also been quick, with just as little evidence, to assert that the Rohingya are prone to radicalisation. But what do those terms entail? Evidence cited to argue for ARSA being a terrorist outfit is often anecdotal, and rarely verifiable. For example, reports and articles alike point to Ata Ullah (the leader of ARSA) being born in Saudi Arabia as evidence of ARSA's identity as a terrorist group, falling prey to violent Orientalist tropes. According to ARSA's own website and social media accounts, the group denies any connections to 'jihadist' groups and defines itself as one fighting for the liberation of the persecuted Rohingya.[3]

What is certain is that ARSA first came to prominence as a result of attacks by the group on military outposts on 9 October 2016. Immediately after the October 2016 attacks by ARSA, the government enforced a state of emergency in Maungdaw and three other townships. Gruesome photos of alleged terrorist atrocities were published widely on social media. The next day, joint counter terrorism operations began and continued, even as organisations on

---

[3] ARSA's official Twitter account, available at https://twitter.com/arsa_official?lang=en (accessed 6 May 2021).

the ground warned that the offensive was a thinly veiled ethnic cleansing replete with extra judicial killings and mass atrocities. By early November, media outlets, including the BBC, reported that attack helicopters were opening fire on civilians in Rohingya townships (BBC 2016). Then, on 25 August 2017, ARSA was officially declared a terrorist organisation, hours before the final 'clearing operations' began in Rakhine.

On 1 September 2017, the Myanmar military declared 370 ARSA militants had been killed; on 12 September, it announced that of the 471 villages targeted for clearance operations, 176 were empty and thirty-four partially abandoned (Associated Press 2017). Satellite imagery revealed razed villages, demolished mosques and burnt fields. Photos from journalists and the Rohingya pointed to the existence of mass graves. Today, almost 6,700 have been killed, countless remain missing, and innumerable Rohingya have been raped, maimed, or injured. According to the UNHCR, an estimated 860,000 Rohingya are currently in refugee camps in Bangladesh (as cited in Relief Web 2020). While it is true that ARSA forces attacked military outposts in Rakhine in October 2016, it is also true that the deaths of nine police officers were weaponised by the Islamophobia of a genocidal state. It is not hard to understand ARSA's turn to violence. Sageman's theory of the roots of radicalisation suggests four elements to the process of joining a terrorist network: a perceived war on one's in-group; moral outrage at some salient major injustice; resonance with personal experiences; and mobilisation by an already politically active network (Sageman 2016). For the ARSA, radicalisation might have been a consequence of all four factors clashing violently, as a result of decades of state-backed oppression of the Muslim minorities in Rakhine. The incentive for ARSA's mobilisation, then, can be seen as the state's failure to be responsive to the needs of the Rohingya, as well as its insistence on creating a constellation in which culture, consciousness and constitution interrelated to strip the Rohingya of belonging. It can be seen, at its root, as a failure of the state, not of religion.

In Myanmar, the Islamophobia that interlinks and interludes military action is, at its root, epistemic in nature. It is fear that transmutes subaltern narratives to create a political binary, leading to one religious tradition taking precedence over another and creating – as its by-product – a human barred from the ontological domain. This particular variant of Islamophobia, as the next section will show, misremembers colonial narratives to justify its own primacy of belonging, lending credence to exclusionary policies at an institutional and national level. It is in this space that the Rohingya become 'Islamist militants' rather than inhabitants of Rakhine, and the junta takes on the role of protecting the rest of Myanmar from 'Islamic terrorism'. Religious figureheads follow, and the masses, gaslit, fall in line.

Genocidal Denial

Genocide, so Stanton (2016) argues, does not end with extermination. To retain legitimacy, regimes, states, or groups that commit genocide must undertake one last step: denial. Actors must erase evidence of atrocities ever being committed and reshape the national memory to forget that the exterminated community ever existed. Immediately after the mass exodus of the Rohingya, the Myanmar government barred independent inquiry into the conflict. UN workers were evicted from Rakhine, and two Reuters reporters jailed for reporting on the atrocities committed by the Tatmadaw (Reuters 2017). Today, there remains, confoundingly, a persistent insistence across a cross-section of Myanmar's state and society that violence either never occurred at all or was justified. When Suu Kyi testified at The Hague, Burmese expatriates protested outside the court; when she returned home, she did so to a hero's welcome. This, to put simply, is genocide denial at a national scale. In the face of overwhelming evidence, how does one explain such indifference?

The academic understanding of Islamophobia thus far has centred on the broad strokes of stigmatisation, marginalisation and intolerance towards Muslims or those perceived to be Muslims. This understanding, while important in its elucidation of impact, falls short of indicating the *nature* of the phenomenon of Islamophobia. As Sayyid (2014) argues, Islamophobia is more than a reflection of attitudes toward Muslims; indeed, increasingly, it manifests as a phenomenon rooted in the political contestation between Muslims and non-Muslims. In Myanmar, and arguably in the rest of South Asia, Islamophobia takes on an added historical and spatial realm, one determined by the specificity of coloniality and national memory. Islamophobia in Myanmar is not any *specific* action, practice, discrimination, or prejudice, but, more accurately, the dissemination of knowledge that subsequently shapes, determines and initiates actions, practices, discriminations and prejudices. It manifests, in essence, as a mobius ideology that continually reinterprets, reinvents, reinvigorates and renegotiates a range of meanings so as to maintain contemporary relevance to further exclusionary practices and policy.

The narrative of the Myanmar state today is a narrative of common history, one where the diverse ethnic groups within Myanmar are a single family of races with a common historical origin, who lived together until colonialism turned one against the other. In this narrative, the Rohingya have changed sides with each change of regime: in 1961, they became a part of the national census, in 2017 they were cast out as terrorists. Each step of that process, however, was mediated by epistemic Islamophobia. When *taing-yin-tha* was codified as the test for citizenship, it was done with the implicit intent of changing the very meaning of citizenship; when Myanmar stopped referring to the Rohingya by name, they did so to erase the history of a people. Inevitably, when these Rohingya – powerless – resisted, their resistance became a hallmark of Islamic extremism rather than political dissent; and the actions of ARSA came to represent the lived traditions of one million Muslims. Islamophobia as it manifests in Myanmar today – and, by extension, in Sri Lanka, India and China – is the product of a post-colonial gaslighting, fuelled by an anachronistic remembering of history, culture and politics. It is a by-product of the conflation of nationhood with religion, and the enforcing of orthodox traditions upon a heterodox population. Understanding Islamophobia today does not just entail how we understand the past, it demands it. Islamophobia in Myanmar does not have a 'start' or a particular source; rather, it is disseminated even as it is constructed, finding resonance across political, social and religious circles as the history of the state gets reinterpreted and reimagined by each successive regime.

Time and again, the crisis in Rakhine has been positioned as a crisis of community, an inability of heterogeneous groups to coexist due to fundamental difference, ethnic or religious. And yet, as this chapter has aimed to show, the crisis in Myanmar is not really a crisis of religion at all. Rather, it is a crisis of narratives, the weaponising of one religion against another, exacerbated by economic and social inequalities. It is, in other words, a crisis of knowledge and power, employed in tandem to construct barriers to Rohingya representation and quarantine belonging to Bamar-Buddhist majorities.

At the most fundamental level, the study of post-colonial societies is a study of ethics; an attempt at dismantling normalised, exclusionary worldviews that have marginalised indigenous, cultural and epistemic traditions. It is, in other words, a study of identity contestation, reformation and erasure. Within the paradigm of post-coloniality, the subaltern is the subject who has been objectified, suppressed and annulled by the empire. In Myanmar, the identity of the Rohingya was transformed and transmuted by readings and re-readings of coloniality by regimes who sought to construct or justify particular programmes of actions, systems of thought, or attitudinal changes. As a result, not only were the meanings of 'Rohingya', 'Burma' and *'taing-yin-tha'* changed, but also the very nature of what constituted a Muslim in Myanmar.

To understand Islamophobia in its entirety demands that we decolonise the phenomenon. It entails being in a narrative relation with pre- and post-colonial traditions, keeping in mind that any relation of this sort is bound to be determined by the powers each party holds in the interaction (Sayyid 2014). The subaltern speaks only when we excavate history in search of *inclusive* truth – an excavation that will be defined by our historical position, our powers and knowledge, and our aspiration and indifference.

For a century, if not more, the Rohingya have languished in silence, their history held captive by the state. To help them, we must first hear them.

Violence, after all, is the stealing of stories, and genocide is its erasure.

References

Allchin, J., (2012), 'The Rohingya, Myths and Misinformation', *DVB*, http://english. dvb.no/analysis/the-rohingya-myths-and-misinformation/22597 (accessed 6 May 2021).

Associated Press (2014), 'Burma Census Is Not Counting Rohingya Muslims, Says UN Agency', *The Guardian*, 2 April 2014, https://www.theguardian.com/world/2014/apr/02/burma-census-rohingya-muslims-un-agency (accessed 6 May 2021).

Associated Press (2017), 'Violence Online Forces Rohingya to Take on Great Risk', *APNews*, 27 October 2017, https://apnews.com/RohingyaExodus (accessed 6 May 2021).

Aung-Thwin, M. (1982), 'Burma before Pagan: The Status of Archaeology Today', *Asian Perspectives* 25(2): 1–21.

Bar-Tal, D. and Antebi, D. (1992), 'Siege Mentality in Israel', *International Journal of Intercultural Relations* 16(3): 251–75.

Baxter, J. (1941), *Report on Indian Immigration*. Rangoon: Superintendent, Government Printing and Stationery, Burma.

BBC (2016), 'Myanmar Army Fires on Rohingya Villages in Rakhine Region', 13 November 2016, https://www.bbc.com/news/world-asia-37968090 (accessed 6 May 2021).

Beech, H. (2019), 'Buddhists Go to Battle', *New York Times*, 8 July 2019, https://www.nytimes.com/2019/07/08/world/asia/buddhism-militant-rise.html (accessed 6 May 2021).

Bischoff, R. (1995), *Buddhism in Myanmar: A Short History*. Kandy: Buddhist Publication Society.

Bridge Initiative (2018), 'The Muslim Bans', https://bridge.georgetown.edu/research-publications/reports/muslimban/ (accessed 6 May 2021).

Buchanan, F. and Charney, M. W. (2003), 'A Comparative Vocabulary of Some of the Languages Spoken in the Burma Empire', *SOAS Bulletin of Burma Research* 1(1): 40–57.

Burmese Rohingya Organization UK (2014), 'Myanmar's 1982 Citizenship Law and the Rohingya'.

Callahan, M. P. (2005), *Making Enemies: War and State Building in Burma*. Ithaca: Cornell University Press.

Cheesman, N. (2017), 'How in Myanmar "National Races" Came to Surpass Citizenship and Exclude Rohingya', *Journal of Contemporary Asia* 47(3): 461–83.

Christie, C. J. (1998), *A Modern History of Southeast Asia: Decolonization, Nationalism and Separatism*. London: I. B. Tauris.

Egreteau, R. (2013), 'Separatism, Ethnocracy, and the Future of Ethnic Politics in Burma (Myanmar)', in Jean-Pierre Cabestan and Aleksandar Pavkovic (eds), *Secessionism and Separatism in Europe and Asia*, 194–211. New York: Routledge.

Fair, C. C. (2018), 'Arakan Rohingya Salvation Army: Not the Jihadis You Might Expect', 9 December 2019, https://www.lawfareblog.com/arakan-rohingya-salvation-army-not-jihadis-you-might-expect (accessed 6 May 2021).

Fortify Rights (2014), 'Myanmar: Abolish Abusive Restrictions and Practices Against Rohingya Muslims', https://www.fortifyrights.org/mya-inv-2014-02-25/ (accessed 6 May 2021).

Grundy-Warr, C. and Wong, E. (1997), 'Sanctuary under a Plastic Sheet: The Unresolved Problem of Rohingya Refugees', *IBRU Boundary and Security Bulletin* 5(3): 79–91.

Human Rights Watch (2012), 'The Government Could Have Stopped This', 31 July 2012, https://www.hrw.org/report/2012/07/31/government-could-have-stopped/sectarian-violence-and-ensuing-abuses-burmas-arakan (accessed 6 May 2021).

Human Rights Watch (2013), 'All You Can Do Is Pray: Crimes Against Humanity and Ethnic Cleansing of Rohingya Muslims in Burma's Arakan State', 22 April 2013, https://www.hrw.org/report/2013/04/22/all-you-can-do-pray/crimes-against-humanity-and-ethnic-cleansing-rohingya-muslims (accessed 6 May 2021).

Human Rights Watch (2018), 'Burma: Scores of Rohingya Villages Bulldozed', February 2018, https://www.hrw.org/news/2018/02/23/burma-scores-rohingya-villages-bulldozed (accessed 6 May 2021).

Ibrahim, A. (2018), *The Rohingyas: Inside Myanmar's Genocide*. Oxford: Oxford University Press.

International Court of Justice (2019), *Verbatim Records, Application of the Convention on the Prevention and Punishment of the Crime of Genocide (The Gambia v. Myanmar)*, 10 December 2019, https://www.icj-cij.org/files/case-related/178/178-20191210-ORA-01-00-BI.pdf (accessed 6 May 2021).

Khalid, M. (2011), 'Gender, Orientalism and Representations of the "Other" in the War on Terror', *Global Change, Peace and Security* 23(1): 15–29.

Kundnani, A. (2014), *The Muslims Are Coming! Islamophobia, Extremism, and the Domestic War on Terror*. London: Verso.

Levitz, E. (2018), 'China Declared Islam a Contagious Disease – and Quarantine 1 Million Muslims', *New York Magazine*, 28 August 2018, http://nymag.com/intelligencer/2018/08/china-muslims-camps-uighur-communist-party-islam-mental-illness.html (accessed 6 May 2021).

Lewy, G. (1972), 'Militant Buddhist Nationalism: The Case of Burma', *Journal of Church and State* 14(1): 19–41.

Ludden, D. (2011), *An Agrarian History of South Asia*. Cambridge: Cambridge University Press.

Myint-U, T. (2019), *The Hidden History of Burma: Race, Capitalism, and the Crisis of Democracy in the 21st Century*. New York: W. W. Norton & Co.

Physicians for Human Rights (2013), 'Massacre in Central Burma: Muslim Students Terrorized and Killed in Meiktila'. Cambridge, MA: PHR.

Relief Web (2020), 'Refugee Response Report 2020', https://reliefweb.int/report/bangladesh/three-years-rohingya-refugee-response-report-2020#:~:text=25%20August%202020%20marks%20three,camp%20in%20Cox's%20Bazar%2C%20Bangladesh (accessed 6 May 2021).

Reuters (2012), 'EU Welcomes "Measured" Myanmar Response to Rioting', 12 June 2012, https://www.reuters.com/article/us-myanmar-violence/eu-welcomes-measured-myanmar-response-to-rioting-idUSBRE85A1HF20120611 (accessed 6 May 2021).

Reuters (2017), 'Two Reuters Journalists Arrested in Myanmar', https://www.reuters.com/article/us-myanmar-journalists/two-reuters-journalists-arrested-in-myanmar-face-official-secrets-charges-idUSKBN1E71CO (accessed 6 May 2021).

Sageman, M. (2014), 'The Stagnation in Terrorism Research', *Terrorism and Political Violence* 26(4): 565–80.

Sageman, M. (2016), 'On Radicalisation', in Shashi Jayakumar (ed.), *State, Society and National Security: Challenges and Opportunities in the 21st Century*, 105–28. Singapore: World Scientific.

San Lwin, N. (2012), 'Making Rohingya Statelessness', *New Mandala*, 29 October 2012,

http://asiapacific.anu.edu.aunewmandala/2012/10/29/making-rohingya-state
lessness/ (accessed 6 May 2021).

Sayyid, S. (2014), 'A Measure of Islamophobia', *Islamophobia Studies Journal* 2(1): 10–25.

Smith, M., Allsebrook, A. and Sharman, A.-M. (1994), *Ethnic Groups in Burma: Development, Democracy and Human Rights*. London: Anti-Slavery International.

Stanton, G. (2016), 'The Ten Stages of Genocide', *Genocide Watch*, https://www.geno
cidewatch.com/ten-stages-genocide (accessed 6 May 2021).

United Nations (1948). *Universal Declaration of Human Rights*.

Walton, M. J. and Hayward, S. (2014), *Contesting Buddhist Narratives: Democratization, Nationalism, and Communal Violence in Myanmar*. Honolulu: East-West Center.

Ware, A. and Laoutides, C. (2018), *Myanmar's 'Rohingya' Conflict*. Oxford: Oxford University Press.

'TURNING SHEEP INTO TIGERS': STATE SECURITISATION OF ISLAM, SOCIETAL INSECURITY AND CONFLICT IN XINJIANG, CHINA

Joanne Smith Finley

Beginning with a summary of the contemporary human rights crisis in Xinjiang, Northwest China, where upwards of one million mostly Muslim Turkic and other minority peoples are extra-judicially detained in internment camps for political 're-education' (Zenz 2019; Reuters 2019), serving long-term prison sentences (Bunin 2019), or in situations of forced labour (Byler 2019; Xu et al. 2020; Zenz 2021; Murphy and Elimä 2021), this chapter assesses how the Chinese state came to this policy juncture. The discussion draws on scholarly and media sources; human rights research; my longitudinal study of Uyghur-Han Chinese relations between 1991 and 2011 (Smith Finley 2013); an analysis of selected violent incidents occurring in Xinjiang between 2012 and 2015 (Smith Finley 2019a); interviews conducted in Ürümchi in September 2016; and conversations and observations conducted in Ürümchi and Kashgar in June-July 2018. While there is evidence that the Arab-descended Hui Muslims in China have also begun to be affected by the religious 'de-extremification' campaign underway in Xinjiang, within a broader PRC state programme to 'Sinicise' religions (Li 2019a; 2019b), this chapter focuses on the Turkic Uyghurs. This group has been disproportionately targeted because of its special status as a peripheral, linguistically and culturally separate people, with a history of two independent states prior to the establishment of the PRC in 1949. While the Chinese government has routinely represented this group as a 'terrorist' and 'extremist' threat since the onset of the US-led 'Global War on Terror' (GWoT) in 2001 (Roberts 2020; Clarke 2018; Rodriguéz-Merino 2019), I have argued elsewhere that in reality it perceives the Uyghurs as a dissident, anti-colonial force which it seeks to suppress by means of state violence and, in the past four years, state terror (Smith Finley 2019b). The state's ultimate goal is to protect the territorial integrity of the Chinese nation, shore up CCP regime legitimacy, and stabilise and secure the northwestern frontier for the purpose of achieving the Belt and Road Initiative (BRI), the global infrastructure development strategy promoting a China-led Eurasian integration that sits at the centre of Xi Jinping's 'China Dream' (Clarke 2020).

Mass Internment for 'Re-education' and 'Thought Transformation' under CCP Regional Party Secretary, Chen Quanguo

The era of mass internment can be dated to the arrival in Xinjiang of new CCP Regional Party Secretary, Chen Quanguo, in late August 2016 and the April 2017 promulgation of the Xinjiang Uyghur Autonomous Region De-Extremification Regulations (XUAR 2017). In late 2017, investigative journalist Megha Rajagopalan published an incendiary report which documented thousands of 'disappearances' of Uyghurs into political re-education centres in Xinjiang since the spring of that year. Their 'crimes', she wrote, ranged from travelling abroad to a Muslim country (or having a relative who had done so) to using Western social media apps; from possessing the wrong content on one's mobile phone to 'appearing too religious' (Rajagopalan 2017). She described one such facility – the euphemistically named Kashgar Professional Skills Education and Training Centre – as . . .

> . . . an imposing compound surrounded by high concrete walls topped with loops of barbed wire. The walls are papered with colourful posters bearing slogans like 'cherish ethnic unity as you cherish your own eyes'. (Rajagopalan 2017)

Once a school, this building now detained Uyghurs and others for months on end, forcing them to study the Chinese language, memorise Chinese laws on Islam and politics, and repeatedly declare how good the Chinese government is to its people. Locals told her that people 'disappear inside that place', becoming wholly unreachable by their family members (Rajagopalan 2017). Rajagopalan's report emerged against the backdrop of the Chinese state's investment since 2015 in a multi-tiered security state that enables 'Orwellian levels' of surveillance (Leibold 2015; Zenz and Leibold 2017). A combination of dystopian technology and human policing, it comprises a grid-style social management system maintained by a network of police and paramilitary troops, with 'convenience police stations' placed every few hundred feet, and armed checkpoints at which ethnically selective checks are made for 'religious content' on Uyghurs' phones (Zenz 2017).

Over the eighteen months following the publication of Rajagopalan's report, a combination of Xinjiang-based scholarship, investigative journalism and human rights research identified a range of eligibility criteria for potential extra-judicial internment in the euphemistically named 'transformation through education centres' (Zenz 2019), including:

- *'Extremist' religious practices*: growing a beard (especially a long one); praying regularly; inviting too many people to one's wedding;

Figure 9.1 'Cherish ethnic unity as you cherish your own eyes: Live together, study together, work together, play together', poster image photographed in Ürümchi, September 2016 (Joanne Smith Finley).

giving children names of Islamic origin; appearing too religious (e. g., wearing veils, headscarves, or long clothes in Muslim style); reciting an Islamic verse at a funeral; washing bodies according to Islamic custom; holding strong religious views; allowing others to preach religion; teaching the Qur'an to one's children; asking an imam to name one's children; attending the mosque regularly; studying or teaching 'unauthorized' forms of Islam; praying at a mosque other than on a Friday (the traditional day of prayer in the Central Asia region); attending Friday prayers outside of one's own village; making the pilgrimage to Mecca (Rajagopalan 2017; Shih 2018; *The Economist* 2018; Kuo 2018; Sudworth 2018; Byler 2018b; Dooley 2018; Denyer 2018)

- *Possessing sensitive digital content (especially 'illegal' religious content) on a mobile phone or computer*: text messages containing religious language; Qur'anic verses or graphics; simple explanations of the Qur'an (in Uyghur, *tabligh*); pictures of women wearing the *niqab*; critical essays or lectures by Uyghur intellectuals (Rajagopalan 2017; Feng 2018; Kuo 2018; Shih 2018; Special Correspondent 2018)
- *Use of Western social media apps or websites*: downloading/using Facebook or Twitter (Rajagopalan 2017)
- *Travelling or studying abroad*, including (but not restricted to) religious study abroad, particularly in a Muslim country; or planning to do so (Rajagopalan 2017; Feng 2018; *The Economist* 2018; Famularo 2018; Sudworth 2018; Dooley 2018; Denyer 2018; Special Correspondent 2018)
- *Links to relatives abroad*: taking or making phone calls to friends and family abroad (especially in one of twenty-six 'sensitive' countries);[1] having a relative who has travelled abroad, particularly to a Muslim country (Rajagopalan 2017; Shih 2018; Kuo 2018; Feng 2018; Sudworth 2018; Samuel 2018; Special Correspondent 2018)
- *Association with 'outsiders'*: talking to foreigners, especially journalists or researchers; affiliation with 'foreign elements' (*The Economist* 2018; Shih 2018)
- *Travelling to inner China* independently for work (Feng 2018; Human Rights Watch 2019)
- *Former criminal conviction*: e. g., language rights campaigner Abduweli Ayup, temporarily re-detained in 2015 after previously serving fifteen months in prison (Rajagopalan 2017; field notes 2018)
- *Association with a current or former convict* (Rajagopalan 2017; field notes 2018)
- *Voicing open criticism*: criticising state policies; asking where one's relatives are (after they were 'disappeared') (Shih 2018; *The Economist* 2018)
- *Insufficient patriotism*: e. g., failing to recite the national anthem in Chinese (*The Economist* 2018)

---

[1] See Table 1 in Human Rights Watch (2018: 15).

- *Illiteracy/poor Chinese language proficiency*: mostly farmers (often illiterate in Chinese and their mother tongue) assumed to have been 'misled by hardened extremists' (Byler 2018b; Dooley 2018; Shih 2018)
- *Insufficient or excessive funds*: failing to pay bills on time (Sudworth 2018); accumulating a suspicious level of wealth (field notes, 2018)

The reports showed that, inside the centres, internees were being kept in overcrowded, unsanitary conditions and fed a starvation diet; forced to study Chinese language, law and policies and to sing patriotic songs; asked to produce self-criticisms; forbidden to speak their mother tongue; and subjected to a coercive secularisation campaign (Shih 2018; Byler 2018a; Special Correspondent 2018; Denyer 2018; *The Economist* 2018; Rajagopalan 2017; Kuo 2018; Dooley 2018). In short, they were expected to 'engrave the [Han Chinese] ancestral land on their hearts' (see Figure 9.2).

In response to those emerging reports, it was initially observed that, although the Xinjiang internment camps shared a mass character and common purpose with twentieth-century concentration camps (quarantining a specific population within the polity), they did not fully reflect the latter's brutality (Roberts 2018: 20). There was then insufficient evidence of a systematic policy of group extermination. Historian Rian Thum nonetheless observed that mass murder and genocide 'do not look like impossible outcomes' (Thum 2018). Reports of physical, psychological and sexual violence and torture became increasingly commonplace (Human Rights Watch 2018; Special Correspondent 2018; Shih 2018; Denyer 2018; Kuo 2018; Sudworth 2018; Al Jazeera 2018; Byler 2018a; ChinaAid 2018; Chao 2019; 101 East 2019; Associated Press 2020; Ingram 2020). At the time of writing, 157 deaths occurring in custody or shortly after release from a camp have been documented, in addition to seven suicides; victims include religious scholars and clerics, intellectuals, university students, businesspeople, artists and writers, teachers, doctors, taxi drivers, a chef, civil servants, security personnel, farmers and herders, factory workers, housemakers and three minors under the age of eighteen.[2] Of course, this represents only the number of *known* deaths; the true figure is likely much higher.

From the end of 2018, state repression of Turkic Muslims entered a new phase involving transfers of the most recalcitrant camp internees – usually young, religious males – to high-security prisons in Xinjiang or inner China (Bunin 2019), while other camp 'graduates' were sent into securitised forced labour (Byler 2019; Xu et al. 2020; Zenz 2021; Murphy and Elimä 2021). Those who remain outside the camps have been terrified into cultural self-censorship through the threat of internment (Smith Finley 2018; Burdorf 2020).

Then, on 29 June 2020, a report was published by investigative journalists with the Associated Press (AP 2020), which significantly shifted the debate.

---

[2] Xinjiang Victims Database, Deaths (2017–), https://shahit.biz/eng/#lists; see also Uyghur Human Rights Project 2019.

Figure 9.2 'Engrave the homeland [Chinese ancestral land] on your heart', poster image photographed in Ürümchi, September 2016 (Joanne Smith Finley).

It supplied evidence of widespread and systematic state suppression of Uyghur births since 2015, based on open-source research (an analysis of the government's own statistics and documents) conducted by the scholar Adrian Zenz (2020)[3] and on AP's interviews with thirty former camp detainees, their relatives and a former camp instructor. The data showed how over the previous four years hundreds of thousands of Turkic Muslim women had been subjected to mandatory pregnancy checks, forcible insertion of intrauterine devices (IUDs), and forced sterilisations and abortions: practices that rose sharply in Xinjiang even as they had fallen to very low levels in China nationwide. Birth control measures had been enforced by leveraging mass internment as threat (to intimidate residents into accepting them) and as punishment: of 484 camp detainees listed in Qaraqash county in Xinjiang, 149 were there for having too many children, according to leaked documents (Associated Press 2020; Shepherd and Patel 2020). Consequently, at the time of writing, the label 'genocide' – unqualified by the modifier 'cultural' – is being discussed by a growing number of scholars, activists, rights advocates, barristers and politicians, as they consider the legal and diplomatic channels that might be pursued to hold the PRC government to account (Smith Finley 2020).[4]

Rights violated by ongoing PRC state campaigns of extra-judicial mass internment, formal incarceration, forced labour, coercive intermarriage and birth suppression, as well as by the broader programme of Sinicisation in Xinjiang, include the right to life, liberty and security (Article 3); the right not to be held in slavery or servitude (Article 4); the right to be free from torture and cruel, inhuman or degrading treatment or punishment (Article 5); the right to equal protection of the law without discrimination (Article 7); the right to be free from arbitrary arrest, detention or exile (Article 9); the right to a fair and public hearing in the determination of criminal charges (Article 10); the right to be free from arbitrary interference with one's privacy, family, home or correspondence (Article 12); the right to leave and return to one's own country (Article 13); the right to seek and enjoy asylum in other countries (Article 14); the right to enter into free, consenting marriage and to found a family (Article 16); the right to own property and not be arbitrarily deprived of that property (Article 17); the right to freedom of thought, conscience and religion (Article 18); the right to freedom of opinion and expression (Article 19); the right to free choice of employment and just remuneration (Article

---

[3] revised version of this report, including corrections, is available here: https://jamestown.org/?attachment_id=86786 (accessed 6 May 2021).

[4] In April 2021, my institution, Newcastle University, hosted a major event titled 'The Uyghur Crisis: Genocide, Ethnocide, or Crime Against Humanity?' at which academics, activists and human rights advocates will share information with international barristers and politicians, with a view to discussing whether a designation of genocide is justified or desirable, and, if so, whether it is possible to prove intent on the part of the Chinese state.

23); and the right to free participation in the cultural life of one's community (Article 27) (United Nations General Assembly 1948).

From Comparative Peace in the 1980s to Renewed Repression in the 1990s

How did the Chinese state come to this extreme policy juncture? If we rewind to the 1980s, we find a very different environment and atmosphere, one enabled by Deng Xiaoping's conciliatory policies that permitted religious, linguistic, educational and cultural freedoms for ethnic minorities. This policy relaxation in 1980–1 sought to build bridges after the excesses of Mao Zedong's Cultural Revolution, during which time minority habits and customs had been persecuted as part of the 'Four Olds' (Dreyer 1968; Catris 2018). It is true that a short burst of violent disturbances greeted the shift, as locals in Kashgar and Aqsu in southern Xinjiang confronted the Han-dominated military, police and Xinjiang Production and Construction Corps (XPCC) to demand improved employment prospects and greater autonomy. The sudden relaxation of minority policy after years of suppression had apparently created an atmosphere of euphoria, and Uyghurs felt encouraged to re-assert their identity. Notably, however, they did not call for political secession within this context of guaranteed freedom of religious belief, and stability soon returned between 1982 and 1987. 1988 brought peaceful protests at Beijing's Central Institute for Nationalities and Xinjiang University in Ürümchi over perceived attitudes of racial discrimination among Han Chinese, with demonstrators calling for 'genuine human rights' and 'nationality solidarity on the basis of equality between nationalities' (Dillon 1995). Again, however, there was no call for secession, and the emphasis on ethnic unity and equality underlined the Uyghurs' willingness to work within the system to improve their situation.

The year 1989 brought a political shift across China, with university students and factory workers protesting in Tian'anmen Square against official corruption and calling for democracy. One of the student leaders was an Uyghur named Örkäsh Dölät (in Chinese, Wu'erkaixi), and Uyghurs increasingly began to conceive of organised political opposition to central rule from this time. Back in Xinjiang, Uyghurs joined with Hui Muslims in Ürümchi in May 1989 in peaceful and violent protest against the book *Sexual Customs*, which was considered to denigrate Islam; while the demonstration focused squarely on the perceived blasphemy of the book's author, the event was experienced differently by Chinese authorities, who represented it as a riot by 'people who opposed the unification of the motherland' (Dillon 1995: 31). By the end of the 1980s, local protest in Xinjiang was coalescing along two main lines: socio-economic inequalities and religio-cultural differences (and related racial discrimination).

The Baren incident of April 1990 in Kashgar prefecture, south Xinjiang, was a distinct turning point, unfolding within a politically sensitive context for the Chinese government. Nationally, it followed violent riots in another borderland territory, Tibet (1988–89) and the repression of the pro-democracy protests at Tian'anmen Square in Beijing (June 1989). Internationally, it occurred in the midst of the collapse of the Soviet Union and the imminent declaration of Kazakh, Uzbek and Kyrgyz independent states across the border. While the PRC state narrative at the time represented the Baren incident as a premeditated, 'counter-revolutionary' armed uprising, since 2001 it has re-cast this event retrospectively as a 'terrorist' incident. Meanwhile, alternative accounts hold that the event began as a peaceful demonstration against official restrictions on religious activities, which escalated into a violent riot when met with state force (Rodriguéz-Merino 2019). Either way, it seems inarguable that the force with which the state responded to the situation was wholly disproportionate; 1,600 Uyghurs were killed by anti-riot troops, tanks and fighter planes (Vicziany 2003). In the aftermath of this event, heavy restrictions on religion were introduced, involving mosque closures and a requirement that imams pledge loyalty to the PRC government. These new controls over Islam and accelerated police repression in the form of 'Strike Hard' campaigns against separatism and 'illegal religious activities' created an atmosphere described as 'more and more stifling for young Uyghurs', throwing some into despair so that they became susceptible to recruitment by the Turkestan Islamic Party (TIP), a fringe group based outside of China (Castets 2015b: 109).

A combination of internal and external factors led to rising ethno-political aspirations across the 1990s, particularly among young Uyghur males, who were inspired by the 1991 collapse of the Soviet Union and the subsequent formation of independent Central Asian states. Simultaneously, Uyghurs became increasingly dissatisfied with the heavy religious restrictions imposed after Baren and with the growing socio-economic inequalities between local people and incoming Han Chinese settlers (Smith 2000). The situation came to a head in 1997. A religious crackdown had been launched in 1996, following the assassination of an Uyghur government official in Kucha, held to be a 'collaborator'.[5] The crackdown is widely believed to have led directly to the 1997 Ghulja (in Chinese, Yining) demonstration in north Xinjiang, which began peacefully but ended in violence. Suggested triggers include multiple arrests of *taliplar* (religious students) who opposed the state's appointments of 'politically loyal' *mollas*, disrupted mosque gatherings during Ramadan, and arrests of Uyghur women as they prayed in a private house (Vicziany 2003: 250–1); the forcible dispersal by Chinese police of a group of women praying at a mosque (Steele and Kuo 2007: 8); and a

---

[5] Personal communication with local party official, May 1996; see also Beckley (1997) and Bellér-Hann (2002: 78). In response, the CCP issued Document No. 7, containing urgent recommendations that the Han Chinese be moved in to stabilise unrest and that the Uyghurs lose the right to study religion abroad. *Sing tao jih pao*, Hong Kong, 5 March 1997, in Summary of World Broadcasts (Asia Pacific), 6 March 1997, FE/2860 G/3.

government ban on the Uyghur cultural gathering known as the *mäshräp* (then taking the form of all-male moral/religious gatherings) (Gladney 2002: 267). Like the Baren incident before it, the Ghulja demonstration was met with disproportionate force: an estimated 400 Uyghurs were shot dead by state agents (Vicziany 2003), and local witnesses affirmed that one in ten men 'disappeared' in its aftermath (field notes, 2002). In the years that followed, channels for dialogue were progressively foreclosed, leaving little to no political space for Uyghurs to engage with the state (Clarke 2015).

A key reason for the shift in state policy back to religious repression in the 1990s is neatly summarised by a commentary published in a Hong Kong newspaper in 1995:

> Some local personalities say that in Mao Zedong's era, there was tight control over religious belief, so national secessionism was well under control; in recent years, however, because the authorities have adopted a relaxed policy towards religious belief, the instigators have often conducted secessionist activities in the name of religion.[6]

The implication was that Chinese authorities saw a direct link between the practice of religion and the growth of aspirations to Uyghur independence; at the very least, they believed that would-be separatists might seek to employ religion as a tool to mobilise secessionist activity. In their view, therefore, only by tightly controlling religion could that outcome be avoided.

The Uyghur Islamic Revival

In Xinjiang, as in other parts of the Islamic world, the attempt by an atheist majoritarian state to restrict religious practice was experienced as a threat to personal and group identity and moral framework; it gave rise to a movement of religious defence (Akbaba and Taydas 2011: 274–7). This unfolded in a context where globalising forces and Deng's Open-Door economics had aided the flow of traditionalist Islamic ideologies into Xinjiang since the start of the 1980s and where an Uyghur Islamic revival was already underway as result of this increased mobility and contact with the wider Islamic world (Smith Finley 2013: 235–93; Harris and Isa 2019: 62–3; Harris 2020). The following extract from my field diary documents the dramatic change in piety that took place within Uyghur society between 1996, when I completed long-term fieldwork in the region, and my return in 2002:

> Six years earlier, you would barely have seen a soul going into the mosque on a non-Friday, just the odd bearded elder. What a difference now! Some men were already inside when I got there [. . .] Men drifted in continuously until about

---

[6] *Lien ho pao*, Hong Kong, 11 October 1995, in SWB (Asia Pacific), 28 November 1995, FE/2472 G/12.

12.45; unlike in the mid-90s, these were not only men in their sixties in long coats, hats and *ötük* [Central Asian leather boots]; there was an equally large number of young men, ranging from teenagers to those in their thirties, as well as some younger boys taken in by fathers and grandfathers. The middle-aged men were conspicuous in their relative absence [. . .] Of course, this generation had grown up during the Cultural Revolution [and so had not been educated in the Arabic script, nor in prayer rituals].

Aq Meschit, Ürümchi, on a Monday in Summer 2002 (field notes, 2002)

In my interviews with local Uyghurs, conducted during the summers of 2002 and 2004, a diversity of reasons for the Islamic revival emerged; importantly, it was clear that the process had been peaceful and cathartic rather than violent or extremist, as current state discourses suggest. Explanations provided by respondents coloured the revival in many hues, giving meaning to a popular Uyghur saying: 'All five digits on one hand are not the same' (Smith Finley 2013: 281). Some characterised it as a form of local, symbolic opposition to the national and global oppression of Muslims and identified with the plight of the Palestinians in the context of Israeli settler colonialism. They shared with other Uyghurs a feeling of victimhood created by domestic Chinese oppression, combined with an empathy for similarly 'oppressed' peoples in the Middle East. This found expression in a sense of global Islamic solidarity and the visible demonstration of opposition through the symbolic vehicle of Islamic practice (Smith Finley 2007). Others saw it as a response to failed development, with state economic projects having failed to bring equal benefit to Uyghurs, and desired to return to the social egalitarianism promoted by the Islamic faith (and previously experienced under Mao). Still others considered it a response to the frustrated ethno-political aspirations of the 1990s – a route for spatial and psychological escapism from Han Chinese domination. A fourth group described it as a reaction against forces of modernity (channelled to Xinjiang via Chinese development) and a return to cultural 'purity' – a process also documented by Maris Boyd Gillette (2002) in her study of Islamic revival among Hui Muslims in Xi'an.

But perhaps the most important theme to emerge was the notion of Islam as a vehicle for personal and national reform – a route to salvation at both the individual level (saving the self) and the group level (saving the Uyghur nation). Here, respondents identified their former religious laxity as the reason for the political plight of their ethnic group; 'harm' done on a personal level became intimately entwined with harm done at the national level (Smith Finley 2013: 281–4; see also Harris and Isa 2019: 71–2). This process is reminiscent of the reaction of some Arabs to their defeat in the 1967 Six Day War with Israel, who concluded that they were 'inadequate believers who had not lived up to the ideals of Islam and therefore deserved their fate [. . .] Muslims needed to be better Muslims [. . .] if God was to spare them further calamity' (Piscatori 1986: 26). Empirical data gathered in Xinjiang in the 2000s thus strongly suggested that, for many Uyghurs, Islam was not the root cause of disaffection in an ideological sense, but rather a response. Islam, as a symbol of resistance against perceived Muslim oppression (at domestic and global levels), as an egalitarian ethos, as a pure and moral religio-cultural system, as a spatial and psychological outlet, and as a path to personal and group redemption was providing respite from a host of pre-existing political, cultural (inter-ethnic) and socio-economic disaffections linked to failed state policies.

'Tipping Points'

If the crackdown following the 1997 Ghulja demonstration was a 'turning point' in the sense of an 'ethno-political anti-climax' for Uyghur male youths aspiring to national independence (Smith 2000) and an acceleration of the Islamic revival that had begun to spread across Uyghur society, 2001 was a definite 'tipping point'. Following the Twin Towers incident, Chinese authorities saw the perfect opportunity to subscribe to the US-led 'Global War on Terror' (GWoT) discourse, which it subsequently used to justify its own introduction of 'counter-terror' measures in Xinjiang (Roberts 2020; Clark 2018; Rodriguéz-Merino 2019). The Chinese state's incitement of Han nationalism against an internal 'Other' – the alleged threat of Uyghur Islamic extremism – created a 'fear factor', damaging both Uyghur-state and Uyghur-Han inter-group trust and 'hardening boundaries' (Kanat 2016; Clarke 2015; Tobin 2020). State agents now increasingly employed preventative or pre-emptive methods of control, while continuing to deploy disproportionate force when reacting to events it now classified as 'terrorist' (formerly, 'counter-revolutionary' or 'splittist' – the Chinese designation for 'separatist') (Clarke 2010: 547–50). Following 9/11, around 3,000 Uyghurs were detained on separatism charges, in a context where very little violence had occurred in the region since the 1997 Ghulja demonstration and none would until the occasion of the 2008 Beijing Olympics (Millward 2009). Pre-emptive policing treated all suspected separatists as potential 'terrorists' and led, for instance, to annual police round-ups of Uyghur youths on the anniversary of the 1997 Ghulja disturbances (Vicziany 2003: 252), as well as to the detention and relocation of all Uyghur and Tibetan residents of Beijing and Shanghai prior to the 2008 Olympic games (Millward 2009: 349; Roberts 2018: 10). As one scholar observed, in the post-2001 period, the Chinese state has tended to 'overreact and to see terrorism even where it does not exist [. . .] if the police or other state organs see manifestations of Uighur culture and Islam that look as if they could be potentially terrorist, they are apt [to] tread on them unnecessarily' (Mackerras 2014: 248). When, in 2004, the state's crackdown on 'illegal religious activities' was joined by a move to phase out Uyghur-medium education, it was clear that Beijing had turned both Uyghur Islam and the Uyghur language into national security threats. In doing so, it evidently hoped to reduce inter-ethnic tensions by limiting religious practice and weakening Uyghur identity – seen as 'unpatriotic' and a threat to the territorial integrity of the motherland (Meyer 2016: 4–5). From the Uyghurs' viewpoint, however, repression of the mother tongue, Uyghur-medium education and Uyghur Islam was experienced as a direct threat to the group's sense of 'societal security' (Waever et al. 1993) – indeed, to the very survival of the Uyghur nation.

The second 'tipping point' came in 2009, the year of the initially peaceful Ürümchi protest against the state's handling of the murder of Uyghur migrant workers in a factory in Shaoguan, Guangdong province (Millward 2009). After the protest organisers had been arrested and removed and the remaining protestors had met rough handling by state security forces, the protest descended into violence, leaving almost 200 people dead, of whom a majority were Han Chinese. The breakdown of trust between Uyghurs and Han, precipitated by post-2001 state discourses that stereotyped and excluded Uyghurs as Islamic 'terrorists', was clearly visible during the Ürümchi riots. There were harrowing scenes in which angry young Uyghur men attacked Han civilians, including men, children and even pregnant women (Palmer 2013). Uyghur households refused safe haven to Han neighbours; Uyghur doctors refused to treat Han patients; and *vice versa* (Smith Finley 2011). The violence flagged a re-orientation along ethnic lines, in response to ethnically differentiated policies (Thum 2009). Moreover, the disproportionate state force wielded both during and following the riots dealt a final blow to relations between Uyghurs and Han, and between Uyghurs and the state. As a retired Uyghur state employee reflected to me in 2016: 'Well, we all know that the government is working only for them [Hans] – that was made very clear during and after 7.5 [5 July 2009]'. She and others confirmed reports of a rush among Uyghurs to move out of Han districts of the city, and *vice versa*, in the months following the event (Smith Finley 2019a).

Accelerated Securitising Practices since 2009

In the wake of the 2009 Ürümchi riots, the Chinese state introduced reforms that allowed for the unrestricted local use of force without central permission (Odgaard and Nielsen 2014: 542–3; 545). This period saw the systematic securitisation and exclusion of *all* Uyghurs, without exception, leading to unanimous dissatisfaction within the Uyghur community towards the state (Tohti 2014; Roberts 2018). Uyghur travellers to inner China now found it nearly impossible to find accommodation and were forced to rely on 'no-show motels', illicit hostelries, or kinship and friendship networks: 'We can't stay anywhere but with our own' (Palmer 2013; see also Rollet 2019). From around 2012, the Chinese state increasingly moved to outlaw mundane, everyday Islamic practices, apparently on the basis that Islamic piety is in itself 'extremist'; the move recalled China's '20 lost years' (Maoist period, late 1950s – late 1970s) when 'attacks directed against the politicisation of Islam [. . .] gave way to the critique of Islam itself' (Castets 2015a: 230). Bans were levied on beards, veils and Islamic names for newborn children. Students who had studied religion abroad without permission could no longer have their diplomas recognized in Xinjiang. Imams were frequently harassed. These were all actions that 'tend to pour oil on the fire' (Castets 2015a: 241; 243–4). Most damaging of all was the introduction of highly intrusive religious policing, according to a new state maxim: 'One village, one police station; one household, one police officer' (Zenz and Leibold 2017). From 2012 onwards, a new army of assistant police were routinely used in large-scale sweep and search operations in rural homes, a practice experienced as highly invasive by locals. Uyghur economics professor Ilham Tohti, currently serving a life sentence on alleged 'separatism' charges, had this to say on the strategy shortly before his arrest in 2014:

> Personnel making visits to the villages and households include cadres, unemployed people whom the government hires, even some young ruffians, people on government subsidies, police officers, special weapons and tactics (SWAT) officers, and so on. I absolutely could not put up with people like this randomly breaking into my house. (Tohti 2014)

In 2014, under the auspices of a 'People's War on Terror', the state spent USD 2 million establishing a network of informers and surveillance cameras in the southern oasis of Yäkän (Yarkand) so as to facilitate house-to-house searches for books or clothing that betrayed 'conservative' religious beliefs and the identification of 'separatists, terrorists and religious extremists'. This category now included women in veils or burqas and young men with long beards (Denyer 2014).

Violence in Southern Xinjiang, 2012–15

Not coincidentally, a wave of retaliatory and mostly spontaneous violent incidents rocked Xinjiang between 2012 and 2015, particularly in those southern oases worst affected by intrusive religious policing. These incidents were rarely premeditated,[7] and few were consistent with globally accepted definitions of 'terror' (Roberts 2018; Smith Finley 2019a). Rather, they were impromptu protests at perceived incidences of state violence, whether economic (land seizures, see Byler 2018b) or religio-cultural (unjust arrest of religious students; a family's defence against state intrusion into their home and violation of the Islamic female modesty code known as *purdah*, or, in Uyghur, *namähräm*). One example of state violence in this context is the 2012 police raid on an 'unsanctioned' religious school in Khotän to 'flush out

---

[7] There were notable exceptions, e. g., the 2014 Maralbeshi market incident (Hoshur 2014) and the 2015 Sogan Colliery attack in Aqsu prefecture (Hoshur and Lipes 2015), both of which appear to have been premeditated, pre-planned attacks on Han Chinese civilians. These were apparently motivated by local anger about Han in-migration and related resource and labour competition.

illegal preachers', which resulted in the death of an eleven-year-old boy and the hospitalisation of twelve other children with severe burns (Musha and Gao 2012). A second example is the pre-emptive police shooting of twenty-two alleged Islamic 'terrorists' in Qarghiliq in 2013, when a group of men believed to have 'worked on a farm during the day and prayed at night' were surrounded and killed (Hoshur 2013c). Examples of angry retaliations to state violence include:

- The 2013 Lukqun attack on police/government establishments in Turpan prefecture, resulting in more than forty-six deaths – a response to the imprisonment of nineteen local Uyghurs for alleged crimes linked to 'religious extremism' (Hoshur 2013a)
- The 2013 murder of Abdurehim Damolla, imam at the Kazihan Mosque, Turpan – the imam had angered the local community by calling the Lukqun attackers (above) 'terrorists' in an echo of state discourse, failing to acknowledge their frustrations at unfounded allegations of 'religious extremism'; he had earlier advocated government policy discouraging the wearing of religious beards and headscarves (Hoshur 2013b)
- The 2013 Ayköl incident, when a crowd attempted to de-arrest Uyghurs being detained outside a mosque during Eid al-Fitr (the end of Ramadan) in Aqsu prefecture – security forces opened fire on the crowd (Hoshur 2013b)
- The 2013 Seriqbuya incident – in which police and so-called 'community workers' broke into an Uyghur home, forced the Uyghur women inside to unveil and demanded the menfolk shave off their beards – resulted in several deaths and the burning down of the house (Hoshur, Qiao and Hai 2013)[8]
- The 2013 Hanerik protest march against the detention of Mettursun Metseydi, imam of an unauthorised mosque, who had drawn large crowds by condemning the government's religious restrictions[9] as 'a humiliation' – paramilitary police stationed on an overpass opened fire on the marchers, some of whom were armed with makeshift weapons, leaving sixty dead (Jacobs 2013)
- The 2014 protest outside a government building in Kucha over the arrest of two dozen girls and women who had refused to remove their headscarves – at least two protestors were killed (Denyer 2014)

---

[8] While the state later reported that said community workers had stumbled across terrorists making explosives and 'lethal weapons', earlier Chinese media accounts had stated that the occupants were undertaking lessons in reading the Qur'an when state agents made entry (Grammaticas 2013).

[9] The restrictions included fines for taxi drivers who carried veiled passengers; a prohibition on doctors treating veiled women; and a requirement to remove veils during police checks.

- The 2014 attack on a police station in Elishqu, Yäkän, in response to restrictions imposed during Ramadan and the extra-judicial police killing of an Uyghur family of five, following forced entry into their home and an attempt to remove the women's veils – fifty-nine protestors were shot dead, initially (Hoshur, Sulaiman and Yang 2014)[10]

All these incidents have two things in common: firstly, local people's shared indignation and anger at what they experienced as over-zealous state restrictions on ordinary, everyday Islamic practices and invasive policing considered to violate the privacy of their homes and the honour of their womenfolk. As Alim Adurshit, Security Chairman at No. 14 village, observed in response to the 2014 Yäkän attack: 'There has been a lot of pent up frustration over house-to-house searches and checking on headscarves during this Ramadan' (Hoshur, Sulaiman and Yang 2014). Secondly, all incidents were handled with disproportionate and lethal state force. Local statements given to the press following the 2013 Hanerik protest march indicate the level of rage provoked by this use of force. As one Uyghur professor described it, 'People here are just boiling over with anger', while a taxi driver declared: 'The Chinese killed our brothers in the street like they were dogs [. . .] we will have our revenge' (Jacobs 2013).

Local Responses to the State Securitisation of Islam

In interviews conducted in the regional capital Ürümchi in 2016, my long-term, urban-based respondents expressed a range of reactions to heightened securitisation practices. When asked whether state discourses on religious extremism and state practices of security were justified, the consensus was that, while a tiny minority of Uyghurs may have succumbed to radical ideas, most deplored violent methods. R2, a retired state employee, and S, an intellectual, observed that what they (as nominal rather than pious Muslims) called 'wrong-headed forms of Islam' had come in from Saudi Arabia, while two professionals, A and H, expressed similar concerns that some southerners had recently adopted 'extreme behaviours', such as refusing to walk on asphalt roads built by 'unclean' Han Chinese labourers. At the same time, all emphasised that 'such behaviour [a desire to self-segregate] does not make those people terrorists'. While they said that they 'support state efforts to stamp out [genuinely] extremist ideas' (this pertaining to the period prior to the current phase of 'de-extremification' and mass internment), R2 noted with evident sympathy: 'Some Uyghur sheep have been forced by circumstance to turn into tigers'. This development was also mentioned by a Uyghur public security officer, R, who confirmed that (in 2016) a small

---

[10] Uyghur exiles now refer to this incident as the Yarkand Massacre of 2014 and estimate that between 1,000 and 3,000 Uyghurs were killed by security forces in the days that followed (Hoshur 2014a; Tohti Arish 2019).

number of exiled Uyghurs were fighting alongside jihadis in Syria. However, R was keen to underline that those individuals were 'not ideologically committed to holy war; it is simply a means to a local, political end – those men will return to free Xinjiang'.

Responses to heightened securitisation included fear, humiliation, exhaustion, paranoia, (black) humour and anger. R2 complained that the all-pervasive surveillance of Uyghurs tarred them with the same brush as alleged 'extremists', claiming fearfully: 'There are eyes and ears everywhere'. Z, who now worked as a security guard (increasingly the only tenable employment option for Uyghur men of a certain age), spoke of the deep humiliation that he felt when obliged to conduct bag and body checks on Uyghur residents, and how he would tell them: 'Please forgive me'. Uyghur public security officer, R, described his exhaustion at the impact of securitisation practices on his profession: 'There's only one kind of police in Xinjiang now – political police (in Uyghur, *siyasiy saqchi)'*. Since 2009, he explained, 'everything is checked, everywhere, at all times'; he even disclosed how the police role is itself securitised, with no public security personnel permitted to travel abroad for fear that they might pass sensitive information on to foreigners. R2, meanwhile, described the sense of paranoia that had taken grip of the Uyghur community: 'No one trusts anyone. Everyone is scared and looking out for their families. No one wants any trouble. It is always better to have one less issue than one more (in Chinese, *duo yishi buru shao yishi)'*. She expressed the sheer relief she had felt after retiring from her state work unit: 'Now, I never have to worry about politics again!' Paranoia was also clearly visible in A's behaviour. This professional, having enthused rather artificially about government policies as we chatted in a public restaurant and then in her home during our first meeting, drove me far out of Ürümchi into the mountains for the second; only then did she feel safe enough to speak directly: 'I have much in my heart I want to say, but I can't say any of it. Well, I can say it, but no one must hear it. If the [government's] policies are fine, then why am I afraid of speaking?' She and others coped with the constant paranoia by employing black humour. As we walked in the mountainous outskirts of the city, A joked about how 'unsafe' she felt in the absence of security forces, then pointed to two golden inflatable lions set before a real estate office and declared: 'We have these to protect us here . . . and I like these better!' She then told of a female friend's darkly humorous retort to the news that local authorities planned to install CCTV cameras above the front door of every home: 'Well, they'd better not put one in the bedroom!' Perhaps most concerning was the sense of anger among current and former state employees (in Uyghur, *khizmätchilär*), who speak fluent Chinese and are ostensibly among the structurally most integrated of citizens. In a conversation between two retired state employees, R2 warned Q that she had better not consider visiting Kashgar with me – a foreign visitor – at that time, as she would be likely to fall under suspicion. Q, however, reacted with righteous indignation:

Why on earth *shouldn't* we show the south to our English friend? What's wrong with that? We won't hurt anyone! And if anyone says we can't, then damn his mother!' [in Chinese, 去他妈的 Qu ta ma de] Fine! Take the bad ones [in Uyghur, *äskilär*] away, we agree with that! But we are not all bad. Every people has good and bad individuals. Why can't they just treat the bad ones with suspicion and leave the rest of us alone?

As the above responses demonstrate, by 2016, the Chinese state's ethnicised security practices had ended up alienating even its most trusted cohort of Chinese-speaking Uyghurs attached to state organs.

Religious Securitisation and Cycles of Violence

In Xinjiang, there is a dynamic relationship between state tolerance (or repression) of religion and waves of Islamic revival and religious defence – a dynamic seen across the entire Muslim world. At least one version of events holds that the Baren incident of 1990 was a local protest against official restrictions on religious activities, while it is generally agreed that the Ghulja 1997 demonstration was a response to the state's criminalisation of religious studies held in unofficial fora. After 1997, the state accelerated its crackdown on religion such that, in the opinion of Uyghur exile activist Erkin Alptekin,[11] Uyghurs were forced to become separatists despite their natural inclination to avoid violence (their self-ascribed proclivity to behave like docile 'sheep'). In the early 2000s, Rudelson and Jankowiak noted the negative effects of repressive religious policy on Uyghur attitudes towards the state, particularly in the south of the region:

> Anti-Han sentiment is far stronger in Kashgar than elsewhere, mainly in response to the government's own efforts to curtail Islamic practices there. Instead of seeing Islam as a channel through which local Uyghurs are able to express social and political frustrations [. . .] the government chooses to perceive it as the cause of those frustrations, which in turn gives rise to actions that further exacerbate the situation. (2004: 316)

Discontent grew throughout the 2000s, as the state appropriated the GWoT discourse in order to re-characterise Uyghurs as potential Islamist terrorists, and exploded during the 2009 Ürümchi riots, when the state failed to justly handle the murder of Uyghur migrant workers by Han Chinese co-workers in Shaoguan. However, instead of addressing the root cause of the protest-turned-riot, the government chose to increase religious repression further, introducing intrusive religious policing from 2012 and launching the 'People's War on Terror' in 2014 – a campaign that fully outlawed

---

[11] Son of Isa Yusuf Alptekin, General Secretary of the National Assembly of the Turkish Islamic Republic of East Turkestan (TIRET) in Kashgar, 1933–4.

everyday Islamic practice. It was in this context that Ilham Tohti, Uyghur economist – and bridge between the Uyghur ethnic group and the Chinese government – observed: 'Every time something happens, the government responds with one word: pressure. High pressure, high pressure, and even greater pressure. This leads to greater resistance and more conflict' (cited in Meyer 2016). Tohti was not alone in doubting the state's hardline approach; some Xinjiang Han were also unconvinced. A Han doctor in Qarghiliq county, commenting on an incident in 2012 where nine Uyghurs stabbed to death ten Han Chinese and injured five others before being shot dead by police, explained:

> I think the sense of dissatisfaction and resistance is a direct result of the govern-ment enforcing a high-pressure policy on Uyghur people [. . .] I have a very good relationship with my Uyghur colleagues at the hospital [. . .] I don't want to see this kind [of] thing happen, but I also don't want to see excessive controls on the local Uyghur people [. . .] If the [harsh] policy continues, there will be more of this kind of thing in the future. (Hoshur and Abdilim 2012)

The Han doctor's prediction was correct, and local violence peaked during the period between 2012 and 2015.

Conclusions

The Chinese state's successive decisions to progressively crack down on 'illegal religious activities' throughout the 1990s, to adopt an Islamophobic GWoT discourse after 2001 (during a period of comparative peace) and to make war on everyday Islamic practice more broadly since 2009 has achieved an effect opposite to what the CCP claimed to seek. Far from maintaining regional stability, state securitisation of religion strengthened an Islamic revival already underway in the context of Open-Door econom-ics and increased human mobility and global flows, heightened societal insecurity in both Uyghur and Han communities and stoked inter-ethnic conflict to the greatest degree seen in Xinjiang since 1949. It was this dynamic of religious repression – and religious defence – that led to the cycles of violence observed in Xinjiang between 2012 and 2015. Socio-economic inequalities between local people and incoming Han settlers were already a factor in regional unrest. Chinese state patronage of the Xinjiang Han is of long standing (Cliff 2015) and, as detailed above, had already given rise to peaceful calls for ethnic equality by the start of the 1980s. Yet, comparative research on the causes of Muslim rebellion worldwide demonstrates that, while socio-economic inequalities often provide the structural conditions for rebellion, they are generally insufficient on their own to engender militant action. Rather, Muslims across national contexts become violently militant when they are (a) denied meaningful access to state political institutions; and (b) faced with indiscriminate repressive state policies (Hafez 2003: 9–19). In particular, religious repression and discrimination by a majoritarian state (those in power) against a minority (the powerless), in a context where the majority culture is protected, creates an antagonistic and divisive atmosphere, leading to the formation of grievances and movements of religious defence (Akbaba and Taydas 2011: 274–7). This has also been the case in Xinjiang.

The Chinese state seized on the cycles of violence between 2012 and 2015 and since April 2017 has used them to justify its assertion that Uyghur society must be 'de-extremified'. It has set out to do this via a campaign of mass internment for political 're-education', formal incarceration, forced labour and a concomitant project to raze Uyghur mosques and shrines – uprooting Uyghur culture and breaking their connection to the land (Thum, cited in Kuo 2019; Thum 2020; Ruser, Leibold, Munro and Hoja 2020). Looking at the current scenario in Xinjiang, it is hard not to conclude that the Chinese state has manoeuvred itself into an impossible corner: where can the state go from here? Official discourses reveal chilling metaphors about 'eradicating the virus' of Islam (Human Rights Watch 2018), spraying chemicals to 'kill all the weeds' (Special Correspondent 2018) and conducting a 'thought liberation movement' (Yi Mu 2018). But how is it possible to eradicate a person's inner identity, culture and faith? All the indications are rather that this programme could radicalise internees and turn them into extremists. As one Han 'relative' recruited to the cadre homestay programme that identifies individuals for internment confided to anthropologist Darren Byler: 'I don't know what will happen if we ever let the Uyghurs out . . . ' (2018b: 9–10). This is a valid concern: one potential outcome of internment is a further escalation of local grievances and the resumption of violence once inmates have the renewed freedom and ability to perpetrate that violence (see also Roberts 2020). Some anecdotal evidence already exists in support of this possibility. One of the few detainees released from the camps, Omurbek Eli, told journalists that Chinese authorities 'are planting the seeds of hatred and turning [detainees] into enemies. This is not just my view – the majority of people in the camp feel the same way' (*The Economist* 2018). The BBC's China Editor wrote similarly that former camp inmates interviewed by his team were all 'burning with resentment' (Sudworth 2018). Outside the camps, meanwhile, the pervasive security presence may have smothered dissent, but 'many quietly seethe at the daily indignities of racial profiling' (Feng 2018). An Uyghur exile in Turkey, whose mother and extended family in Xinjiang were prevented from attending her wedding after Chinese authorities refused them passports, told the press: 'Don't misunderstand me, I don't support suicide bombers or anyone who attacks innocent people [. . .] But in that moment [. . .] I was so pissed off that I could understand how those people could feel that way' (Rajagopalan 2017).

As things stand now, China's treatment of the Uyghurs – both in and outside of the camps – has progressed beyond Stage 3 (Discrimination) on

Allport's 'Ladder of Prejudice' to reach Stage 4 (Physical Attack). Indeed, by the UN's (1948) definition, it meets all five criteria for the crime of genocide (Klimeš and Smith Finley 2020). It did not have to be this way. Xinjiang has known two periods of relative peace under CCP rule: the 1950s – the early years – when state nationality policies were progressive and included public rejection of 'Great Han chauvinism' (attitudes of Han superiority), respect for local religious practices and the provision of mother-tongue education for Uyghurs; and the 1980s, when religion resurfaced after the ravages of the Cultural Revolution, and Uyghurs enthusiastically participated in the rebuilding of their mosques during the 'golden period' of Deng Xiaoping's conciliatory minority policies. But it is hard to imagine how a return to comparatively relaxed ethnic relations could be possible in the aftermath of mass internment. It would require an official acknowledgement that current policies of securitisation have failed, as well as a commitment to some sort of reconciliation process, perhaps like the one established by South Africa's Government of National Unity to deal with abuses that occurred under Apartheid. There will be a significant level of social and psychological damage to repair in Turkic communities, which perhaps can only be done by studying the patterns, causes and consequences of state violence since 2009. As Priscilla Hayner writes in her seminal work on truth commissions,[12] state terror and abuse leave behind a powerful legacy:

> Where there was torture, there are walking, wounded victims. Where there were killings [. . .] there are often witnesses to the carnage, and family members too terrified to fully grieve. Where there were persons disappeared [. . .] there are loved ones desperate for information. Where there were years of unspoken pain and enforced silence, there are often a pervasive, debilitating fear and, when the repression ends, a need to slowly learn to trust the government, the police, and armed forces . . . (2002: 4)

Truth commissions, as a form of transitional justice, can in addition to establishing the truth also lead to governments taking actions to repair or address damages, or to promote national reconciliation and conflict resolution. Examples include lustration, the process that removes persons from public employment based on their affiliation with the prior abusive regime (as in Eastern Europe); the purging from security forces of individuals with a record of human rights abuses (El Salvador); granting access to former state security files (Eastern Europe); repairing the financial and psychological damage done to victims and communities; and, perhaps most importantly, making institutional or policy changes to prevent further abuses in the future (Hayner 2002: 11–14).

---

[12] Hayner (2002) considers in detail the five most significant truth commissions to date, those held in Argentina, Chile, El Salvador, South Africa and Guatemala, as well as a further sixteen commissions elsewhere.

However, truth commissions are always officially sanctioned and empowered by the state and have usually only taken place where a state was in political transition, for example, from authoritarian to democratic rule. Their key function is to investigate politically motivated or politically targeted repression used to maintain or obtain power and weaken political opponents (Hayner 2002: 17). As Goodhart notes, authoritarian rulers have long insisted that human rights do not appeal to people outside of 'the West' because rights are incompatible with their values or cultures (Goodhart 2018: 412). China is no exception, having designed its own concept of 'human rights with Chinese characteristics' in 2011. Given the increasingly authoritarian nature of Chinese rule in general, and its settler-colonial policies and practices in Xinjiang in particular, there is currently little likelihood that the CCP will countenance such a move, even assuming it does decide to slowly dismantle the re-education camps, release prisoners and decommission forced labour.

References

101 East (2019), *Uighurs: Nowhere to Call Home*, Documentary film, https://www.alja-zeera.com/programmes/101east/2019/01/uighurs-call-home-190131085421513.html (accessed 6 May 2021).

Akbaba, Y. and Taydas, Z. (2011), 'Does Religious Discrimination Promote Dissent? A Quantitative Analysis', *Ethnopolitics* 10(3/4): 271–95.

Al Jazeera (2018), 'Academics Condemn China over Xinjiang Camps, Urge Sanctions', 27 November 2018, https://www.aljazeera.com/news/2018/11/academics-con-demn-china-xinjiang-camps-urge-sanctions-181127015605193.html (accessed 6 May 2021).

Associated Press, 'China Cuts Uighur Births with IUDs, Abortion, Sterilization', 29 June 2020, https://apnews.com/269b3de1af34e17c1941a514f78d764c (accessed 6 May 2021).

Beckley, N. (1997), 'China's Muslims Sharpen their Knives against Peking', *The Independent*, 5 March 1997.

Bellér-Hann, I. (2002), 'Temperamental Neighbours: Uighur-Han Relations in Xinjiang, Northwest China', in Günther Schlee (ed.), *Imagined Differences: Hatred and the Construction of Identity*, 57–81. Hamburg: Lit Verlag.

Bunin, G. A. (2019), 'From Camps to Prisons: Xinjiang's Next Great Human Rights Catastrophe', *Living Otherwise*, 5 October 2019, https://livingotherwise.com/2019/10/05/from-camps-to-prisons-xinjiangs-next-great-human-rights-ca-tastrophe-by-gene-a-bunin/ (accessed 6 May 2021).

Burdorf, H. (2020), 'A Police State Going into Hiding', *Living Otherwise*, 31 January 2020, https://livingotherwise.com/2020/01/31/a-police-state-going-into-hiding/ (accessed 6 May 2021).

Byler, D. (2018a), '"As If You've Spent Your Whole Life in Prison": Starving and Subdued in Xinjiang Detention Centers', *SupChina*, 5 December 2018, https://supchina.com/2018/12/05/starving-and-subdued-in-xinjiang-detention-centers/ (accessed 6 May 2021).

Byler, D. (2018b), 'Violent Paternalism: On the Banality of Uyghur Unfreedom', *The Asia-Pacific Journal* 16(24:4), 15 December 2018.

Byler, D. (2019), 'How Companies Profit from Forced Labor in Xinjiang', *SupChina*, 4 September 2019, https://supchina.com/2019/09/04/how-companies-profit-from-forced-labor-in-xinjiang/ (accessed 6 May 2021).

Castets, R. (2015a), 'The Modern Chinese State and Strategies of Control over Uyghur Islam', *Central Asian Affairs* 2(3): 221–45.

Castets, R. (2015b), 'La Chine face au terrorisme islamiste' [China Faces Islamist Terrorism], *Questions internationales* 75: 105–9.

Catris, S. E. (2018), 'A New Cultural Revolution?' Paper presented to the Symposium on China's Mass Incarceration of Uyghurs, George Washington University, 27 November 2018.

Chao, S. (2019), 'Exposed: China's Surveillance of Muslim Uighurs', *Al Jazeera*, 1 February 2019, https://www.aljazeera.com/blogs/asia/2019/01/exposed-china-surveillance-muslim-uighurs-190130011449217.html (accessed 6 May 2021).

ChinaAid (2018), '20 Prisoners Mentally Break Down in Chinese Detention Camp', 5 April 2018, https://www.chinaaid.org/2018/04/20-prisoners-mentally-break-down-in.html (accessed 6 May 2021).

Clarke, M. (2010), 'Widening the Net: China's Anti-Terror Laws and Human Rights in the Xinjiang Uyghur Autonomous Region', *The International Journal of Human Rights* 14(4): 542–58.

Clarke, M. (2015), 'China and the Uyghurs: The "Palestinization" of Xinjiang?' *Middle East Policy* 22(3): 127–46.

Clarke, M. (2018), 'China's "War on Terrorism": Confronting the Dilemmas of the "Internal-External" Security Nexus', in Michael Clarke (ed.), *Terrorism and Counter-Terrorism in China: Domestic and Foreign Policy Dimensions*, 17–38. Oxford: Oxford University Press.

Clarke, M. (2020) 'Beijing's Pivot West: The Convergence of *Innenpolitik* and *Aussenpolitik* on China's "Belt and Road"?' *Journal of Contemporary China* 29(123): 336–53.

Cliff, T. (2016), *Oil and Water: Being Han in Xinjiang*. Chicago: University of Chicago Press.

Denyer, S. (2014), 'China's War on Terror Becomes All-Out Attack on Islam in Xinjiang', *Washington Post*, 19 September 2014.

Denyer, S. (2018), 'Former Inmates of China's Muslim "Reeducation" Camps Tell of Brainwashing, Torture', *The Washington Post*, 16 May 2018.

Dillon, M. (1995), 'Xinjiang: Ethnicity, Separatism and Control in Chinese Central Asia', *Durham University East Asian Papers* No. 1.

Dooley, B. (2018), '"Eradicate the Tumours": Chinese Civilians Drive Xinjiang Crackdown', *AFP*, 26 April 2018, https://www.yahoo.com/news/eradicate-tumours-chinese-civilians-drive-xinjiang-crackdown-051356550.html (accessed 6 May 2021).

Dreyer, J. T. (1968), 'China's Minority Nationalities in the Cultural Revolution', *China Quarterly* 35: 96–109.

The Economist (2018), 'Apartheid with Chinese Characteristics: China Has Turned Xinjiang into a Police State Like No Other', 31 May 2018, https://www.economist.com/briefing/2018/05/31/china-has-turned-xinjiang-into-a-police-state-like-no-other (accessed 6 May 2021).

Famularo, J. (2018), '"Fighting the Enemy with Fists and Daggers": The Chinese Communist Party's Counter-Terrorism Policy in the Xinjiang Uyghur Autonomous Region', in Michael Clark (ed.), *Terrorism and Counter-Terrorism in China: Domestic and Foreign Policy Dimensions*, 39–73. Oxford: Oxford University Press.

Feng, E. (2018), 'Crackdown in Xinjiang: Where Have All the People Gone?' *Financial Times*, 5 August 2018, https://www.ft.com/content/ac0ffb2e-8b36-11e8-b18d-0181731a0340 (accessed 6 May 2021).

Gillette, M. B. (2000), *Between Mecca and Beijing: Modernization and Consumption among Urban Chinese Muslims*. Cambridge: Cambridge University Press.

Gladney, D. C. (2002), 'Xinjiang: China's Future West Bank?' *Current History* 101(656): 267–71.

Goodhart, M. (2018), 'Constructing Dignity: Human Rights as a Praxis of Egalitarian Freedom', *Journal of Human Rights* 17(4): 403–17.

Grammaticas, D. (2013), 'Doubts over China Government Claims on Xinjiang Attack', *BBC News*, 26 April 2013, http://www.bbc.co.uk/news/world-asia-china-22319579 (accessed 6 May 2021).

Hafez, M. M. (2003), *Why Muslims Rebel: Repression and Resistance in the Islamic World*. Boulder: Lynne Rienner.

Harris, R. and Isa, A. (2019), 'Islam by Smartphone: Reading the Uyghur Islamic Revival on WeChat', *Central Asian Survey* 38(1): 61–80.

Harris, R. (2020), *Soundscapes of Uyghur Islam*. Bloomington: Indiana University Press.

Hayner, P. B. (2002), *Unspeakable Truths: Confronting State Terror and Atrocity*. London: Routledge.

Hoshur, S. and Abdilim, M. (2012), 'Immigration Tensions Led to Attack: Anger over Fewer Opportunities May Have Driven Uyghurs to Go on a Killing Spree', *Radio Free Asia*, 29 February 2012, http://www.rfa.org/english/news/uyghur/attack-02292012184547.html?searchterm=None (accessed 6 May 2021).

Hoshur, S. (2013a), 'Xinjiang Violence More Serious Than Reported', *Radio Free Asia*, 27 June 2013, http://www.rfa.org/english/news/uyghur/violence-06272013230950.html (accessed 6 May 2021).

Hoshur, S. (2013b), 'Imam Stabbed to Death After Supporting Crackdown Against Uyghurs', *Radio Free Asia*, 16 August 2013, http://www.rfa.org/english/news/uyghur/imam-08162013200309.html (accessed 6 May 2021).

Hoshur, S. (2013c), 'Death Toll in Xinjiang Police Shootout Climbs as Exile Group Blasts Raid', *Radio Free Asia*, 27 August 2013, http://www.rfa.org/english/news/uyghur/crackdown-08272013212441.html (accessed 6 May 2021).

Hoshur, S. (2014a) '"At Least 2,000 Uyghurs Killed" in Yarkand Violence: Exile Leader', *Radio Free Asia*, 5 August 2014, https://www.rfa.org/english/news/uyghur/yarkand-08052014150547.html (accessed 6 May 2021).

Hoshur, S. (2014), '22 Killed in Farmers' Market Attack in Xinjiang's Kashgar Prefecture', *Radio Free Asia*, 18 October 2014, http://www.rfa.org/english/news/uyghur/attack-10182014194433.html (accessed 6 May 2021).

Hoshur, S., Long, Q. and Nan, H. (2013), 'Xinjiang Violence Leaves 21 Dead', *Radio Free Asia*, 24 April 2013, http://www.rfa.org/english/news/uyghur/maralbeshi-04242013190839.html (accessed 6 May 2021).

Hoshur, S., Sulaiman E. and Yang F. (2014), 'Dozens of Uyghurs Shot Dead in Riots in Xinjiang's Yarkand County', *Radio Free Asia*, 29 July 2014, http://www.rfa.org/english/news/uyghur/reports-07292014102851.html (accessed 6 May 2021).

Hoshur, S. and Lipes, J. (2015), 'Death Toll in Xinjiang Coal Mine Attack Climbs to 50', *Radio Free Asia*, 30 September 2015, http://www.rfa.org/english/news/uyghur/attack-09302015174319.html (accessed 6 May 2021).

Human Rights Watch (2018), '"Eradicating Ideological Viruses": China's Campaign of

Repression Against Xinjiang's Muslims', September 2018, https://www.hrw.org/sites/default/files/report_pdf/china0918_web.pdf (accessed 6 May 2021).

Human Rights Watch (2019), 'China's Algorithms of Repression: Reverse Engineering a Xinjiang Police Mass Surveillance App', 1 May 2019, https://www.hrw.org/report/2019/05/01/chinas-algorithms-repression/reverse-engineering-xinjiang-police-mass-surveillance (accessed 6 May 2021).

Ingram, R. 'Confessions of a Xinjiang Camp Teacher', *The Diplomat*, 17 August 2020, https://thediplomat.com/2020/08/confessions-of-a-xinjiang-camp-teacher/ (accessed 6 May 2021).

Jacobs, A. (2013), 'Over News of Clash, A Shroud of Silence in Xinjiang', *New York Times*, 26 August 2013, https://www.nytimes.com/2013/08/27/world/asia/over-news-of-clash-a-shroud-of-silence-in-xinjiang.html (accessed 6 May 2021).

Kanat, K. B. (2016), 'The Securitization of the Uyghur Question and Its Challenges', *Insight Turkey* 18(1): 191–218, http://file.insightturkey.com/Files/Pdf/kanat-18-1-web.pdf (accessed 6 May 2021).

Klimeš, O. and Smith Finley, J. (2020) 'China's Neo-Totalitarian Turn and Genocide in Xinjiang', *Society and Space*, 7 December, https://www.societyandspace.org/articles/chinas-neo-totalitarian-turn-and-genocide-in-xinjiang.

Kuo, L. (2018), 'My Soul, Where Are You? Families of Muslims Missing in China Meet Wall of Silence', *The Guardian*, 13 September 2018.

Kuo, L. 2019, 'Revealed: New Evidence of China's Mission to Raze the Mosques of Xinjiang', *The Guardian*, 7 May 2019.

Li, W. (2019a), 'Eradicating Mosques Through . . . Merger', *Bitter Winter*, 9 May 2019, https://bitterwinter.org/eradicating-mosques-through-merger/ (accessed 6 May 2021).

Li, W. (2019b), 'Imam from Gansu: "The State Has Hurt Muslims' Feelings"', *Bitter Winter*, 20 May 2019, https://bitterwinter.org/imam-from-gansu-the-state-has-hurt-muslims-feelings/ (accessed 6 May 2021).

Mackerras, C. (2014), 'Xinjiang in 2013: Problems and Prospects', *Asian Ethnicity* 15(2): 247–50.

Meyer, P. K. (2016), 'China's De-Extremization of Uyghurs in Xinjiang', *New America International Security Program Policy Paper*, June 2016, https://www.newamerica.org/international-security/policy-papers/china-de-extremization-uyghurs-xinjiang/ (accessed 6 May 2021).

Millward, J. A. (2009), 'Introduction: Does the 2009 Urumchi Violence Mark a Turning Point?' *Central Asian Survey* 28(4): 347–60.

Murphy, L. T. and Elimä, N. (2021), 'In Broad Daylight: Uyghur Forced Labour and Global Solar Supply Chains.' https://www.shu.ac.uk/helena-kennedy-centre-international-justice/research-and-projects/all-projects/in-broad-daylight.

Musha, J. and Shan, G. (2012), 'Dozen Children Injured in Police Raid', *Radio Free Asia*, 6 June 2012, http://www.rfa.org/english/news/uyghur/raid-06062012173326.html (accessed 6 May 2021).

Odgaard, L. and Nielsen, T. G. (2014), 'China's Counterinsurgency Strategy in Tibet and Xinjiang', *Journal of Contemporary China* 23(87): 535–55.

Palmer, J. (2013), 'The Strangers: Blood and Fear in Xinjiang', *Chinafile*, 25 September 2013, http://www.chinafile.com/reporting-opinion/postcard/strangers (accessed 6 May 2021).

Piscatori, J. P. (1986), *Islam in a World of Nation-States*. Cambridge: Cambridge University Press.

Rajagopalan, M. (2017), 'This Is What A 21st-Century Police State Really Looks Like', *Buzzfeed*, 18 October 2017, https://www.buzzfeed.com/meghara/the-police-state-of-the-future-is-already-here?utm_term=.wvW1NkOQw#.td4om9yG2 (accessed 6 May 2021).

Reuters (2019), '1.5 Million Muslims Could Be Detained in China's Xinjiang: Academic', 13 March 2019, https://www.reuters.com/article/us-china-xinjiang-rights/15-million-muslims-could-be-detained-in-chinas-xinjiang-academic-idUSKCN1QU2MQ (accessed 6 May 2021).

Roberts, S. R. (2018), 'The Biopolitics of China's "War on Terror" and the Exclusion of the Uyghurs', *Critical Asian Studies* 50(2): 232–58.

Roberts, S. R. (2020), *The War on the Uyghurs: China's Internal Campaign Against a Muslim Minority*. Manchester: Manchester University Press.

Rodríguez-Merino, P. A. (2019), 'Old "Counter-Revolution", New "Terrorism": Historicizing the Framing of Violence in Xinjiang by the Chinese State', *Central Asian Survey* 38(1): 27–45.

Rollet, C. (2019), 'Airbnb Listings in China Are Littered with Racist Discrimination', *Wired*, 3 May 2019, https://www.wired.co.uk/article/airbnb-china-uyghur-muslim (accessed 6 May 2021).

Rudelson, J. and Jankowiak, W. (2004), 'Acculturation and Resistance: Xinjiang Identities in Flux', in Frederik Starr (ed.), *Xinjiang: China's Muslim Borderland*, 299–319. New York: M. E. Sharpe.

Ruser, N., Leibold, J., Munro, K. and Hoja, T. (2020) 'Cultural Erasure: Tracing the Destruction of Uyghur and Islamic Spaces in Xinjiang', Australian Strategic Policy Institute, 24 September, https://www.aspi.org.au/report/cultural-erasure.

Samuel, S. (2018), 'China Is Treating Islam Like a Mental Illness', *The Atlantic*, 28 August 2018, https://www.theatlantic.com/international/archive/2018/08/china-pathologizing-uighur-muslims-mental-illness/568525/ (accessed 6 May 2021).

Shepherd, C. and Pitel, L. (2020), 'The Karakax List: How China Targets Uighurs in Xinjiang', *Financial Times*, 17 February 2020, https://www.ft.com/content/e0224416-4e77-11ea-95a0-43d18ec715f5 (accessed 6 May 2021).

Shih, G. (2018), 'China's Mass Indoctrination Camps Evoke Cultural Revolution', *Associated Press*, 18 May 2018, https://apnews.com/6e151296fb194f85ba69a8babd972e4b (accessed 6 May 2021).

Smith, J. (2000), 'Four Generations of Uyghurs: The Shift towards Ethno-Political Ideologies among Xinjiang's Youth', *Inner Asia* 2(2): 195–224.

Smith Finley, J. (2007), 'Chinese Oppression in Xinjiang, Middle Eastern Conflicts and Global Islamic Solidarities among the Uyghurs', *Journal of Contemporary China* 16(53): 627–54.

Smith Finley, J. (2011), '"No Rights without Duties": *Minzu pingdeng* [Nationality Equality] in Xinjiang since the 1997 Ghulja Disturbances', *Inner Asia* 13: 73–96.

Smith Finley, J. (2013), *The Art of Symbolic Resistance: Uyghur Identities and Uyghur-Han Relations in Contemporary Xinjiang*. Leiden: Brill Academic Publishing.

Smith Finley, J. (2018), 'Now We Don't Talk Anymore: Inside the "Cleansing" of Xinjiang', *Chinafile*, 28 December 2018, http://www.chinafile.com/reporting-opinion/viewpoint/now-we-dont-talk-anymore (accessed 6 May 2021).

Smith Finley, J. (2019a), 'The Wang Lixiong Prophecy: "Palestinization" in Xinjiang and the Consequences of Chinese State Securitization of Religion', *Central Asian Survey* 38(1): 81–101.

Smith Finley, J. (2019b), 'Securitization, Insecurity and Conflict in Contemporary

Xinjiang: Has PRC Counter-Terrorism Evolved into State Terror?' *Central Asian Survey*, 38(1): 1–26.

Smith Finley, J. (2020), 'Why Scholars and Activists Increasingly Fear a Uyghur Genocide in Xinjiang', *Journal of Genocide Research*, https://doi.org/10.1080/146235 28.2020.1848109 (accessed 6 May 2021).

Special Correspondent (2018), 'A Summer Vacation in China's Muslim Gulag: How One University Student Was Almost Buried by the "People's War on Terror"', *Foreign Policy*, 28 February 2018, http://foreignpolicy.com/2018/02/28/a-summer-vaca tion-in-chinas-muslim-gulag/ (accessed 6 May 2021).

Steele, L. and Kuo, R. (2007), 'Terrorism in Xinjiang?' *Ethnopolitics* 6(1): 1–19.

Sudworth, J. (2018), 'China's Hidden Camps: What's Happened to the Vanished Uighurs of Xinjiang?' *BBC News*, 24 October 2018, https://www.bbc.co.uk/news/ resources/idt-sh/China_hidden_camps (accessed 6 May 2021).

Thum, R. (2009), 'The Ethnicization of Discontent in Xinjiang', 2 October 2009, *The China Beat Blog Archive 2008–2012*, 574, http://digitalcommons.unl.edu/chinabeat archive/574 (accessed 6 May 2021).

Thum, R. (2018), 'China's Mass Internment Camps Have No Clear End in Sight', *Foreign Policy*, 22 August 2018, https://foreignpolicy.com/2018/08/22/chinas-mass-internment-camps-have-no-clear-end-in-sight/ (accessed 6 May 2021).

Thum, R. (2020) 'The Spatial Cleansing of Xinjiang: Mazar Desecration in Context', *Made in China Journal*, 24 August, https://madeinchinajournal.com/2020/08/24/the-sp atial-cleansing-of-xinjiang-mazar-desecration-in-context/.

Tobin, D. (2020), *Securing China's Northwest Frontier: Identity and Insecurity in Xinjiang*. Cambridge: Cambridge University Press.

Tohti Arish, A. (2019), 'Yarkand Massacre: Another Painful Memory of Uighur People', 29 July 2019, https://uhrp.org/news-commentary/yarkand-massacre-another-painful-memory-uighur-people (accessed 6 May 2021).

Tohti, I. (2014), 'Ilham Tohti Says', *China Change*, 16 September 2014, https://china change.org/?s=ilham+tohti+says&submit (accessed 6 May 2021).

United Nations General Assembly (1948), *Universal Declaration of Human Rights*, https:// www.un.org/en/universal-declaration-human-rights/ (accessed 6 May 2021).

Uyghur Human Rights Project (2019), 'UPDATE – Detained and Disappeared: Intellectuals Under Assault in the Uyghur Homeland', 21 May 2019, https://uhrp. org/press-release/update-%E2%80%93-detained-and-disappeared-intellectuals-under-assault-uyghur-homeland.html (accessed 6 May 2021).

Vicziany, M. (2003), 'State Responses to Islamic Terrorism in Western China and Their Impact on South Asia', *Contemporary South Asia* 12(2): 243–62.

Xinjiang Uyghur Autonomous Region (2017), 'XUAR Regulations on De-Extremification', 30 March 2017, http://www.chinalawtranslate.com (accessed 6 May 2021).

Xu, V. X., Cave, D., Leibold, J., Munro, K. and Ruser, N. (2020), 'Uyghurs for Sale: "Re-education," Forced Labour and Surveillance Beyond Xinjiang', *Australian Strategic Policy Institute*, Policy Brief 26, March 2020, https://www.aspi.org.au/ report/uyghurs-sale (accessed 6 May 2021).

Yi, M. (2018), 'A Thought Liberation Movement is Underway Across the Great Land of Xinjiang', 9 October 2018, republished from Tianshan.net, http://news.sina.com. cn/c/2018-10-09/doc-ihkvrhpt4037609.shtml (accessed 6 May 2021).

Zenz, A. and Leibold, J. (2017), 'Xinjiang's Rapidly Evolving Security State', *China Brief* 17(4), https://jamestown.org/program/xinjiangs-rapidly-evolving-security-state/ (accessed 6 May 2021).

Zenz, A. (2019), '"Thoroughly Reforming Them towards a Healthy Heart Attitude": China's Political Re-Education Campaign in Xinjiang', *Central Asian Survey* 38(1): 102–28.

Zenz, A. (2020), 'Sterilizations, IUDs and Mandatory Birth Control: The CCP's Campaign to Suppress Uyghur Birthrates in Xinjiang', *The Jamestown Foundation*, Washington, https://jamestown.org/product/sterilizations-iuds-and-mandatory-birth-contr ol-the-ccps-campaign-to-suppress-uyghur-birthrates-in-xinjiang/ (accessed 6 May 2021).

Zenz, A. (2021), 'Coercive Labor and Forced Displacement in Xinjiang's Cross-Regional Labor Transfer Program', https://jamestown.org/wp-content/uploads/2021/03 /Coercive-Labor-and-Forced-Displacement-in-Xinjiangs-Cross-Regional-Labor-Tr ansfers-A-Process-Oriented-Evaluation.pdf?x11163.

INDEX

EU representative:
Easy Access System Europe
Mustamäe tee 50, 10621 Tallinn, Estonia
Gpsr.requests@easproject.com